Cultural Difference and Social Solidarity

Cultural Difference and Social Solidarity: Solidarities and Social Function

Edited by

Scott H. Boyd and Mary Ann Walter

CAMBRIDGE
SCHOLARS
P U B L I S H I N G

Cultural Difference and Social Solidarity: Solidarities and Social Function,
Edited by Scott H. Boyd and Mary Ann Walter

This book first published 2014

Cambridge Scholars Publishing

12 Back Chapman Street, Newcastle upon Tyne, NE6 2XX, UK

British Library Cataloguing in Publication Data
A catalogue record for this book is available from the British Library

ISBN (10): 1-4438-5549-9, ISBN (13): 978-1-4438-5549-5

TABLE OF CONTENTS

Social Function

PREFACE

This book is the second in a series that arises from the activities of the Cultural Difference and Social Solidarity Network, an international network formed in 2010 by Scott H. Boyd at Middle East Technical University—Northern Cyprus Campus, and Paul Reynolds at Edge Hill University in the UK. Part of the mission of CDSS is to promote international collaboration and exchanges of perspectives and research in the sometimes contradictory, sometimes conflicting areas of social differences and diversities and social cohesion and solidarity. In the context of a world where religious, nationalist, ethnic, gender, and political differences (amongst others) appear prominent and deeply contested, strategic attempts at social solidarity, such as multiculturalism, are open to critical questioning. The network seeks to develop international linkages to encourage learning from different bodies of scholarship, knowledge, and arguments that might provide for fruitful dialogues as to the balance and consistency of solidarity and difference in the democratic societies we seek to participate in making. Whilst the network has no formal political affiliation, many of its members have very broadly similar values in seeking to advance thinking that respects difference and diversity and explores how it can be juxtaposed with solidarity in democratic and communal ways rather than through authoritarian and oppressive strategies based on hierarchy, prejudice, pathology, inequality, and injustice.

The hope is that by promoting collaborative international research and creating spaces (in text, conferences, workshops, or seminars) for exchanging knowledge and perspectives, fruitful dialogue and critical thinking can be encouraged. Though it is an academic network, it seeks to provide argument and evidence that may also provoke thinking and action in the political domain. As a network it has a particular interest in encouraging diverse academic voices. This involves constructive intellectual dialogues from different parts of the globe, and the support and encouragement of younger researchers as the future thinkers of solidarity and difference on a global stage.

This book is one of a number of initiatives from within the network since its inception. Most of the authors attended the second annual conference in 2012, and each responded to our call to contribute a book chapter based on their current research. All contributions were taken through an editorial process, and additional contributions were commissioned where they enrich the collection. The collection is not, as such, a conference proceedings volume. It arises from the conference as starting point for sharing research, ideas, and points of view, but the priority of the editors and the network leaders is to produce texts that stand alone as contributions to scholarship in the area.

We offer our thanks to each contributor for taking the time to contribute to this text. We would also like to thank all the participants, past and present, for their support of the Cultural Difference and Social Solidarity Network, and particularly those whose comments on the original papers enriched their final forms. We would also like to thank Paul Reynolds and John McSweeney for their time in reviewing various types of submissions and helping to organise our events and discussions, and Özlem Ezer Boyd and Ben Walter for their help and patience. Lastly, we would like to thank Middle East Technical University–Northern Cyprus Campus for its hospitality and on-going support of this project.

INTRODUCTION

PAUL REYNOLDS

Solidarity has a curious absent presence in social theory and analysis. Whilst the concept of solidarity would seem to be a critical feature in any form of collective community, organisation, or association, it is often used as either a descriptor or a characteristic of competing models of social cohesion and communality in society. It is regarded as a characteristic of societies or communities to be aspired to, rather than a central explanatory concept. Social and political theorists of society have used other concepts and ideas that do the work of providing the conceptual basis for explaining the way societies work and how they change. Lawrence Wilde observes:

> 'Solidarity' seems to have been confined to the realm of rhetoric while serious theoretical work has concentrated on other aspects of political association such as democracy, nationalism, community, multiculturalism and human rights In essence, solidarity is the feeling of reciprocal sympathy and responsibility among members of a group which promotes mutual support. As such it has subjective and emotional elements, and this helps to explain its conceptual neglect.... (2007, 171)

Yet as a characteristic of contemporary societies, solidarity is often elusive and subject to contestation, requiring constant remaking, particularly in the contemporary context of social diversity, political and religious difference, and the development of more subjective and diffuse cultures, identities, and "lifeworld" conditions. For much of the political and intellectual focus on solidarity is based on how a solidarity that is not composed of oppression, police enforcement, and exclusionary values can be composed alongside patterns of social and cultural diffusion and diversity. Mason (2000), for example, subsumes these challenges within the broad question of how communities foster belonging as a normative commitment, which stresses how shared moral, cultural, and political values and a sense of belonging within a community are critical to any notion of solidarity in society. Turner and Rojek (2001, 68), in contrast, subsume much of their debate on solidarity to considerations of theories of power and social order and the necessity of a focus on "the non-contractual element of contract (that is common values, collective sentiments) which underpins everyday reciprocities and relations." This alternate focus on normative commitments and moral values or politics, order, and the distribution of power is a central axis for studies that focus on solidarity. Hence much of the best work that engages the idea of solidarity is necessarily trans-disciplinary, including philosophical, legal, social, cultural, and political dimensions.

This is not to claim an easy contradiction between solidarity and difference. Audre Lorde (1997) observes that "it is not our differences that divide us. It is our inability to recognise, accept, and celebrate those differences." However, the characteristics of social cohesion and social diversity have often given rise to contested politics and struggles for liberty, rights, and justice. This is particularly the case where identities or interests in society make their claims to recognition, rights, and economic redistribution where they are denied under the extant social and political settlement. Davina Cooper frames the political tension well when she observes:

> [Diversity politics] goes beyond the conditional liberal promise bestowed on minorities of toleration, providing their differences are kept from affecting others. . . . The space of diversity politics is one in which social diversity is valued and celebrated. . . . The space of diversity politics raises questions and embraces diverging opinions about the desired place of collective identities within society . . . is a new hegemony worth seeking or are all hegemonies however radical they appear in theory, disastrous to the pursuit and maintenance of a freer, more enabling society? (2004)

Solidarity as an idea is both critical to understanding social and political cohesion and the balance of cohesion and diffusion that emerges at any given political moment from whatever social, cultural, political, and economic order and whatever moral and political discourses are engaged. Yet it has often been assumed, or subsumed, in debates around identities, social divisions, and the exercise of power in making order in contemporary society, and so is insufficiently theorised in itself.

If Wilde's "feeling of reciprocal sympathy . . . responsibility . . . mutual support" is the essence of solidarity, it is clear that solidarity works at different levels and different contexts. Solidarity is both a characteristic of any society, community or association, yet also a quality of relationships at social, community, and interpersonal levels. Social identities and interests seek to represent solidarity in their political struggles; social institutions have solidarity as a necessary feature of their operation; communities have solidarity as a feature of their capacity to have shared moral and political commitments and draw lines of inclusion and exclusion; and social relations are measured and understood in part by the solidarity they engender. Solidarity covers a range of relationships, from political affiliation, commitment, and participation to identification, recognition, and cultural engagement, through to interpersonal constructions of intimate and emotional relations. Crow (2002, 1), one of the most common primer texts on solidarity, neatly frames his discussion with theoretical concerns around order, function, and division and balances of change and continuity; solidarities from family through community to political organisation; and solidarities deconstructed into causes, contexts and consequences in seeking to present a general understanding of "how people strive to come together and act as a coherent and united force" that illustrates the range of relationships and dynamic debates around solidarity.

Whilst these different articulations of solidarity are important to disentangle in their specificity, solidarity has common threads across these different levels. It speaks to some form of communality, whether through political ideology, moral values, tradition, orthodoxy and culture, or shared interests and identification. Also, importantly, as the title of this volume suggests, it is a central *social function*. The functionality of solidarity has been central to its use in social theory and philosophy, and provides some of the central tensions in exploring the concept of solidarity.

Wilde (2007, 2013 and in Chapter One below) provides a comprehensive genealogy of the concept of solidarity, and shows that in a sense, the earliest sociologists showed considerable awareness of the importance of solidarity in understanding social cohesion at times of substantial social, economic, and political change. Solidarity emerges as a conceptual expression of moral and social cohesion in nineteenth century French social theory, most prominently in the work of Emile Durkheim. For Durkheim (1984), solidarity is tied to the idea of a functional society, where social institutions function to maintain moral boundaries that signify shared values and belonging. Durkheim used the distinction of organic and mechanical solidarity to assert that forms of solidarity, composed through changing social institutions, varied in different forms of society with different divisions of labour—agrarian or industrial. Regardless of that diversity, solidarity remained a necessary feature for the function of those societies. Durkheim's concern was that the organic social binds and common moral values produced by social institutions in agrarian societies were more subject to failure in industrial societies where social and community interdependence was more estranged (or anomic). The division of labour under capitalism brought pressure to bear on social institutions to carry and propagate shared values and promote shared experiences. The failure of social institutions to adapt to these new social conditions produced anomie and the disintegration of solidarity.

Durkheim's solidarity is a solidarity for a functional society, where the assumption of Durkheim's science is that social progress is being decoded and functionality is a necessary good in any social collective. This has been the prevailing paradigm within which solidarity has been seen: promoting coherence over division without necessarily questioning whether solidarity is necessarily to be valued in itself, or whether solidarity is being promoted in conditions on inequality, oppression, and injustice. Hence despite its socialist roots, solidarity has been a somewhat conservative concept in sociological analysis, necessarily exploring change as measured against functionality or patterns of dysfunction in social systems.

It is perhaps this association that saw the decline of focus on solidarity in conflict-based theories of Marxism or feminism, where failures in the maintenance of solidarity are often a property of emerging social divisions that cause social and political dysfunction to effect structural change. Strategies for social solidarity are viewed with suspicion for their apologia for existing social ills and their focus on retaining the existing functions in society and the institutions that facilitated them. Particularly with the post-Second World War scepticism for the enlightenment project and social progress as a given, the conservative association of solidarity with functionality went against the eruptions of post-modern and identity politics.

In the context of the family, for example, the functions of the reproduction of labour, patriarchy and gendered division, authority relations, heteronormative sexuality, and moral and social conservative culture values all became subject to criticism and resistance where radical positions outlined the terms of oppression, exploitation, inequality, and injustice they could involve. From these struggles, since the 1960s, has emerged more diverse family forms that reflect rejections of these functions—though the family as a form still retains functional elements in how people express their belonging and relate to other social institutions. What has changed is that functionality, whilst still critical in the political and policy debates, is set against the politics and cultural specificities of diverse populations, often with difficult outcomes, as the attempts to develop multicultural politics in Europe have to some extent illustrated (see Hasan 2010, Parekh 2000, and Taylor 1994 for a representation of the debates).

Solidarity is a critical feature of the integrity, social, and moral capital as well as the political stability and legitimacy of any society, both as a social function and beyond that as a principle, idea, objective, or critical concept. Hence this text seeks to both explore questions of solidarity in both contemporary conceptual and empirical studies, and in doing so emphasize its importance in social analyses.

Studies of solidarity give rise to a number of important questions about how the concept is understood and articulated, the first being the general question of a solidarity for what. In particular, what forms of social system are social institutions charged with producing solidarity for, and are they desirable social systems? A combination of pernicious ideology, appeals to nationalist fervour, racist moral boundaries, and the utilisation and enhancement of the policing functions of the state to crush dissent produced solidarity in Nazi Germany. This is certainly not a strategy for solidarity that would appeal to many. There is the question of solidarity as functional to what form of community, with what levels of in/equality, in/justice, or oppression/freedom. The balance of solidarity that is necessary for social functions might involve a trade off with levels of undesirable characteristics such as injustice.

Secondly, what priority has solidarity? How far is solidarity a social priority? Solidarity is not a uniformly understood or desired property, and neoliberals, for example, would see solidarity in minimal terms in relation to participation in the market and social institutions that encourage a general sense of order and community. This is very different from the notion of solidarity as an expression of shared values and resources, and participative politics and cultural sharing.

Thirdly, through what mechanisms does solidarity occur and what social institutions promote solidarity? There are clearly traditional structures that do so, such as religious institutions, but what about other and more recent social institutions, such as the mass media or the World Wide Web and social networking?

Related to the mechanism is the means. There are questions of whether solidarity is achieved through ideological or repressive means, by social and political institutions that seek to encourage participation and recognition or conformity and hierarchical order.

Lastly, do we consider solidarity as position and/or strategy and/or goal? Discussions of solidarity often conflate three understandings of how solidarity is conceived: as the communality and shared values of particular identities and interests and how their exercise of solidarity represents their politics within wider society; as strategic politics that seeks to bind together a collective approach to social, cultural, and political change; and as the goal of a society that is considered healthy, inclusive, and empowering to all its component populations.

These sorts of questions speak to a form of solidarity that is constituted on a social and community level, as this introduction has observed, solidarity spans the social and cultural, the "lifeworld." Private and intimate contexts within social institutions such as family, religious organisation, public leisure and entertainment, and the urban setting and public spaces offer considerable "lifeworld" practices that bind people together in their everyday experiences. Solidarity in the big picture of ideological representations, hegemonic strategies or the workings of social and cultural institutions, are only effective in the context of their impact percolating into the intimate lived experience of people.

For Wilde (2013), these private and intimate contexts of solidarity in relationships like love and friendship serve to augment notions of collectivity, community, civil society, and public life. The value of this insight is that it cautions against always assuming a big picture or top-down dynamic when solidarities percolate from intimate spheres of association and through organisation and association within the civil strata. In the last thirty years, much of the debate around solidarity in society has been around what mechanisms produce what level of solidarity and what level of individual commitment is the best balance in mature economies.

In a number of different forms, from libertarianism through conservative republicanism to "new" social democracy, neoliberal politics have pushed back the frontiers of the public and the collective, through the mechanisms of individuation, privatisation, the commodification of social life, and consumerism as the principal dynamic in social life. Under such ideological and political regimes, solidarity is found in the limited notion of self-interest extended to family and intimates, and crucially in participation in markets that provide goods, services, and experiences and representative architectures that bring people together under a competitive yet communal ethos to defend liberal freedoms and conservative traditions. These traditions retain the fundamentals of a liberalism that has forgotten its enlightenment roots for a crude utilitarian parody that supports economic life as "civilization." They are porous to new ideas and particularly new sciences and technologies, but only insofar as they further reinforce privacy, individuality and market benefits or leave minorities in the margins. What this leaves is a simultaneous framing of politics towards individuated subjects whilst acknowledging the power of globalisation and the growth of an interconnectedness, particularly amongst global business and financial interests in the twenty-first century (this is explored in De Beer and Koster 2009).

The power of neoliberalism is that it has colonised or dissolved much of the language and culture of social democratic and socialist politics. Collectivism is consigned to history by its association with the "failed" projects of communism, socialism, and traditional statist social democracy, though this general malaise has arguable exceptions, for example in Chavez's Venezuela. For those on the left, a viable, feasible, and persuasive idea of solidarity around collective values is essential to revivifying debate around the public and the civil in contemporary politics. The agenda for scholarship into the different dimensions of solidarity is thus fertile and in need of critical thinking.

The Text

This book seeks to explore different dimensions and cases in considering solidarity as a social function and bring to the fore the critical value of the concept of solidarity in understanding contemporary societies. The first section focuses on solidarity itself, and begins with Lawrence Wilde's exercise in retrieving the origins of the concept of solidarity in French social thought in the nineteenth century and exploring their contemporary relevance. Identifying solidarity as a product of early engagements between socialist and Christian thought, Wilde explores three competing models: Pierre Leroux's ethico-inclusive model, a more radical redemptive model advocated by Louis-Auguste Blanqui, and the class struggle model that emerges in the work of Marx and Engels. Wilde's argument is that solidarity has become subsumed within the dominant and traditional Marxist model of class politics and has not surmounted the problems he identifies of an inability to account adequately for the failures of Stalinism and policing regimes as a consequence of actually existing communist revolutions in the twentieth century, and for the diversity of social divisions and identities in its focus on class determinations. Wilde is drawn towards a radical humanist politics in which collective solidarity on national and global levels is central, and argues that a return to Leroux's ethico-inclusive account of solidarity would be a valuable contribution to theorising social and political change.

John McSweeney takes a different approach to theorizing solidarity, through a critical discussion of the later Foucault's augmentation of his concerns with a critical politics of difference with a politics of *parrhesia*, which focuses on the truth teller and, in this context, the act of telling the truth about difference. McSweeney sees Foucault's elaboration of a notion of care of the self deriving from cynicism and providing a reframing of his politics of difference to sustain socio-political solidarity. The combination of the aesthetics of the care of the self and the speaking to truth of *parrhesia* leads to a politics that uncover the pernicious effects of ordering structures in society and offers the possibility of solidarity in the act of recognising difference through shared experience of how that difference is experienced as difference, and as subjectivities that are demystified and therefore understood. This is a solidarity of being outside of formal structures in order to change them and recognise the value of that common experience in relation to injustice, regulatory regimes and social ordering that produces hierarchy and "othering." For McSweeney, the enterprise of truth telling and in doing so expressing care for self and other together is a fruitful basis for a contemporary solidarity.

David Stoop draws from a different intellectual tradition, the critical theory of Theodor Adorno. Stoop's focus is on the problems of any conception of solidarity that seeks to account for the identitarian logic that underpins reconciliation between difference and solidarity in initiatives such as multiculturalism. This identitarian logic neither recognises criticisms of its own traditions in identity representation, nor accounts for the material contexts within which solidarity struggles are played out. Stoop explores Adorno's concept of non-identity and his negative dialectics as a means for opening up a space for a different, non-identitarian notion of difference and solidarity. Stoop is clear that this exploration does not produce an easily translated analysis into a politics of solidarity, but sees value in the critique of alienation and objectification, instrumental reason and the structuring principles of contemporary societies that Adorno offers. From a different position to McSweeney, the shared experience of oppression is central to the prospects for solidarity that respects the autonomy of the individual.

In my chapter I draw from another intellectual tradition, that of Alisdair MacIntyre and his rearticulation of Aristotelian virtue ethics, to explore the value of solidarity ingrained in the practice of politics as a means of developing solidarity. Despite the dissonances between MacIntyre's pessimistic response to the amoral banality of modern capitalist societies, features of his philosophy provide the prospects for a disciplining of current radical and Marxist politics. He draws out and focuses on the necessity of recognising the importance of practices as collective activities, the problems of institutional organisation and bureaucratic and managerial logics, and the importance of understanding traditions of politics and values and being wary of abstractive logics as guides for political thought and action. I offer this in a provisional essay, which seeks to put solidarity at the centre of radical and Marxist theory and politics, but also to anchor it and concrete processes and activity through the importance of practice as a foundation for politics.

Finally for this section, Zuzana Klímová turns from social analysis to literary theory to explore the social function of postcolonial literature in the 1960s and the second decade of the twenty-first century. Klímová's analysis is of postcolonial literature's rearticulation of the aesthetic function of literary creation. Central to postcolonial literature is the notion of counter-discourse against colonial and imperial truths and representations and particularly the impact of such traditional readings in producing "others" in prejudicial and pejorative forms. Klímová writes against the traditional apolitical reading of literature and locates postcolonial literature as a counterpart to political struggles and the assertion of political independence. Klímová traces the development of postcolonial literature over the last six decades and its articulation of an aesthetic politics that has an impact on the emergence of a postcolonial world and creates the space for debates as to how postcolonial literature attacks, but sometimes is contradictory in sustaining, the colonial past within its discourse. Klímová's chapter is less explicit in its discussion of solidarity but has an important contribution to debate in thinking about the different mechanisms by which solidarity is produced, and focusing upon the literary dimension.

The first section provides different theoretical approaches to the conception and exploration of solidarity, and approaches that depart from the traditional and dominant perspectives within which debates about solidarity take place. Their particular focus and critical thinking are valuable in themselves, and also add to the extant literature and encourage broader and new approaches to thinking about solidarity. The second section, sub-titled "social function," seeks to explore particular cases in which solidarity is constituted. The cases are remarkable by their diversity in global location, level of association, focus on cultural, political and policy contexts, and different approaches to analysis. As such, they provide a diverse set of cases from which different aspects of the problems of making and remaking solidarity can be explored.

Sibylle Heilbrunn, Leima Davidovich, and Leah Achdut provide a case study of Israel in exploring questions of solidarity. Writing against European sociological conceptions of exploring the tendencies to the collapse of solidarity and social cohesion through migration, globalisation, and modernising processes, they point to a distinction in looking at solidarity in Israel. Focusing on immigrant populations from the former Soviet Union and Ethiopia and the extant Palestinian population, they explore how the three populations experience the processes of social cohesion, using surveys and official statistical sources. Their research shows variance in the levels of social cohesion and the interrelationships and "trade off patterns" that these populations are subject to and experience. This exploration of social cohesion provides evidence that the migrants from the former Soviet Union are most integrated and the Palestinians least so, and joins a significant body of literature that challenges current Israeli political strategies in respect of solidarity and managing difference within the Israeli state.

Claire Farrugia provides a different and far smaller case study, that of the African Village Market in Sydney, Australia. The market provides a space for communal meeting, social enterprise, and the fostering of community. This community provides the material for an ethnographic study that explores the meaning making of solidarity within the African diaspora. Farrugia emphasizes the practice of solidarity through sharing practices within the market that bind the community together. Within the context of reducing public funding for such spaces, Farrugia explores the complex interrelations between the practising of solidarity alongside the recognition of differences within the African diasporic community as a means of recognising the value of such a space.

Simona Zavratnik moves from an example of solidarity made constructively within community to the complexities of solidarity and identity in the Slovene context. Zavratnik looks at Slovenia's management of migration and incorporation of different ethnic minorities, and particularly at how these approaches deal with the contentious issues left from the conflicts that emerged in the former Yugoslavia (of which Slovenia was a part) in the 1990's. The focus of this analysis is on how statehood and the emergence of a distinct national identity challenged migration and ethnic diversity, particularly in respect of immigrants deemed to be "less desirable." Broadening the case within the context of European trends and data, Zavratnik suggests that public perception is an important variable in how states respond to migration and ethnic diversity, raising the issue of the relationship between a political responsiveness to public opinion *contra* the formation of public opinion by which states seek to maintain their power and conception of social cohesion.

Finally, Burcu Şentürk explores how state action can dissolve the solidarity in a community. Focusing on urban policies in Turkey, Şentürk focuses on the slum dwellers of the Ege district in Ankara, and how they were formed by migration from rural areas as the economy modernised. These slum districts are characterised by homogenous political orientation, lived experience, and ethnic and religious identities. The similarities, collective needs and struggles of this emergent community reinforced their solidarity, but are then eroded by strategic policies that seek to redistribute slum dwellers to other parts of the city and fragment the political polarisation of the development of these communities, and the impact of urban reformation projects. This eroded the sense of community solidarity and the politics of communality that solidarity produced.

These cases provide apt illustrations of the importance of solidarity as a social function and how solidarity is in various ways made or challenged. They have in common a clear understanding that social solidarity is inherently political (Scholz 2008), and whilst solidarity is not only produced by the state, the state in direct and indirect ways makes important contributions to the maintenance or erosion of solidarities in society and community as well as interests and identities in society.

This modest contribution to scholarship signposts some of the fertile possibilities for thinking about solidarity in the twenty-first century, whether measuring the value of existing ideas and strategies, such as multiculturalism, or exploring what new forms of social and cultural institutions might produce solidarity, such as new information technologies, or exploring whether cosmopolitanism or other concepts should now take up the running in opening the imagination to the possibilities of society where belonging, shared commitments and political, economic, and cultural resources coincide with the space to be different in diverse social forms, organisations and constructs.

References

Cooper, Davina. 2004. *Challenging Diversity: Rethinking Equality and the Value of Difference*. Cambridge: Cambridge University Press.

Crow, Graham. 2002. *Social Solidarities: Theories, Identities and Social Change*. Buckingham: Open University Press.

De Beer, Paul and Koster Ferry. 2009. *Sticking Together or Falling Apart?: Solidarity in an Era of Individualization and Globalization*. Amsterdam: Amsterdam University Press.

Durkheim, Emile. 1984. *The Division of Labor in Society*. London: MacMillan.

Hasan, Rumy. 2010. *Multiculturalism: Some Inconvenient Truths*. London: Politicos.

Lorde, Audre. 1997. *Our Dead Behind Us: Poems*. London: WW Norton and Company.

Mason, Andrew. 2001. *Community, Solidarity and Belonging: Levels of Community and their Normative Significance*. Cambridge: Cambridge University Press.

Parekh, Bhikhu. 2000. *Rethinking Multiculturalism: Cultural Diversity and Political Theory*. Houndsmill: Palgrave.

Rorty, Richard. 1989. *Contingency, Irony, and Solidarity*. Cambridge: Cambridge University Press.

Scholz, Sally J. 2008. *Political Solidarity*. University Park, PA: Pennsylvania State University Press.

Taylor, Charles. 1994. *Multiculturalism: Examining the Politics of Recognition*. Edited and Introduced by Amy Gutmann. New Jersey: Princeton University Press.

Turner, Bryan and Chris Rojek. 2001. *Society and Culture: Principles of Scarcity and Solidarity*. London: Sage.

Wilde, Lawrence. 2007. "The Concept of Solidarity: Emerging from the Theoretical Shadows?" *British Journal of Politics and International Relations* 9:171-181.

—. 2013. *Global Solidarity*. Edinburgh: Edinburgh University Press.

SOLIDARITIES

CHAPTER ONE

THREE FORMS OF NINETEENTH CENTURY WORKING CLASS SOLIDARITY AND THEIR CURRENT RELEVANCE

LAWRENCE WILDE

The concept of solidarity was first developed by the French social thinker Pierre Leroux in *De L'Humanité*, published in 1840 (Wilde 2013, 20-22). It was one of a cluster of terms, such as "socialism" and "communism," which emerged, first in France and Britain and quickly elsewhere, to express the hopes of the rapidly growing working class for a more just social order (Bestor 1948, 259). The association of solidarity with socialism became common in France in the 1840s, culminating in the emergence of *Solidarité Républicaine* in November 1848, the first mass socialist party which had over 350 branches with 30,000 members within months. It won over two million votes at the legislative assembly election of May 1849, with 200 deputies adopting the title of *démoc-socs*, or social-democrats (Pilbeam 2000, 190-1). It was not until much later in the century that the concept of solidarity came to be adopted by sections of the liberal bourgeoisie. Emile Durkheim brought it into the realm of academic social science with the publication of *The Division of Labour in Society* in 1893, while Léon Bourgeois, leader of the Radical Party, popularised a liberal appeal to class reconciliation when he published *Solidarité* in 1896.

In this chapter I identify three forms of solidarity advocated by various nineteenth century socialist movements, with "socialist" used in a broad sense to cover all the doctrines and movements that combined firm rejection of the capitalist economic system with a commitment to some form of egalitarian and democratic alternative. They all acknowledged the need for some form of united action against the prevailing social system, but there were distinct differences when it came to identifying the groups that were to be mobilised, the scope of their activities, and the nature of their social goals. The first three sections will look critically at each of the forms in turn—the ethico-inclusive, the redemptive, and the class struggle perspectives—while the concluding section will consider their impact on twentieth century politics and their possible relevance for social struggles of today.

Ethico-Inclusive Solidarity

The concept of solidarity developed by Leroux can be characterised as "ethico-inclusive" because it demanded social and political inclusion and was expressed in explicitly ethical terms. In Book 4 of *De L'Humanité* Leroux conceived the "mutual solidarity of humans" as the alternative to the shortcomings of the Christian virtue of charity. Rather than helping others out of duty to God without enquiring into the reasons for their misfortune, people ought to express the love of God through embracing their fellow human beings in mutually supportive relations (Leroux 1985, 157-72). While acknowledging the positive contribution of Christianity to morality in the past, he argued that the time had come for a new religion of Humanity in which the love of God was expressed as love for the God in ourselves and others (Leroux 1985, 158 and 165). Although Leroux condemned the enslavement of workers in the new industrial system and declared the bourgeoisie, with its rampant individualism, to be "the enemy," he opposed violent revolution and consistently supported peaceful agitation for social, economic and political reform (Bakunin 1976, 96). This model of solidarity associated the needs and aspirations of the working class with the common good of the whole society. The workers were conceived broadly as all those who laboured to make a living, including independent urban workers and poor peasants. In this conception, the demand for social inclusion followed the spirit of the great French Revolution of 1789 with its appeal for "liberty, equality, fraternity."

Although Leroux was wary of specifying the forms that the socialism of the future might take, it is possible to form a clear picture of the guiding principles of the ethico-inclusive form of solidarity, outlined in France by Leroux and other socialists such as Louis Blanc, and by some leaders of the Chartist movement in Britain such as James Bronterre O'Brien, Ernest Jones and Julian Harney (Maw 2008, 201-26; Claeys 1987, 158-62; Thompson 1998, 111-30). They denounced the exploitation that flowed from an unregulated market economy, and demanded the full social and political inclusion of the urban and rural working class. The organisation of working class solidarity varied, including producer and consumer cooperatives, craft-based trade unions, and political agitation for assistance for workers and for full democratic rights. In France, the most specific plan for an alternative to competitive capitalism was the system of "social workshops," first set down by Louis Blanc in *L'Organisation du travail* in 1839. These were to be state sponsored cooperatives in which the solidarity of the workers in each workshop was to develop into solidarity between all the workshops in the same industry, culminating in a wider solidarity between all the various industries in the country (Blanc 1841, 84). Blanc called his vision for the future socialist society "a vast system of solidarity" (Blanc 1841, 142). Crucially, the workshops would be the vehicle to give substance to the demand for the right to work, which proved, as shall see, too dangerous for the propertied classes to tolerate. The commitment to peaceful change meant that the proponents of this model of solidarity often sought the cooperation of those in positions of power and influence, in the somewhat naïve belief that the development of more cooperative social system would be accepted as the rational course of action. In the 1845 introduction to *L'Organisation du travail* Blanc explicitly addressed his work to the rich, appealing to them that the cause of the poor was also "your cause" (Sewell 1997, 235).

The Chartists addressed their demands for democratic rights directly to Parliament by presenting three massive national petitions between 1839 and 1848, only to be met with disdain. Although this mass movement had a "physical force" element to it, the large majority of those involved pursued reforms within legal limits. Indeed their respect for observing legality was shown when the sole Chartist Member of Parliament, Feargus O'Connor, withdrew his motion to discuss the last great Chartist petition in 1848 when the House of Commons administrators cast doubt on the validity more than half of the four million signatures (Roberts 1999, 112-3). At the same time the last great national demonstration of 80,000 Chartists passed off peacefully at Kennington Common in London, but in the months that followed almost 300 leaders were arrested and imprisoned, and the movement collapsed (Thompson 1984, 328-9).

The ethico-inclusive model of solidarity consistently exhibited an ethical commitment to social inclusion. We have seen that Leroux grounded his commitment to social solidarity in an egalitarian interpretation of Christianity, while Blanc described socialism as "the gospel in practice" (Blanc 1966, 257). This Christianity was not that of the established churches, which they regarded as corrupting the liberational essence of the religion, but it built on the moral intuition of those educated in the Christian tradition. There was also a tradition of non-Christian "deistic" religion among followers of Charles Fourier and Henri de Saint-Simon that argued for social justice (Pilbeam 2000, 39-53). This was developed further by Auguste Comte and his "religion of humanity" and was influential in the development of social liberalism as well as Durkheim's commitment to social solidarity (Durkheim 1968, 62-63; Wernick 2001). In the Chartist movement, as Dorothy Thompson has pointed out, it is clear from speeches and writings that most Chartists were Christians "of one sort or another" (Thompson 1986, 260). Even in the secular socialist tradition, inspired by cooperative thinkers such as Robert Owen and William Thompson in the 1830s, a strongly moralistic rhetoric was employed to claim justice and entitlement for the working class (Claeys 1987, 64-5).

The commitment to internationalism was also typical of the ethico-inclusive model of solidarity. Leroux himself argued, in an address to his fellow printers in 1851, that solidarity should be rooted in workplace associations that would transcend national boundaries, introducing "the true human society" which "makes all men solidary while rendering them free" (Sewell 1997, 274). This internationalism was an important feature of early socialism, marked by the formal establishment of The Society of Fraternal Democrats, comprising members from a number of European countries, in 1846. Its programme, formulated by the English socialist, Julian Harney, declared that "our moral creed is to receive our fellow-men without regard to country, as members of one family–the human race, and as citizens of one commonwealth–the world" (Braunthal 1967a, 66).

In both Britain and France, however, the commitment to peaceful political progress placed the socialist leaders and their movements in jeopardy at times of political crisis. The suppression of the Chartist movement in Britain set back the development of independent working class political activity for over 30 years. The French case is perhaps more instructive for understanding the difficulties faced by those who preached a peaceful path to socialism. The revolution of February 1848 ushered in a Provisional Government that included Louis Blanc, and a somewhat watered-down version of his national workshops was introduced. Although the majority in the Provisional Government intended the workshops to be little more than a temporary act of charity to rescue workers from destitution in a time of particularly severe distress, the wording of the decree itself conveyed a radically different message. As William Sewell notes, the decree established the workshops not on the basis of charity but on the solemnly proclaimed right of all citizens to labour. The workers were convinced that it had established the right to labour as a fundamental right of man (Sewell 1997, 246). It appeared that a major step had been taken towards the triumph of the principle of solidarity over the principle of charity. However, the general election in April returned a conservative majority and Blanc was removed from the new government, which, on June 21, decreed the dissolution of the workshops. Thousands of workers in Paris took to arms in a rebellion that lacked leadership and clear goals, and in four days of fighting approximately 1500 workers were killed and 12,000 arrested and imprisoned (Sewell 1997, 272). The violent suppression of the workers' uprising was followed by closure of many socialist clubs and publications, and eventually by the abolition of universal male franchise. Nevertheless, this was not the end of the ethico-inclusive approach to solidarity. Despite this, *Solidarité Républicaine* continued to attract members and electoral support, but the state intensified its repression. Most of the social democratic leaders were arrested at various times during the Second Republic and many of them fled France even before Louis-Napoleon assumed total control in December 1851. The new dictator immediately imposed a ban on all socialist and labour organisations that was tightly enforced until the late 1860s. This quickly led to the marginalisation of the ethico-inclusive model of solidarity.

Despite the difficulties of pursuing peaceful tactics in the face of acute economic exploitation and political oppression, one outstanding example of ethico-inclusive working class solidarity deserves mention. This was the support of British cotton workers for the anti-slavery movement in the American Civil War, which involved an enormous self-sacrifice. When the Civil War broke out in 1861 the Northern states set up a naval blockade to prevent the slave-owning Confederacy from exporting its principal product, cotton. As almost 80 per cent of the cotton imported into Lancashire and Scotland was from the Confederacy, mass unemployment and poverty soon developed. Nevertheless, the workers campaigned hard to prevent the British government to break the blockade and effectively declare war on the USA, which it was urged to do by the cotton owners and other manufacturers. They also pleaded with President Lincoln to make the freeing of the slaves the goal of the conflict. Thanking them for their courageous support, Lincoln noted that they could have secured work and food if the blockade had been broken, but "they could not allow their instinct to override their conscience" (Foner 1981, 88).

Redemptive Solidarity

The redemptive approach to solidarity viewed the existing social order as totally oppressive and corrupt, and sought deliverance through complete revolutionary transformation. The leading advocate of this approach in France was Louis-Auguste Blanqui, who spent a lifetime gathering disciplined groups of conspirators together, including many years in jail as a result of his insurrectionary activities (Braunthal 1967a, 46-7). Blanqui saw the role of these revolutionary groups as inspiring the proletarians - workers and peasants alike—"the desire to redeem themselves from servitude" (Blanqui 1832a). This redemptive urge, spontaneous and explosive, rejected the idea of building mass movements of workers in trade unions or legal political parties. In practice, the solidarity developed in this model was primarily that of the small, disciplined revolutionary group, aiming to create a solidaristic society after the forces of oppression had been destroyed. Typically, these groups were high on apocalyptic rhetoric and low on the details of what forms the transition to "freedom" might take. This conspiratorial approach was by no means restricted to France, gaining support among opponents of the highly authoritarian Russian state (Venturi 1983) and also in Italy and Spain (Woodcock 1977, 307-75).

The followers of Blanqui were the major political force at work in the great rebellion that produced the Paris Commune of 1871 (Braunthal 1967a, 153-5; Horne 2002, 290-303). The solidarity of the Commune rested on a shared sense of the betrayal of Paris by the government of the new Third Republic, the injustices of the past, and a conviction that a more just society could be created without privileged elites. The Communards were to pay a high price for their defiant stance. After ten weeks of independence, between March 18 and May 28, the Army of the national government marched from Versailles to destroy the Commune, slaughtering an estimated 25,000 people in the process (Horne 2002, 418; Edwards 1972, 158). Many others were exiled and not allowed to return to France until the amnesty of 1880. As Robert Gildea has commented, the repression handed to the workers "a founding myth of the heroism, martyrdom and promised redemption of the working class that trumped all others" (Gildea 1996, 44). The ferocity of the state suppression of the revolutionary working class was decisive in marginalising appeals to a social republic forged out of compromise with the ruling class (Sewell 1999, 275-6). Working class solidarity in the early years of the French Third Republic expressed itself in revolutionary rather than reformist terms, for despite the extension of representative democracy, militant workers were unwilling to trust parliament and the state.

In Europe as a whole, anarchism became the principal vehicle for the redemptive model of solidarity. One of its leading proponents, Mikhail Bakunin, committed himself early in his career to the idea of sweeping away all institutions of power in order to achieve freedom, famously declaring that "the passion for destruction is a creative passion, too!" (Bakunin 1973, 57). The redemptive nature of his conception of solidarity is well illustrated by his response to the defeat of the Commune, in which he pledged his commitment to a liberty that would "shatter all the idols in heaven and on earth and will then build a powerful new world of mankind in solidarity, upon the ruins of all the churches and all the states" (Bakunin 1973, 262). After talking about the massacre of the Communards as the crucifixion of "humanity itself," he promises that the coming international revolution, "expressing the solidarity of all peoples, shall be the resurrection of Paris" (Bakunin 1973, 264-5). Bakunin rejected what he termed "Marxian solidarity," arguing that it was "decreed" from top down, but he extolled the watchword of solidarity as "the confirmation and realisation of every freedom, having its origin…in the inherent social nature of man" (Bakunin 1973, 284-5).

The determination of the anarchists to maintain their anti-authoritarian purity was such that they abstained from constitutional politics and from trade union trade union activity that restricted itself to bargaining for better pay and conditions. This was to prove decisive in limiting the effectiveness of anarchism as a movement, leaving the major organisations of the working class in the hands of reformists or Marxists. In practice, the political abstentionism of anarchism did not lend itself to the development of solidaristic mass movements, with the important exception of Spain (Woodock 1977, 335-375). However, besides the solidarity within and between anarchist groups, attempts were made to reach out to other groups pursuing socialistic goals, and Bakunin and his followers played an important role in the First International between 1868 and 1872. It represented thousands of workers from across Europe and North America, and had some notable successes in supporting labour struggles (Braunthal 1967a, 113-6). However, from the outset it was beset by doctrinal, tactical and organisational differences. In the aftermath of the repression of the Commune it looked likely that the groups preaching political abstentionism would gain a majority in the General Council, and Marx engineered the relocation of the Council to New York and effectively ended the brief but spectacular life of the International (Braunthal 1967a, 116- 94) The anarchists continued to hold International Congresses, but their strength diminished as masses of workers began to organise in socialist parties that were willing to engage with existing political institutions. When the Second International was inaugurated in Paris in 1889, the old differences between anarchists and socialists quickly resurfaced. At the Zurich Congress of 1893 a number of Marxists proposed that future membership of political organisations be restricted to those committed to political action, which meant that "the workers" parties should make full use of political and legal rights in an attempt to capture the legislative machine and use it in the interests of the working class and for the capture of political power (Braunthal 1967a, 251). The motion passed, effectively excluding the anarchists, and the decision was upheld three years later at the London Congress.

Perhaps the most significant mass movement embodying the idea of redemptive solidarity was revolutionary syndicalism, which developed among craft-based trade unions in France in the 1890s and reached a dominant position in the national labour federation, the CGT (*Confédération Générale du Travail*), between 1902 and 1912. At its height the unions embracing revolutionary syndicalism totalled no more than 400,000 members, but its militancy was formidable and its fierce hostility to all forms of political practice was unremitting (Ridley 1970, 63-79). Its dual purpose was to promote workers' immediate interest through industrial action, and, more importantly, to pursue the final emancipation of the proletariat from the despotism of capitalist democracy by means of the general strike. Typically, there were no details of what the transformed society would look like in the event of a successful general strike, and the growing acceptance of the pursuit of reforms as the only practical way forward led to a dissipation of the revolutionary purity of the movement (Ridley 1970, 153-5). The clearest expression of revolutionary syndicalism's apocalyptic commitment was George Sorel's *Reflections on Violence*, first published in 1906, in which he extolled the virtues of the "terrible nature of the revolution" and "its character of absolute and irrevocable transformation" (Sorel 2009, 154). For Sorel, the proletariat's task was to prepare itself for "the great battle," not to make plans for the post-revolutionary society. The workers should concentrate on the sole aim of "expelling the capitalists from the productive domain" (Sorel 2009, 161). His defence of revolutionary violence eschewed all ideas of social reform or reconstruction; the myth of the general strike was sustained by the emotional power of redemption.

The dangers of an approach that condemned representative democracy as corrupt and was deliberately vague about its social goals quickly became apparent. The French movement provides alarming examples. For a number of years before the outbreak of the First World War Sorel associated with extreme right wing monarchists, taking nationalistic, anti-Semitic and anti-democratic positions, and although he tired of this line by 1914, his work was later appropriated by sections of Italian fascism (Wilde 1986). One of Sorel's followers, Georges Valois, deserted the anarcho-syndicalists to join the extreme Right, founding the first fascist group in France in 1925 before swinging back to syndicalism (Ridley 1970, 236). Another friend of Sorel, Hubert Lagardelle, who once defended revolutionary syndicalism as the only way forward for the working class in debate with Emile Durkheim (Lukes 1973, 542-6), became an adherent of

Italian fascism in the 1920s. He served in the Vichy government in France as Minister for Labour in 1942-43, creating a fascist charter of labour with the slogan "Solidarity, Duty, Sacrifice" (Ridley 1970, 237-238).

The Class Struggle Approach

The "class struggle" approach to solidarity was first advocated by Karl Marx and Friedrich Engels in the *Communist Manifesto* of 1848. They portrayed the development of history as a succession of class struggles, culminating in the final clash between the bourgeoisie and the working class, or proletariat (Marx and Engels 2010a, 67-8). In this view, the proletariat did not refer to all oppressed groups but only to those workers who depended entirely on selling their labour power (Marx and Engels 2010a, 77-9). They might make alliances with other groups such as peasants or the self-employed, but it was their historic task to win the battle for democracy, seize state power, and, by taking production into social ownership, create a classless society free from oppression and exploitation (Marx and Engels 2010a, 86). Communists were not supposed to form a separate party opposed to other working class parties, but were to offer leadership in the struggle against the bourgeoisie, while recognising that this was always an international struggle (Marx 2010a, 79-80). In practice, this meant supporting the emerging trade union movements and working class political parties and campaigns while always pointing to the ultimate goal of taking production into social control. In his work with the First International he invoked solidarity as the "basic principle" of the movement, arguing that "we will only be able to attain the goal we have set ourselves if this life-giving principle acquires a secure foundation among the workers of all countries" (Marx 2010c, 325).

In Marx's lifetime the working class formed a majority of the population only in Britain, and nowhere was full political democracy achieved. Marx argued that it was entirely possible for workers to achieve their goal "by peaceful means" in countries with liberal political institutions, but it would require revolutionary force to achieve democracy in those that did not permit legal opposition (Marx 2010, 324). In the years following Marx's death in 1883 Engels reiterated the strategy of democratic struggle where possible and clandestine organisation where necessary (Wilde 1999, 198-200). Socialism could be won only through the mass mobilisation of the working class in political struggle and the seizure of state power. Furthermore, to replace capitalism as an international system, "united action of the leading civilized countries" was one of the first conditions for success (Marx and Engels 2010a, 85). By the time of Engels' death in 1896, socialist parties had established themselves in most European countries and they formed part of the Second International, while trade unions were nationally organised and beginning to reach out to the mass of unskilled workers. This strategy offered a middle way between the ethico-inclusive and redemptive approaches. Its goal was a classless communist society, but it resolutely refused to argue for this in moral terms. It was also, if necessary, prepared to use violence to resist coercion by the ruling classes. In contrast to the redemptive model, it sought mass support for a strategy of building a viable social alternative, using all available means, including struggles for reforms, to build a majority that could win state power.

The class struggle model involved dilemmas, some of which were openly discussed in Marx's lifetime. Marx was well aware that engaging in legal forms of political and economic struggles might lead to the dilution of commitment to social revolution, with socialists lured into compromises within the existing social and political structures. He spoke witheringly of the ineffectiveness of the "parliamentary cretinism" of the French socialists in the Second Republic (Marx 2010b, 211), and warned the German socialists against becoming seduced by a "servile belief in the state" and a "democratic faith in miracles" (Marx 2010c, 357). Engels identified a tendency to settle for moderate or even reactionary policy initiatives because radical transformation became viewed as something for the "distant and unforeseeable future" (Engels 1989, 427-8). In other words, the material successes achieved by the working class movements could lull them into settling for piecemeal reform rather than social transformation. With massive resources developing in the form of party buildings, printing presses and publications, social and sporting clubs, there were strong material reasons not to provoke the state authorities (Geary 1989, 128-31). Marx was also aware that most trade union activity focused on winning better pay and conditions for its members rather than destroying capitalism. He urged the unions to act as organising centres for the complete emancipation of the working class, to organise among the unskilled workers and to convince the world that their efforts were not "narrow and selfish" but were aimed at winning freedom for the "downtrodden millions" (Marx 2010c, 91-92). The class struggle approach assumed that in the pursuit of its material interest the working class must threaten the system that reproduced its exploitation, but this was not always obvious in practice.

Another major problem for the class struggle approach was its ambiguous approach to the state. As we have seen, the seizure of state power was considered indispensable, yet in *The Civil War in France* Marx declares that "the working class cannot simply lay hold of the readymade state machinery, and wield it for its own purposes" (Marx 2010c, 206). Accordingly, Marx approved the radical administrative changes undertaken in the brief existence of the Paris Commune, such as the abolition of the standing army, the payment of officials at workers' rates, the election of judges and magistrates, and the election by all citizens of delegates who were fully accountable and subject to recall (Marx 2010c, 209-10). He praised the proposed national model of a federation of Communes that reserved only a "few but important functions" for central government Marx 2010c, 210). However, in a national state these "few" functions would have to include the regulation of national production by a common plan, clearly an enormous and unprecedented endeavour. The important questions of what forms of governance would be adopted and how they would remain accountable were left unanswered.

Marx termed the transition from capitalism to communism the "revolutionary dictatorship of the proletariat" (Marx 2010c, 355), by which he meant it must safeguard itself from usurpation by the old ruling forces, but did this mean that, in a political crisis, democracy itself might be dispensable? This was the interpretation adopted by Lenin when he dissolved the newly elected Constituent Assembly in Russia in 1918, but there is clear evidence not only that this contravened the views on democracy of both Marx and Engels, but also the vast majority of European social democrats. In *The Civil War in France* Marx had written that "nothing could be more foreign to the spirit of the Commune than to supersede universal franchise by hierarchic investiture" (Marx 2010c, 211). Six years after the Commune was suppressed by the newly established Third Republic, Marx expressed his hopes that the bourgeois republic would survive the threat of a *coup d'état* because the threat of another dictatorship was appalling–"no nation can afford to repeat the same stupidities too often" (Marx 1991, 278). Engels was an enthusiastic supporter of electoral politics in Germany, France, Italy and Britain in the early 1890s, and there was a consensus in the Second International that social democracy was an extension of the democratic principle to the social and economic sphere, not its negation (Wilde 1999, 204-5). Lenin's repudiation of representative democracy as "bourgeois democracy" was bitterly denounced by leading social democrats such as Rosa Luxemburg and Karl Kautsky (Luxemburg 1970, 387-95; Kautsky 1983, 123-5). Without democracy there can be no solidarity, and in the communist movement that developed worldwide after the Russian Revolution, solidarity was not a significant concept, replaced instead by "discipline" (Stjernø 2004, 265-7). It is not without irony that the free trade union movement that erupted in Poland in 1980 with the name of

Solidarity should play a decisive role in the collapse of communism in Europe.

Legacy

The class struggle model, with its ambiguities, triumphed within European socialism in the years between Marx's death and the outbreak of the First World War. The major socialist parties in Europe adhered to Marxist programmes and dominated the Second International. Only in Britain, where the Labour Party did not declare a socialist programme until 1918, did reformist socialism seek to engage constructively with social liberalism. The wave of strikes that swept Europe in the years before the war gave the impression of a mighty movement pushing for success in the not-too-distant future, but in reality socialist consciousness was relatively under-developed. Just how far the class struggle model of solidarity had failed to develop that wider commitment to social transformation became clear in 1914 when virtually all the socialist or labour parties of Europe voted to support the war efforts of their respective states. The Socialist International was shattered, destroyed by the determination of its leaders and their followers to put national solidarity above solidarity with the international working class (Braunthal 1967a, 355).

Perhaps no one was more shocked at capitulation of the International than Lenin, who within months declared it to be "dead" and began to campaign for the formation of a new International that would have no room for reformists (Braunthal 1967b, 44). Although he received little support for this position for the first three years of the war, the situation changed when Lenin's party, the Bolsheviks, seized power in November 1917 and quickly dispensed with representative democracy. It was against all the principles of class struggle and even the established policy of his party, which had been dedicated to the establishment of a democratic republic (Braunthal 1967b, 80-91). In a country in which the vast majority of the country were peasants and were the working class formed a small minority, a dictatorship was inevitable. The founding congress of the Third International in Moscow in 1919 under the leadership of the Bolsheviks excluded reformist socialists, provoking a profound worldwide split between revolutionary communists and reformist socialists (McDermott and Agnew 1996, 1-80). In most countries militant socialists joined the newly established communist parties, and dutifully followed the progressive elimination of democracy that developed in Russia during the Civil War and the rise to power of Stalin. The social-democrats continued to adhere to their reformist path, but with little prospects of winning power electorally because of the strength of the communists, with notable exceptions in Sweden and Britain. By the 1960s most of these parties had rejected the goal of replacing capitalism with a qualitatively different socialist society. Lenin's strategy was a clear example of redemptive solidarity, in which the "sell out" of the reformists had to be redeemed by the revolutionary purity of international communism. But in rejecting the progressive nature of representative democracy, now derisively dismissed as "bourgeois democracy," communism had jettisoned the pledge of the *Communist Manifesto* that the proletarian movement is "the self-conscious, independent movement of the immense majority, in the interests of the immense majority" (Marx 2010a, 78).

Despite retreating from the original goal of creating a socialist alternative to capitalism, the socialist and labour movements played a decisive role in securing the establishment of welfare states in Western Europe by the 1960s or 70s. Since the economic crisis of the late 1970s and early 1980s the emergence of economic globalisation driven by doctrinaire free-market neoliberalism has reversed the trend towards social equality and created disturbing new problems of social exclusion (Wilde 2013, 218-54). The phenomenon of neoliberalism has been incisively analysed through the lens of class analysis by David Harvey, who concludes that "if it looks like class struggle and acts like class war then we have to name it unashamedly for what it is" (Harvey 2009, 202). However, does it follow, as he insists, that the immense majority either surrender to its power or "respond to it in class terms?" This seems to me to be a rather desperate appeal to revive modes of struggle and levels of consciousness which no longer reflect the realities of what is possible, at least in the rich countries of the world. With so many productive and extractive industries now based in the less developed countries, there will be struggles that resemble the solidaristic struggles that shaped the historical development of Europe and North America. But there will also be struggles of a new kind, reflecting different coalitions of interests and new forms of consciousness. David McNally provides a good example in showing how, in Bolivia, the development of privatisation policies in the 1980s broke the strength of the established miners' trade union, but in the late 1990s mass movements developed in opposition to the privatisation of water and gas imposed at the behest of the International Monetary Fund. This quickly gave rise to a political movement involving new solidarities between a range of social groups representing peasants, women, public sector and private sector workers, unemployed and indigenous peoples (McNally 2011, 152-61). This was crowned by the decisive election victory of Evo Morales in 2005, and the adoption of redistributive policies and links with other left-wing

Latin American governments that offer a regional resistance to neoliberalism. These new coalitions of resistance express their cause in an explicitly ethical way, demanding respect for the dignity of all and an end to the worst forms of social injustice.

In the affluent states there has been a weakening of the old forms of working class solidarity, expressed in trade union activities and left-wing political parties. Economic globalisation has weakened the capacity of social democratic movements to exert regulatory control over national economies. Neoliberal economic policies have widened the gaps between rich and poor at both global and national levels, pushing social solidarity further out of reach. However, even during the period of neoliberal ascendancy, new forms of solidarity flourished around the new social movements, with struggles against sexism, homophobia, racism and xenophobia asserting rights of recognition and norms of tolerance that point to the need for a more pluralistic solidarity. Environmental movements have shown the necessity of coordinated global action as the only hope for saving the planet from the consequences of global warming, while One World movements demand radical regulatory and redistributive measures to lift billions out of severe poverty. These struggles are mobilised in an explicitly ethical way, with slogans like "make poverty history" bringing attention not only to the billions living in severe poverty in the less developed world, but also to the plight of the new poor in economically "developed" parts of the world. Likewise "we are the 99 per cent" draws attention to the injustice of the enrichment of the few at the expense of the many, while "whose world is it anyway?" demands the creation of social relations in which economics serves the social needs of the immense majority rather than sacrificing them on the altar of profit. This new politics of solidarity reaches back in spirit to the original ethico-inclusive model of solidarity, with inclusion now referring to the global sphere as well as the nation-state. The irrationality of neoliberalism was shown to the world by the financial crisis of 2008, but it continues to exert a stranglehold on national and global politics. If new forms of ethico-inclusive solidarity can break the divisive dominance of neoliberalism, it would open up a new horizon of global solidarity.

References

Bakunin, Jack. 1976. *Pierre Leroux and the Birth of Democratic Socialism, 1797 – 1848*. New York: Revisionist Press.

Bakunin, Mikhail. 1973. *Bakunin on Anarchy*. Edited by Sam Dolgoff. London: Allen and Unwin.

Bestor, Arthur E. 1948. "The Evolution of the Socialist Vocabulary." *Journal of the History of Ideas* 9 (3):259-302.

Blanc, Louis. 1841. *L'Organisation du travail*. Paris: Imprimarie De Dondey-Dupré.

—. 1966. "Socialism." *The Red Republican and The Friend of the People*, (July 1851). London: Merlin Press.

Blanqui, Louis-Auguste. 1832. "Defence Speech." *Louis-August Blanqui Archive*. Accessed December 12, 2012. http://www.marxists.org/reference/archive/blanqui.index.html.

Braunthal, Julius. 1967a. *History of the International, volume 1, 1864-1914*. Washington and New York: Praeger.

—. 1967b. *History of the International, volume 2, 1914-1943*. London: Nelson.

Claeys, Gregory. 1987. *Machinery, Money and the Millennium: From Moral Economy to Socialism, 1815-1860*. Princeton: Princeton University Press.

Durkheim, Emile. 1969. *The Division of Labor in Society*. Translated by George Simpson. New York: The Free Press.

Engels, Friedrich. 1989. Preface to "The Housing Question" by Karl Marx and Friedrich Engels, *Collected Works,* volume 26. London: Lawrence and Wishart.

Foner, Philip S. 1981. *British Labor and the American Civil War*. New York: Holmes and Meier Publishing.

Harvey, David. 2009. *A Brief History of Neoliberalism*. Oxford: Oxford University Press.

Horne, Alistair. 2002. *The Fall of Paris*. London: Pan.

Kautsky, Karl. 1983. "Dictatorship and Democracy." *Karl Kautsky: Selected Political Writings*. Edited by Patrick Goode. London: Macmillan.

Leroux, Pierre. 1985. *De L'Humanité*. Paris: Fayard.

Luxemburg, Rosa. 1971. "The Russian Revolution." *Rosa Luxemburg Speaks*. Edited by Mary-Alice Waters. New York: Pathfinder Press.

McDermott, Kevin, and Jeremy Agnew. 1996. *The Comintern: A History of International Communism from Lenin to Stalin*. Basingstoke: Macmillan.

McNally, David. 2011. *Global Slump: The Economics and Politics of Crisis and Resistance*. Oakland, CA: PM Press.

Marx, Karl. 1991. "Letter to Friedrich Adolph Sorge, 27 September 1877." In *Karl Marx and Friedrich Engels: Collected Works*, volume 45. London: Lawrence and Wishart.

—. 2010a. *The Revolutions of 1848*. London: Verso.

—. 2010b. *Surveys From Exile*. London: Verso.

—. 2010c. *The First International and After*. London: Verso.

Maw, Ben. 2008. "The Democratic Anti-Capitalism of Bronterre O'Brien." *Journal of Political Ideologies* 13 (2):201-26.

Pilbeam, Pamela. 2000. *French Socialists Before Marx*. Teddington: Acumen.

Ridley, F. F. 1970. *Revolutionary Syndicalism: The Direct Action of its Time*. Cambridge: Cambridge University Press.

Roberts, Stephen. 1999. "Feargus O'Connor in the House of Commons, 1847-1852." *The Chartist Legacy*. Edited by O. Ashton, R. Fyson and S. Roberts. London: Merlin.

Sewell, William H. 1997. *Work and Revolution in France: The Language of Labor from the Old Regime to 1848*. Cambridge: Cambridge University Press.

Sorel, Georges. 2009. *Reflections on Violence*. Cambridge: Cambridge University Press.

Stjernø, Steinar. 2004. *Solidarity in Europe: The History of an Idea*. Cambridge: Cambridge University Press.

Thompson, Dorothy. 1986. *The Chartists: Popular Politics in the Industrial Revolution*. Aldershot: Wildwood House.

Thompson, Noel. 1998. *The Real Rights of Man: Political Economies for the Working Class, 1775-1850*. London: Pluto.

Venturi, Franco. 1983. *Roots of Revolution: A History of the Populist and Socialist Movements in Nineteenth Century Russia*. Chicago: University of Chicago Press.

Wernick, David. 2001. *August Comte and the Religion of Humanity: The Post-Theistic Program of French Social Theory*. Cambridge: Cambridge University Press.

Wilde, Lawrence. 1986. "Sorel and the French Right." *History of Political Thought* 7 (2):361-74.

—. 1999. "Engels and Revolutionary Strategy." *Engels After Marx*. Edited by Terrell Carver and Manfred Steger. Pennsylvania: Pennsylvania State University Press.

—. 2013. *Global Solidarity*. Edinburgh: Edinburgh University Press.

Woodock, George. 1977. *Anarchism*. Harmondsworth: Penguin.

CHAPTER TWO

PARRHESIA AND SOLIDARITY:
RETHINKING THE POLITICS OF DIFFERENCE
WITH THE FINAL FOUCAULT

JOHN MCSWEENEY

At the beginning of his 1976 lecture course, *"Society Must Be Defended,"* French philosopher Michel Foucault acknowledged that his excavation of "genealogical fragments" from the history of psychiatry and the prison system appeared to be "leading nowhere" (Foucault 2003, 4). His attempted articulation of sites of difference that might exceed even the subtly differentiated networks of modern power appeared increasingly inadequate. Should he seek to construct upon these genealogical fragments a more substantive site of freedom, his discourse would risk becoming complicit with the unitary discourses of power, which they sought to contest (Foucault 2003, 11). Indeed, he saw that the sites of difference uncovered by genealogy had had to become ever more rapidly, finely and subtly articulated, and to depend increasingly for their construction upon the intellectual's erudition, if they were to be sufficiently sophisticated and genealogically invested to resist the assimilative capacities of contemporary power relations, even for a time (Foucault 2003, 8; see Deleuze 2006, 139). While he determined to go on as far as he could with this project against the odds, the evident difficulties faced by what may aptly be termed his "politics of difference" powerfully anticipated the crisis which would soon engulf his thought. Not only did he face the difficulty of sustaining unstable articulations of difference, of uncertain force, as a locus of political action, but the fact that sites of difference could only hope to remain politically effective by their ever greater and more rapid differentiation undermined the prospects for social solidarity (and collective political action).[1] Possible sites of solidarity must, as it were,

---

1. Solidarity is generally not an explicit theme in Foucault's work. However, in his

deconstruct themselves in favour of an increasingly singular conception of their difference to remain "ahead" of power, fragmenting the space of any possible solidarity or politics. Indeed, Foucault's sense of his position as intellectual dramatized this undermining of solidarity: the philosopher whose *Discipline and Punish* had only recently been taken up and deployed by protesting French prisoners in their cells, now saw himself as pursuing a discourse only properly accessible to the intellectual.[2] Against this backdrop, it is not surprising that Foucault soon lost a significant degree of confidence in the political effectiveness of the activism which had placed him in solidarity with diverse groups and individuals, throughout the 1970s until that time.

I wish to argue, however, that this is not Foucault's last word on the possibility of a politics centred on the valorisation of difference yet capable of supporting socio-political solidarity. His turn to the ancient Greeks in the final period of his work, to determine the genealogical roots of modern subjectivity, is often taken to constitute a retreat from politics into an ethics of the self—either an ethics of the liberal subject inimical to his earlier critique of power, (e.g. Paras 2006) or an aesthetics of the self which gives up on the possibility of politics (e.g. Žižek 1989, 2). Against this, I will argue that Foucault finds, in his final two lecture courses at the *Collège de France*, a framing of the care of the self in the ancient Greek notion of *parrhesia*, which recasts the articulation of one's "difference" as

---

1972 discussion with Gilles Deleuze, Foucault and Deleuze agree that in political action it is always a "multiplicity," or more precisely the individuals who form such a "groupuscule," who speak and act. Moreover, they are not represented by any individual (including the intellectual) or group "consciousness," but arrive at their own knowledge of the situation in which they find themselves (Foucault and Deleuze 1996, 75). Evoked here, then, is the notion of a grouping of diverse individuals who are united solely by a certain solidarity with one another in relation to a given political concern, and who, it is natural to suppose, act in solidarity with others beyond this multiplicity. At a minimum, Foucault's work in this period presupposes a solidarity-in-difference of political actors as the condition of collective political action. Moreover, his analyses of madness, disciplinary power and sexuality reflect aspects both of his own experience of oppression and exclusion and an evident concern with wider, related oppressions and exclusions. Indeed, Foucault's work and activism might be said to be informed by something like Lawrence Wilde's notion of human solidarity as "a feeling of sympathy shared by subjects within and between groups, impelling supportive action and pursuing social inclusion" (See Wilde 2013, 1).
2. Foucault arrives at a form of the Marxist conception of the relation of the intellectual to the masses which he and Deleuze had criticized in their 1972 discussion (Foucault and Deleuze 1996, 74-75).

an implicit act of solidarity and an explicitly political act; that Foucault discovers a politics of difference resonant with the solidarity with the oppressed, excluded, marginalised and "disciplined," which had been a constant of his work throughout his career. The presence of such a conception of subjectivity within the original matrix (genealogical roots) of Western subjectivity holds out the possibility that a similar solidaristic, parrhesiastic practice will prove viable and effective within the matrix of contemporary subjectivity and politics.

Parrhesia

Foucault's analysis of care of the self as an aesthetics of the self—a major theme of his final 1984 publications and interviews, but reflecting the focus of his *Collège de France* lectures only to 1982 (Gros 2005, 507-17)—represents a significant advance upon his work in the mid-1970s. It succeeds in articulating the elaboration, and indeed cultivation, of difference as a locus of subjectivity. Care of the self, in this formulation, genealogically anticipates the structure of Foucault's revised "governmental" conception of subject-power relation of the late 1970s, in which power depends upon the subjectivation rather than the subjection of individuals—that is, it constitutes the individual as free subject (free *and* subjected, subjected *as* "free") rather than merely dominated (Foucault 2007, 87ff). As an aesthetics of the self, care of the self involves the cultivation of a relation to oneself of freeing oneself from oneself, *se déprendre de soi-même* (Foucault 2000a, 8). In other words, rather than attempt to construe sites of difference as the locus of a subjectivity resistant to power, care of the self as an aesthetics of the self involves an experimental, "ascetic" practice (an *"ascesis"*) which aims to discover what it is of oneself that one may do without—what of the self, constituted in the relation to power, may be shown to be inessential to one's subjectivity and thus a function of power (Foucault 2000a, 9; Foucault 1992, 305). Attention to difference, specifically one's experience of one's "self-difference," becomes a locus of the "subtraction" of power from subjectivity. In this reading, the tension in Foucault's analysis lies not so much in any aestheticization of subjectivity as that the ancient Greek "aesthetic" care of the self belongs to the (male) citizen's private preparation for public life, rather than his public, political activity as such. Care of the self aimed at producing the balanced, moderate individual prepared for the vicissitudes of public life, rather than constituting a mode of public life as such. The question remains, then, as to whether the care of the self may be transposed into a contemporary ethico-*political* practice, or remains politically-constrained by its genealogical roots in private subjective practices.

These tensions (and the charge that the final Foucault simply retreats into ethics) are addressed by his discovery, in his 1983 lecture course at the Collège de France, *The Government of Self and Others* (Foucault 2010), of the existence of a broader significance to *parrhesia*, a term which he had previously encountered in relation to spiritual direction. In that context, *parrhesia*, which literally means to "say all," but also had the connotation of speaking frankly or freely telling the truth, described the frank speech of the spiritual director to the directee (Foucault 2005, 366-8). Now, however, Foucault discovers the political significance of *parrhesia*, a significance that becomes fully clear and further radicalized by his discovery of a politicised, parrhesiastic conception of care of the self in the following year's course, *The Courage of Truth* (Foucault 2011).

In *The Government of Self and Others*, Foucault reconstructs two precise notions of *parrhesia* dispersed across numerous texts, which grant the term its political importance and force. First, reflecting usage in later antiquity, he analyses the notion of *parrhesia* previously best known to Foucault readers through *Fearless Speech*, an edition of his 1983 Berkeley lectures established by Joseph Pearson (Foucault 2001). *Parrhesia* here refers to the speech of one to whom an injustice has been done by a powerful person—for instance, the tyrant—who publicly speaks the truth of that injustice to the more powerful person, from a position of weakness, but with courage and at no little risk and danger to themselves. Briefly, the convention of *parrhesia* allowed the powerful person to accept the speech of the parrhesiast without losing face, but it was equally within his power to bring the full force of his ire to bear upon the *parrhesiast*. As such, *parrhesia* was a dangerous, courageous activity that might realistically end in one's death, even as that danger and the courage it demanded was essential to the "weight" granted to the act of *parrhesia* (Foucault 2010, 48ff).

Crucial, for Foucault, then, is that *parrhesia* involves a very real constitution of oneself as the subject of the truth that one speaks, indeed, of a truth that one must speak,[3] binding oneself to it and accepting the consequences of one's frank speech. It involves a commitment of oneself, to the

---

3. The idea that the parrhesiast speaks out of a certain personal-subjective *necessity* (Foucault 2010, 66), even when it places him/her at risk, provides an important resonance with Foucault's acknowledgement of the "biographical" element in his work, of subjective experience (of exclusion, oppression, of constitution as "abnormal" and the passions these experiences give rise to (Foucault 2010, 120ff)) as the matrix of the emergence of the political and will be significant for the subjective intensity of solidarity constituted by *parrhesia*.

point of risking one's life, in a veritable retroactive constitution of one's self as the subject of this truth. Foucault is at pains to distinguish *parrhesia* from other forms of discourse in ancient Greece. He acknowledges that it might involve a certain "dramatics of discourse"—its public confrontation with the powerful is itself a powerful mode of articulating the truth, while its risking of the life of the speaker serves as a powerful "demonstration" or "persuasion" of its truth. Nevertheless, he argues that *parrhesia* was not defined by appeal to any technical methods of rhetoric, demonstration or persuasion, but by a mode of "plain speaking" distinct form them (Foucault 2010, 61-9, esp. at 68). As such, *parrhesia* is not merely any speaking of truth to power, which might be exercised through the methods of rhetoric, demonstration or persuasion, but a distinctive mode of truth-telling. Indeed, insofar as it bears upon the constitution of oneself as a subject, *parrhesia* is a mode of self-constitution, which promises to support a distinctive practice of the self.

The second notion of *parrhesia* analysed by Foucault is earlier, dating from the fourth century BCE, and relates to the political structure of the city-state. In this regard, Foucault cites Polybius that the early Greek city states are characterised by three things: *democratia*, *isegoria*, and *parrhesia*. *Democratia* refers to the participation of all citizens in power, *isegoria* is related to equality of rights and duties, freedoms and obligations, while *parrhesia* is the right of anyone, even one who has no official position, to speak in the assembly. The distinction of *isegoria* and *parrhesia* is of decisive significance, clarifying that the latter is not a straightforward instantiation of a democratic equality of speech. Rather, the right to speak the truth frankly, beyond official channels, prevents democracy from being reduced to its formal functions or de facto practices, either of which might well be inadequate in practice and fail to sustain that equality (Foucault 2010, 71). One might say *à la* Jacques Rancière that democratic equality can be achieved only in its assertion against its putative formal, institutionalised expression (Rancière 1999, 34ff).

Parrhesia is thus a crucial *political* mechanism of the Greek *polis*. It is a right to speak the truth grounded in equality and democratic access to power, which paradoxically exceeds every formal institutional expression of democratic equality, in order to preserve it: "*Parrhēsia* founds democracy and democracy is the site of *parrhēsia*" (Foucault 2011, 300). As Foucault shows via a detailed reading of Euripides' *Ion*, *parrhesia*—although rooted in the rights of citizenship—is a discourse of "ascendancy," of taking "leadership," in which citizens of the "first rank" emerge to confront the *polis* with its truth. In principle, it is democratic in form, precisely because it speaks the truth of and about the polis yet "leaves others the freedom to speak, and allows freedom to those who have to obey, or leaves them free at least insofar as they will only obey if they can be persuaded" (Foucault 2010, 104). It should be noted here, however, that, although *parrhesia* within the assembly is a political right of the citizen, it shares the agonistic structure of the later *parrhesia* of the powerless. Although power is here "constitutional," it is still a question of confronting that power with an uncomfortable truth. There is no guarantee of its acceptance, no guarantee that the parrhesiast within the assembly will be recognised as a democratic leader, rather than condemned as an agitator who speaks falsely in favour of particular interests. Indeed, if rejection of one's frank speech does not bear the dangers of the powerless speaking the truth against the tyrant, it nonetheless could have significant negative consequences for one's standing and influence within the polis.

In this regard, Foucault highlights that such *parrhesia* is marked by the problems that beset a democratic leadership by the "best," (for example, the dominance of leadership by members of the traditional power-holding families, the role of popularity) as well as by the problem concerning how the truth of a citizen's *parrhesia* may be determined (with the threat of the degeneration of the assembly into a cacophony of competing voices and interests). As such, his argument partly bears parallels with Rancière's when the latter highlights the concerted effort of even Plato and Aristotle to ensure that democracy would not disrupt the rule of "best" (the aristocrats) and the "useful" (the wealthy) over the *demos* or mass of the people (Rancière 1999, 61ff). Nevertheless, Foucault's text suggests an important nuance: that democracy depends on the emergence of (parrhesiastic) leaders if it is to sustain the equality enshrined in its institutions, such that the issue is not with the emergence of leadership within democracy as such, but with the politics of that leadership, of how the "best" or "useful" are defined and how access to leadership is effectively controlled.

This problematic is echoed and extended, for Foucault, by the fact that the later notion of *parrhesia* as the speaking of the truth to power both is a generalisation and, arguably, marks a degradation of the *parrhesia* of the democratic assembly. His analysis outlines how over time there is an extension of the right to exercise *parrhesia* beyond the formal context of the assembly, yet that this right emerges in part out of necessity as *parrhesia* comes to be treated with increasing suspicion within the assembly (as degenerating into the voicing of interests rather than a speaking of the truth) and people are increasingly confronted with both a range of forms of power, formal and de facto, other than democracy. *Parrhesia* is inserted within a political field which may extend from democracies that welcome *parrhesia* as their founding principle and guarantee, through democracies that view *parrhesia* with varying degrees of suspicion as disruptive of good democratic governance; to tyrannies, monarchies and oligarchies within which the *parrhesia* of the ruler's advisor concerning his rule is viewed as critical to it,[4] yet within which the powerless may have to resort to the naked courage of telling the truth to the powerful, to attain justice, with all of the risk that such *parrhesia* implies.

A brief consideration of Sally J. Scholz's helpful taxonomy of solidarities and their characteristics will help clarify how the specific spectrum of contexts within which *parrhesia* is inserted and constituted begins to address the ultimate concern of this chapter: Foucault's elaboration of a politics of difference capable of supporting socio-political solidarity (Scholz 2008). Scholz argues that all forms of solidarity have three characteristics: the binding together of individuals into some kind of group, mediation between individuals and a genuine collectivity, and collective responsibility/positive moral obligations. In turn, she distinguishes between social, civic and political forms of solidarity. Social solidarity is characterised by a sense of common identity or a shared experience of oppression. The extent of the obligations arising from social solidarity reflects the intensity of what is shared in common (identity, experience of oppression). Civic solidarity, in turn, is the solidarity of citizens with one another as citizens, its responsibilities being mediated through state apparatuses. Finally, political solidarity is oppositional, involving commitment to challenging an injustice, oppression or situation of vulnerability, and unity here arises from this commitment rather than social or civic bonds and entails the responsibility of action toward the goal of eliminating the given injustice or oppression.

Against this framework, *parrhesia*, as Foucault analyses it, can be understood, at one end of its spectrum, to reflect a complex combination of civic and political solidarity: it is civic insofar as it is an action of the citizen within the democratic assembly in solidarity with his fellow citizens toward the goal of ensuring that the rights of the citizen are protected. It is, moreover, an individual act that mediates the democratic unity of all citizens. Yet it is also a form of political solidarity insofar as it exceeds the channels of the civic per se, in an oppositional act which seeks to realise civic democratic rights and principles (as well as the good of the polis more generally) against actions or decisions which impede their realisation. (It might also be noted that *parrhesia* within the assembly may be motivated by abstract democratic principles or concrete injustices or

---

4. It is beyond the scope of this chapter to discuss Foucault's treatment of this form of *parrhesia* in any detail.

inequalities, such that its roots may lie in civic, political or social factors.) At the other end of the spectrum, where *parrhesia* is practiced outside of political structures as a speaking of truth to power, it will derive from experience of oppression or injustice, and thus bear a certain political force, but remain circumscribed by the one-to-one form of the parrhesiastic relation. The injustice suffered by the parrhesiast may well reflect a broader political issue, or at least a wrong wrought by a ruler upon a citizen. However, in Foucault's analysis, there is no suggestion that an ancient Greek parrhesiastic intervention has, or is intended to have, any broader import or wider political impact. It is circumscribed as an exchange between individuals, which addresses a specific injustice. (Indeed, this circumscription is important in facilitating the powerful person's acknowledgement of an injustice, insofar as it suggests an instance of the inappropriate exercise of power, rather than the raising of fundamental questions about the form and extent of that power.) Nonetheless, this form of *parrhesia* reveals the intensity of its subjective motivation and, potentially, that an intense "social" motivation may well lie behind it. This form of *parrhesia* is grounded in the passion of the one wronged for justice, a passion which may not simply be the passion of a wronged individual as such, but a passion for the rights that ought to follow upon being a citizen. What is not clear from Foucault's 1983 lectures is how the individual's *parrhesia* outside of structures of power can exemplify an explicit solidaristic politics of difference. This, however, is a question addressed by Foucault's deepened examination of this form of *parrhesia* in the following year's lecture course.

Via Ethical Parrhesia to the Cynics

The Courage of Truth, Foucault's 1984 lecture course at the Collège de France, shows how, from the fourth century BCE, *parrhesia* came to constitute a distinct mode of care of the self. In addition to the transformations in the notion already discussed, he argues that suspicion concerning the manner in which *parrhesia* allows all to speak unscrupulously on behalf of their interests, led to it being increasingly re-figured, more safely, as a form of telling the truth *about oneself*, that is, about one's existence within the *polis*. It thus increasingly came to function as a dimension of care of the self rather than a directly political act. In this respect, *parrhesia* is increasingly transposed from a political into an ethical practice, in which critique of politics may arise but is, at best, indirect. For Foucault, Socratic dialogue is the instance *par excellence* of such an ethical, parrhesiastic truth-telling directed toward care of the self. Socrates' dialogic practice adds immeasurable depth to the notion of constituting oneself as a subject of *parrhesia*,[5] yet it is also marked by ambiguity: Socrates' acceptance of the depoliticization of *parrhesia* risks aligning him too closely with the societal order that he wishes to criticize. As Frédéric Gros puts it, Socrates undoubtedly sets out "to disturb the good (or false) conscience" of his fellow citizens. But "apart from his mania for interminable discussions, he adopts a rather orderly and traditional way of life" (Gros 2011, 351). And, indeed, for Foucault, Socrates' practice exemplifies the tensions in ethical *parrhesia*. One key tension, upon which Foucault focuses, emerges from the relation between life and logos in ethical *parrhesia* and bears upon the problem of politics. Via a reading of Plato's *Laches*, Foucault argues, that, ultimately for Socrates, one cannot arrive at a reasonable understanding of courage, or the virtues more generally, and thus that care of the self commits us to an ongoing struggle to *relate* our existence to *logos*, that is, to reason (Foucault 2011, 121ff). The deep point here is that insofar as *parrhesia* has become a telling the truth about oneself, and thus a practice directed in the first instance toward oneself, the truth of one's *parrhesia* could only be properly established via the rationality of the parrhesiastic *logos* in the dialogue with oneself. (Even in his encounters with others, Socrates attempts to have them convince themselves of the rationality of his arguments.) Thus, when adequate rational understanding proves elusive, Socrates can only demonstrate the truth of his *parrhesia* (and thus support others in caring for themselves) by giving form to this self-care in his existence. If speech and life are thus connected, Foucault argues that this connection constitutes only a harmony of these two elements. That is, one's life remains an *external* proof of the truth of one's *logos*, any political implications of one's *parrhesia* remaining subtly external to one's ethical truth-telling. (Foucault thus arrives at an implicit critique of his earlier appeal to the care of the self as an ethics of the self—which had centred on Socrates to a significant degree—recognising the political limit of a practice defined primarily in terms of a personal-subjective practice.)

By contrast, Foucault goes on to argue that the Cynic way of life (some elements of which are to be found, to a degree, in Socrates' practice) is a direct test of truth, of what is truly necessary to human life (Foucault 2011, 171).[6] In a life of poverty and refusal of attachment, which invites

---

5. Foucault devotes almost five lectures to examining Socratic *parrhesia*, including an analysis of Socrates attitude towards his death in parrhesiastic terms, an analysis rendered poignant by Foucault's own impending death (Foucault 2011, 73ff).
6. It should also be noted that no less than is the case with other of his works (as discussed later in this chapter), Foucault reads the Cynics from a specific perspective, for specific ends, with the potential for distortions and productive

rejection and abuse, the Cynic interrogates the truth of human existence by living the accepted principles upon which society and societal life are based, but takes them to their extreme, logical conclusions, revealing both their limits as rational principles and/or the limits of their deployment within society (Foucault 2011, 232). For example, the notion of the "true life" in Greek culture is variously grounded in principles of non-concealment, purity, conformity to nature, and sovereignty. Taking these principles literally, Foucault argues, the Cynics led an absolutely public and shameless life, purified of wealth and attachment, in a radically animal fashion, and in a radical, uncompromising commitment to exercising sovereignty over that life (by refusing submission to the sovereigns and sovereignties of social life). The Cynic life thus becomes a "scandal", "the grimace of the true life," and the "broken mirror" (Foucault 2011, 227, 270) in which people are confronted with the contradictions and inconsistencies of their way of life—in brief, the Cynic life confronts society with its truth: "Cynic courage of truth consists in getting people to condemn, reject, despise, and insult the very manifestation of what they accept, or claim to accept at the level of principles" (Foucault 2011, 234). As such, the Cynic's life no longer simply corroborates the truth of his logos, but is the locus of the interrogation of that truth. It is thus at once a care of the self *and* fundamentally political. On the one hand, it interrogates the principles by which one's self is constituted, aiming to determine what is essential to human life and what is detrimental to it. On the other hand, it not only pursues this interrogation publicly but does so as an explicit examination of the principles that underpin life in the polis, an examination, moreover, which confronts their fellow citizens and those in power with that examination.

It is beyond the scope of this chapter to do justice to Foucault's rich and detailed analysis of the Cynic life and Cynic practice. However, it will be important to highlight several features of the Cynic courage of truth, which are critical for Foucault, enabling him to evoke a radically refigured politics of difference (supportive of social solidarity), in continuity with fundamental impulses of his work from the early 1970s. These features are: one's life as matrix of the Cynic philosophical gesture, the articulation of one's difference as a mode of truth-telling, care of the self as simultane-ously a care for others, and the importance of the philosophical tradition to this philosophical life.

First, Cynic *parrhesia*, like all forms of *parrhesia*, involves a binding of oneself to the truth one has told and a constitution of oneself as the

---

readings that this generates.

subject of that truth, with all of the courage that this requires and all of the risk it entails. (The precise quality and force of Cynic *parrhesia* arises from the juxtaposition of a genuine care of the self with a radical commitment to telling, or rather living, the truth of one's life.) However, more than this, in Cynic *parrhesia*:

> In all meanings of the word, one "exposes" one's life. That is to say, one displays it and risks it. One risks it by displaying it; and it is because one displays it that one risks it. (Foucault 2011, 234)

Foucault certainly intends here to contrast "lived" Cynic *parrhesia* with "discursive" Socratic *parrhesia*. However, more than this, he suggests that risking one's life is not simply an intentional philosophical gesture, but that one's life is the matrix of any such philosophical gesture; that a subjective experience of the contradictions of the principles of life in the polis is the root of the Cynic's practice and that the Cynic is impelled to expose their very self because of the contradictions in the would-be "good" life, which they experience. As such, Foucault draws implicit parallels with his own preoccupations with questions such as madness and sexuality, which he acknowledges are rooted in his "biography." Foucault was somewhat circumspect concerning his interest in madness, suggesting in a 1978 interview that he has had a "complex relationship" to it (Foucault 2000b, 244), while in a later interview he stresses only the significance of his brief professional experience of working in a psychiatric institution (Foucault 1988, 10). However, his *History of Madness* points additionally to a profounder question of the relationship of madness to reason, as its condition of possibility and potential point of destruction, with this question finding clear echoes in Foucault's personal history in this period (see Macey 1993, 27ff). The "exposure" of Foucault's life in his concern with sexuality is rather more evident, especially from the early 1980s where he wrote and gave interviews about the gay movement, its significance, and his participation in it.[7] In other words, part of the commitment of the care of self must be this exposing of oneself, of how one's life and self reveals the limits, and of the distortions and injustices of society's rational principles, with the risks that one will be deemed mad, abnormal, and so on.

Second, Foucault argues that, for the Cynics, exposing and risking one's life points to the possibility of a different world. Specifically, he

---

7. In the early 1980s, Foucault also spoke about the importance of one's "passions" as the ultimate, obscure ground of political action and which makes one's "existence a work" (Foucault 1996, 313, 317; Veyne 1997, 227).

suggests that the Cynics pursuit of another life (*vie autre*) is a critique of a Platonism which tends to prioritise "*the* other world" (*l'autre monde*) of the Forms and "*the* other life" (*l'autre vie*) of the soul which it supports. Instead, the Cynics pursuit of an "other life" *within* (immanent to) the life of the polis, causes the possibility of an "other world" (a different world) in the here and now to loom up. That is, the Cynics live the difference of their existence from that supposed to derive from the principles of life in the polis (Foucault 2011, 319-20). As such, they demonstrate the existence of other possibilities of how given principles might be enacted, as well as the manner in which these principles in practice are typically circumscribed, interpreted and distorted by other unspoken principles and prejudices. In this way, they point to the contingency of the current sociopolitical order and open spaces of difference. In other words, Cynic parrhesiastic truth-telling is not a matter of arriving at the truth of what is, or of the essence of a thing—a truth of the same (Foucault 2011, 314). It rather involves, as Foucault puts it, "an essential position of difference" (Gros 2011, 356).[8] To tell the truth is both to tell the truth of one's difference (from the normal, the same, etc.), and to point to the possibility of a different life. In this manner, Foucault finds in the Cynics a parallel (and genealogical antecedent) to his own attempt to valorise difference in relation to politics.

As seen, Foucault's work in the 1970s threatened to become ever more fragmentary and (tactically) ever more marginal, raising questions about its status, viability and ultimate value. Later in the 1970s, as he sought to reorient his work, Foucault admitted that even his earlier more substantial histories were each written from a particular perspective—they were not strictly true in the usual academic sense. Rather, they were, he proposed, "fictions" that might become true, if the new possibilities of thought and experience they opened up came to be true in people's lives and integrated into knowledge (Foucault 2000b, 243-5). He had in mind for instance the way in which his history of madness had profoundly influenced thinking on mental illness among a wide diversity of professionals, academics and ordinary people, while remaining a work which undoubtedly was written from a certain perspective, with certain emphases which would not meet the standards of neutrality and comprehensiveness more typically required of academic arguments. In this manner, Foucault was able to re-establish the relation of his work to truth. However, it remained outside of truth, having in itself an indeterminate status—his work might prove to be

---

8. This expression is found at the end of the manuscript of Foucault's final lecture at the Collège de France in 1984. However, due to time constraints it was not delivered as part of the lecture.

merely subjective or distorted, and there exist no criteria to arrive at a judgment on this question. Indeed, even when effective in changing how people think, his work could be considered to have had merely a distorting influence on thinking about a given question, such that the idea that it had "become true" would constitute a denigration of the notion of truth. Now, in light of the Cynics, Foucault can argue that his work participates in a significant tradition of truth-telling, and give density and weight to the notion that "there is no establishment of the truth without an essential position of difference" (Gros 2011, 356).

Third, while the Cynic aims at care of the self, two factors relate him to others. In the first instance, the Cynic always has a duty to "supervise" others:

> The Cynics have a much greater task, responsibility, and merit with regard to the whole of humanity since, to the best of their ability, they exercise supervision (*episkopountes*) over all men, observing what they do, how they spend their life, what they care for, and what they neglect contrary to their duties. (Foucault 2011, 312)

In turn, then, both in his self-care and in his concern with others, he is always interested in what is essential to being human and thus he is primarily concerned with that, in others and in their lives, which has to do with humanity as such. And thus his care of himself and his concern with others are one and the same thing. As Foucault puts it, "it is his own solidarity with humankind which is questioned, which is the object of his care . . . when he looks at how men act and spend their lives" (Foucault 2011, 312). This interpretation resonates with Foucault's own view that, for all of its roots in specific experiences of marginalisation, exclusion, etc., his project is not a matter of transforming personal experiences into discourse, but of touching upon broader structures and issues, which make possible a certain "transformation" in others (Foucault 2000b, 244).

Fourth, and following on from this point, although the lived life is the primary locus of truth-telling, Cynicism, at the same time, stands in complex relation to philosophy and the philosophical life. Philosophy is a preparation for the Cynic life of taking care of oneself; and to do so one must study what is really essential for existence and live life according to the principles that one formulates. Cynicism is thus simultaneously "inside and outside philosophy"—a characteristic of it which, Foucault suggests, makes it particularly interesting to him (Foucault 2011, 237). Not least, it can be argued that Foucault here finds a resolution to the problem of the relation of the intellectual to others, which afflicted his thought in the mid-1970s. His analysis of Cynic life and practice, suggests a framework in which lived *parrhesia* has priority over philosophical reflection upon it. Even if philosophy is generally considered necessary to the Cynic life, it is secondary to it; it may help deepen the Cynic's ability to live the truth of himself and the polis, but the parrhesiastic life is not something accessible exclusively or primarily to the philosopher. In this sense, there is a fundamental equality between the philosopher and any other parrhesiast—an equality grounded in the exercise of *parrhesia*. And indeed, philosophy is granted a particular configuration in relation to this equality: it is rooted in lived experience, yet potentially directs it, insofar as philosophy aims to uncover the principles, structures, exclusions, and so on, which traverse and condition lived experience and which prompt the felt need for the parrhesiastic care of the self in the first place. Moreover, if Cynicism is simultaneously "within and outside philosophy," then equally we might say that philosophy, in an important sense, moves repeatedly outside itself. It is repeatedly drawn outside itself—its paradigms, methods and certainties are repeatedly ruptured by the *parrhesia* of experience.

Parrhesia and Solidarity

The preceding analysis suggests that Foucault's analysis of Cynic care of the self supports a rich reframing of his earlier politics of difference, capable of sustaining socio-political solidarity. His genealogical methodology had threatened to fragment the spaces of subjective and collective resistance, while his aesthetic conception of care of the self remained constrained to a freeing oneself from oneself—and thus to a kind of blind, negative and potentially inward-looking approach to the truth of one's subjectivity. Now, however, the parrhesiastic telling of the truth of one's difference (from the socio-political order of the same) is a constitution of the self as a subject of truth. While both the aesthetic care of the self and *parrhesia* reveal the contingency and distortions of the "ordering" structures, discourses and principles that shape lives, as well as the unspoken, additional relations which give them their specific qualities and force, there is a decisive shift in tone and emphasis. The focus is no longer precisely on subtracting power from subjectivity, or of constructing one's life as a work of art which one hopes may inspire others to do the same. Rather it is a matter, in the first instance, of the subject laying claim, in a confrontation with power, to the right to and the possibility of a different life. Critical here, for the construction of a politics, is the difference between the primacy of a being given over to an "artistic" process, which ultimately yields a certain self-freeing subjective relation to oneself, but never quite arrives at a defining constitution of the subject, and the (alternative)

primacy of a constituting of oneself as subject of one's difference and the
possibilities for a different life that it holds. The latter embodies a direct
political commitment and confrontation, while fully respecting the com-
plication of one's "Self-difference."

In turn, several features of Foucault's analysis together clearly point to
the potential for solidarity within such a politics. (Foucault tends to focus
on the material at hand, rather than explicitly linking that material to his
own practice.) First, as we have seen, Foucault argues that, while *parrhesia* arises from the subjective experience of one's difference, it is always
concerned with how that subjective experience reflects and bears upon
broader human experience in relation to the principles of life in the polis.
He is explicit that lived Cynic *parrhesia* is always in solidarity with
broader human experience, that one cannot distinguish care of the self and
care for others—and we saw how this accords with Foucault's own practice throughout his career. Second, such *parrhesia* arises, moreover,
precisely out of an experience of exclusion, marginalisation or the many
subtle constraints imposed by the socio-political order. It is a demand for
justice, freedom, and the right to the possibility of a different life. Third,
the further conjunction of *committing* oneself and *exposing* one's life suggests something of the intensity of parrhesiastic practice and the solidarity
it embodies. For this conjunction not only suggests a radical, practical
commitment and risking of oneself, but that one is willing to expose the
particularities and peculiarities of one's own self and personality, of laying
bare what may well be deemed one's "madness," "abnormality," etc., to
care for oneself and others.

Many of the features of socio-political solidarity are thus met: a connection with others grounded in a sense of shared experience or commonly
suffered injustice, a real commitment to the other in which one risks oneself, a (nonetheless) individual practice which mediates collective
concerns. In addition, if the earlier *parrhesia* of the assembly existed at the
limit of the polis, exceeding formal democratic possibilities of intervention, so too, in a more general sense, is parrhesiastic care of the self a
politics that by definition exceeds the limits of the socio-political, in order
to realise its ideals. The solidarity arising from *parrhesia* is the solidarity
of risking standing outside of formal structures and modes of action, to
transform them. Indeed, Foucault tends to hold together the different senses of *parrhesia* he uncovers to generate the density of the term's meaning.
Thus, it is important to locate Cynic *parrhesia* as representing one end of
the spectrum of possible forms of *parrhesia* outlined in 1983. In this respect the civic-political solidarity embodied in the *parrhesia* of the
assembly stands in relation to the political solidarity of Cynic *parrhesia*,

both sharing a complex relation to the outside of the political. Once more this suggests something of the depth of solidarity implied by *parrhesia*: that one is willing to place oneself outside of the normal, available spaces of civic-political action to care for self and others. At the same time, Foucault's attention both to the *parrhesia* of the assembly and Cynic *parrhesia* outside of such formal structures of power, suggests a more comprehensive political stance, willing to engage with formal political structures and practices where possible and relevant; a politics which is committed to standing with the victims of injustice, exclusion, etc., but which does so within a commitment to the democratic project.

Finally, Foucault's revised conception of the place of philosophy in relation to *parrhesia* suggests the contours of the solidarity of the intellectual with others. The intellectual is a fellow traveller with non-intellectuals, who no less than them must live the truth of his/her existence. Philosophy may enable people their practice of *parrhesia*, but in no way is a quasi-Marxist avant-garde of political practice. Indeed, as seen, philosophy becomes refigured as a repeatedly interrupted and re-invented discourse, through its relation to the primacy of lived *parrhesia*.

There remain undoubtedly questions about the strengths and weaknesses of Foucault's framing of political practice in terms of *parrhesia*, not least the viability of re-animating the parrhesiastic impulse in a modern context (see, for example, Marzocca 2013). However, what cannot be doubted is that he succeeds in finding a renewed articulation of his own practice which reflects his career-long passionate solidarity with others, in difference. And, indeed, what Foucault's analysis highlights is that crucial to this or any such politics is the willingness to commit and risk oneself in a living of the truth of one's experience and of the "order" of one's society, for oneself and others. A fundamental challenge of Foucault's final lecture course is precisely this: what or how much are we willing to risk to tell the truth of our society and thus take care of ourselves and others?

References

Deleuze, Gilles. 2006. "On the New Philosophers (Plus a More General Problem)." In *Two Regimes of Madness: Texts and Interviews 1975-1995*, 139-47. New York: Semiotext(e).

Foucault, Michel. 1988. "Truth, Power, Self: An Interview with Michel Foucault (conducted by Rex Martin)." In *Technologies of the Self: A Seminar with Michel Foucault*, 9-15. Edited by Luther H. Martin *et al.* Amherst: The University of Massachusetts Press.

—. 1992. *The Use of Pleasure: The History of Sexuality*. Volume 2. Translated by Robert Hurley. London: Penguin.

—. 1996. "Passion According to Werner Schroeter." In *Foucault Live, Collected Interviews 1961-1984*, edited by Sylvère Lotringer, 313-21. New York: Semiotext(e).

—. 2000a. "What is Enlightenment?" *Ethics: Essential Works of Foucault 1954-1984, Volume 1*, edited by Paul Rabinow, 303-319. London: Penguin.

—. 2000b. "Interview with Michel Foucault (conducted by D. Trombadori)." In *Power: Essential Works of Foucault 1954-1984, Volume 3*, edited by Paul Rabinow, 239-297. New York: The Other Press.

—. 2001. *Fearless Speech*. Edited by Joseph Pearson. New York: Semiotext(e).

—. 2003. *"Society Must be Defended": Lectures at the Collège de France, 1975-76*. Edited by Mauro Bertani and Alessandro Fontano. Translated by David Macey. London: Allen Lane.

—. 2005. *The Hermeneutics of the Subject: Lectures at the Collège de France, 1981-1982*. Edited by Frédéric Gros, trans. Graham Burchell. New York: Palgrave Macmillan.

—. 2007. *Security, Territory, Population: Lectures at the Collège de France, 1977-1978*. Edited by Michel Senellart. Translated by Graham Burchell. New York: Palgrave Macmillan.

—. 2010. *The Government of Self and Others: Lectures at the Collège de France, 1982-1983*. Edited by Frédéric Gros, trans. Graham Burchell. New York: Palgrave Macmillan.

—. 2011. *The Courage of Truth, The Government of Self and Others II: Lectures at the Collège de France, 1983-1984*. Edited by Frédéric Gros. Translated by Graham Burchell. New York: Palgrave Macmillan.

Foucault, Michel, and Gilles Deleuze. 1996. "Intellectuals and Power." In *Foucault Live, Collected Interviews 1961-1984*, edited by Sylvère Lotringer, 74-82. New York: Semiotext(e).

Gros, Frédéric. 2005. "Course Context." In *Michel Foucault, The Hermeneutics of the Subject: Lectures at the Collège de France, 1981-1982*, edited by Frédéric Gros and translated by Graham Burchell, 507-50. New York: Palgrave Macmillan.

Macey, David. 1993. *The Lives of Michel Foucault*. New York: Vintage Books.

Marzocca, Ottavio. 2013. "Philosophical Parrêsia and Transpolitical Freedom." *Foucault Studies* 15 (February):129-147.

Paras, Eric. 2006. *Foucault 2.0: Beyond Power and Knowledge*. New York: The Other Press.

Rancière, Jacques. 1999. *Dis-Agreement: Politics and Philosophy*. Translated by Julie Rose. Minneapolis and London: University of Minnesota Press.

Scholz, Sally J. 2008. *Political Solidarity*. Philadelphia: Penn State University Press.

Veyne, Paul. 1997. "The Final Foucault and his Ethics." In *Foucault and his Interlocutors*, edited by Arnold I. Davidson. Chicago: University of Chicago Press.

Wilde, Lawrence. 2013. *Global Solidarity*. Edinburgh: Edinburgh University Press.

Žižek, Slavoj. 1989. *The Sublime Object of Ideology*. New York and London: Verso.

CHAPTER THREE

DIFFERENCE, SOLIDARITY AND NON-IDENTITY: A NEGATIVE DIALECTICAL APPROACH TOWARDS SOLIDARITY

DAVID CHRISTOPHER STOOP

The history of the word solidarity is usually traced back to the French Revolution, even though it has its roots in Roman law, where it referred to the liability of a joint-debtor, the *obligatio in solidum* (Zoll 2000, 17-18). In the *Dictionnaire de l'Académie Françoise*, published in 1694, the word *solidité* (which later transformed into *solidarité*) is still defined in this legal sense: "Solidité refers in practical terms also to a commitment or obligation with several debtors, where each of them has to pay for the others the whole sum they owe together" (Académie Française 1694, 485).[1]

The concept of solidarity began to transcend the purely legal framework and acquired a strong political meaning in the aftermath of the French Revolution. The importance of solidarity and its close relation to the idea of fraternity is apparent in many early documents of the working-class movement, such as the "Provisional Constitution of the International Workers Association" (1864) that proclaims the "Solidarity among workmen of various professions within each land, and of the fraternal union of workers of different countries" (quoted according to Schieder 1974, 578). In the nineteenth century, early socialist thinkers such as Pierre Leroux or Charles Fourier drew upon solidarity as a political concept and discussed it in relation to workers' struggles (Wildt 1999, 209-215; Metz 1999).

But the concept has also received attention from the developing academic discipline of sociology. Auguste Comte, one of the "founding fathers" of modern sociology, used the term solidarity to describe the

---

1. Unless otherwise noted, all translations are my own.

cohesiveness of social groups (Comte 1985, 80). His approach has been adopted and extended by Emile Durkheim, who differentiates "mechanic" and "organic" solidarity. According to Durkheim, mechanic solidarity can be defined as "a more or less organised entity of beliefs and collective feelings shared by all members of the group" (Durkheim 1926, 99), whereas organic solidarity is described as a result of the division of labour in modern forms of production: "The more division of labour, the more everyone depends upon society. The activity of each individual is as individual as it is specialised" (Durkheim 1926, 101). With his account of solidarity, Durkheim explicitly formulates a problem that is still in the centre of every discussion about solidarity: How is it possible to reconcile individual freedom and collective duties?

Accounts of solidarity often focus on the question of social, moral and political cohesion and they consequently involve a strong notion of identity that is either derived from social belonging, a moral consensus, or a common political interest. Solidarity is then interpreted as a mutual obligation amongst equals. But as such, it also necessarily produces coercive effects towards the members of the solidarity group and exclusions towards those who are not included as equals.

In contrast to accounts of solidarity that rely on a positive notion of identity, I will draw upon Theodor W. Adorno's concept of negative dialectics to suggest a politics of non-identity as a possible way to avoid the opposition between individual freedom and solidarity. Negative dialectics first of all provides a logic of philosophic concepts that is closely linked to a critique of knowledge. I will, however, argue that it is also of great value in a narrower political context. As Adorno himself admits, the concept of negative dialectics seems to be contradictory since dialectics from Plato to Hegel always arrived at a positive through the negation of the negation.

In a first sense, dialectics suggests nothing else but that things do not vanish into their concept. From this, dialectics deducts a law of movement in contradictions. But in contrast to the dialectics of Hegel, the contradiction of negative dialectics is derived from non-identity and it does not establish any positive meaning: Negative dialectics is defined as the "consistent consciousness of non-identity"[2] (Adorno 2003b, 17). It acknowledges that concepts (*Begriffe*) can never fully grasp the complexity of being which resists any attempt to identify or represent it. But insofar concepts are an integral part of thinking, the problem of identification reaches into thought itself: "to think means to identify"

---

2. Quotes from Adorno's *Negative Dialektik* are translated on the basis of the translation provided by Dennis Redmond (Adorno 2001).

(Adorno 2003b, 16). In fact, identification is at the heart of Western logic which is based on the *tertium non datur*, the exclusion of the third. According to Adorno, traditional (Marxist) dialectics fails to grasp the non-identical because it is not radical enough in its negativity and falls back to the principle of identity:

> What is positive in itself is fetishized from the vernacular, in which human beings praise what they positively would be, finally to the bloodthirsty phrase of the positive forces. By contrast what is to be taken seriously about the unwavering negation is that it does not lend itself to the sanctioning of the existent. The negation of the negation does not make this revocable, but proves that it was not negative enough. (Adorno 2003b, 162)

According to Adorno, the conflict between the system of identity and the non-identical takes the form of a contradiction because "every one which does not suborn itself to the unity of the dominating principle, according to the measure of the principle, does not appear as a polyvalence which is indifferent to this, but as an infraction against its logic" (Adorno 2003b, 58). Adorno is in strong opposition to the logic of identification, but he also rejects the idea that the non-identical could be expressed as a positive. There are two dimensions to this: On the side of concepts, the non-identical can never be grasped in identifying terms. A constellation of concepts can provide insights, but the richness of being and becoming is ultimately inaccessible to concepts. On the side of materiality itself, the system of identifications and the reality of what Adorno calls the "administered society" prevent any autonomous positive form of non-identity. Adorno explicitly describes the system of identification in relation to the Marxian understanding of exchange value (abstract labour) and he understands it as a structuring force which is imposed on (while dialectically reproduced by) the individuals.

If postmodern theorists such as Gilles Deleuze criticise dialectics for milling everything into the contradiction, Adorno explicitly agrees that the dialectical method leads to an impoverishment of experience. But, as he argues, this impoverishment "proves itself to be entirely appropriate to the abstract monotony of the administered world. What is painful about it is the pain of such, raised to a concept" (Adorno 2003b, 18). The cult of the positive and the immediate is a sign of an insufficient reflection of the state of the world. Adorno argues against the idea of immediacy with reference to Bergson (but the argument equally applies to Deleuze):

Bergson created, in a *tour de force*, a different type of cognition for the sake of the non-conceptual. The dialectical salt was washed away in the undifferentiated flow of life; that which was materially solidified was dismissed as subaltern, instead of being understood along with its subalternity. Hatred of the rigid general concept produced a cult of irrational immediacy, of sovereign freedom amidst unfreedom. (Adorno 2003b, 20)

To sum up his argument, Adorno suggests that positive difference (which he does not deny) can in current society only be expressed as a contradiction, as the one that is non-identical in a system of identifications. It is exactly at this point, where solidarity is established as solidarity between non-identicals, between violations of the logic. But this solidarity needs to find its expression in negative critique. A non-identifying solidarity can therefore only be established as a *negative solidarity.*

The concept of negative dialectics has been criticised from different angles. One of the most widespread suspicions is that it leads to a "vicious cycle" (Hardt/Negri 2009, 97). According to Antonio Negri and Michael Hardt, the dialectical method "[. . .] accounts for the fact that Horkheimer and Adorno can see no way out, leaving humanity doomed to the eternal play of opposites" (Hardt/Negri 2009, 96-97). Negri and Hardt contrast the rigidity of dialectics with Spinoza's idea of an "always excessive imagination" that constitutes a "real material force" (Hardt/Negri 2009, 99). They argue that the multitude can fully rely on its own productive capacities. It does not depend on the *Empire* and consequently only needs to abolish (or to flee from) it. This *nomadic* conception of resistance is entirely different from the Marxian understanding of social transformation by which Adorno's analysis is informed.

The difference between the proletariat and the multitude is that the latter goes "through" the *Empire* without transforming itself in a way that could be differentiated from the constant forms of becoming postulated by Negri and Hardt. The multitude is essentially free already. The proletarian revolution envisioned by Marx on the other hand does not only abolish capitalism, but also the proletariat as a product of the capitalist mode of production. In the process of revolution, the proletariat has to become a non-proletariat to overcome its alienated existence (Reitter 2010). In a similar way, Adorno's dictum that "there is no right life in the wrong one" (Adorno 2003a, 43) expresses the deep conviction that alienated forms of social relations in capitalist societies necessarily produce deformed subjectivities which are unable to build sincere cooperations. The difference between a negative dialectical approach and the immanent conception of Negri and Hardt is that the latter assume that what they call "biopolitical commons" can exist outside the capitalist mode of production, whereas Adorno insists that there is no immediate access to the good life because all of its expressions are mediated by the context of "total delusion" (*Verblendungszusammenhang*) of the alienated society. Positive forms of solidarity therefore become possible only in the aftermath of negative solidarity.

Another influential criticism of dialectics has been provided by Jürgen Habermas, who criticised Adorno's scepticism by pointing out that the pessimism of his theory is accompanied by an underlying romantic hope for a "dialectical leap." In Habermas' view, the individualist conception of autonomy provided by Kant, which he sees at work in Adorno's theory, needs to be replaced by an inter-subjective ethics that transforms the Kantian self-legislation into a cooperative project (Habermas 1996, 48-49). According to Habermas, the "discursive turn" of the categorical imperative helps to solve the moral problem of how to include the Other: "It [the categorical imperative, D.S.] is replaced by the discourse-principle 'D,' according to which norms are only valid if they could be agreed upon in a practical discourse by everyone concerned" (Habermas 1996, 49). Although Habermas' inter-subjective ethics and the idea of an "unrestrained discourse" (Habermas 1995, 60) seemingly include the Other in a communicative process, it has been questioned what kind of Otherness is implied in his theory. Habermas has been criticised (especially from a feminist perspective) for relying on an abstract and universal conception of the Other. The figure of the universal Other is a necessary part of his inclusive concept of justice, but at the same time it reduces the concrete other to an abstraction of Otherness. It is therefore unable to grasp the other in its concrete specificity and consequently hides the non-identical behind an implicit universal concept. In order to incorporate the acknowledgement of the concrete individual into discourse ethics, Seyla Benhabib consequently argued that the perspective of political justice that bases on the "generalised Other" needs to be complemented by a perspective that acknowledges the "concrete other" as a singularity with unique experiences, wishes and desires. The perspective of the concrete other is concerned with personal care, love, friendship and intimacy rather than abstract rights (Benhabib 1987, 92). It is, however, unclear how and to what extent the acknowledgement of the concrete other, which is expressed through personal care, can function as an inclusive concept.

Adorno on the other hand insists that the theory of non-identity points towards an all-encompassing inclusion. In an attempt to re-articulate Adorno's "Post-Kantian indefinite task in a suitable altered form," Pensky (2008, 52) arrives at the judgement that "citizenship interpreted via the language of basic rights would allow for no exclusions whatsoever." This conclusion resembles Adorno's aphorism that "tenderness would be solely what is most crude: that no-one should starve any longer" (Adorno 2003a, 178). But Pensky's re-articulation is illusionary insofar as he rejects the negative dimension of Adorno's theory and approaches the problem in purely moral terms. Pensky does not explain how basic rights could be granted in a world of capitalist nation states, where rights are enforced by nations and consequently often melt down to slightly extended citizen-rights. In this context, truly universal rights are possible only as a negation of the exclusionary logic of the nation-form. Habermas, Benhabib and others implicitly assume that the "free discourse" or the "deliberative pub-lic" is at least "in the making", if not already in existence. But the rejection of the "dialectical leap" leads to a certain ignorance of discourse ethics towards its own condition of possibility.

The perspective of negative dialectical solidarity acknowledges and criticises the fact that the structuring principles of capitalist democracy ultimately undermine the very possibility of deliberation. There is no free discourse in the administered society and the acknowledgement of the other is constantly undermined because the individuals encounter each other as competitors: as losers, profiteers and bystanders of exploitation and oppression.

However, the question arises whether the critique formulated by Ador-no is possible if the context of delusion is as total as he depicts it. In order to understand Adorno's concept of alienation and resistance, it is neces-sary to take his notion of *experience* (*Erfahrung*) into consideration. Adorno draws upon a Hegelian understanding of experience as a dialecti-cal process of *becoming-conscious* (*Bewusstwerdung*) in which both the object and the consciousness itself are transformed. Defined in this way, experience is sharply differentiated from pure sensation, which leaves the consciousness unchanged.

This difference has most strikingly been pointed out by Walter Benjamin, who argued that the dissipation of attention and the fact that communication in modern society is more and more dominated by a series of shocks lead to a poverty of experience: "The replacement of the older *relation* by *information* and information by *sensation* reflects the increasing poverty of experience." (Benjamin 1972, 189) The lack of experience is a lack of remembered experiences. Drawing upon the trauma-theory of Freud, Walter Benjamin describes this lack of experience as the result of protective mechanisms of the consciousness against an overload of stimuli:

The high amount of shock-moments amongst impressions, the constant necessity of the consciousness to act as a protection against sensational
stimuli and the success with which it operates prevent impressions from
becoming part of *Erfahrung* [experience] and they fulfil more and more the
term *Erlebnis* [experience in the sense of experiencing an event, D.S.].
(Benjamin 1972, 193)

Adorno himself discusses experience in close relation to *Bildung*,
which is "nothing else but culture to the side of its subjective appropriation" (Adorno 1979, 92). *Bildung* is the experience of culture. But as
Adorno argues, the extension of the humanist ideal of *Bildung* under capitalist conditions leads to a situation where the lack of resources (most
importantly *Muße*, leisure time) makes it impossible for the individual to
appropriate culture. At the same time, culture itself is commodified and
transformed into a mere product of culture industry. The lack of experience proclaimed by Adorno in his *Theorie der Halbbildung* is therefore
also a result of the lack of concrete occasions for experiences. The alienated totality of society does not only undermine the subjective conditions,
but also the objective possibility of experience.

It is therefore only as a negative, as a lack of experience, that experience points to the possibility of a better world. This experience of non-
experience is what constitutes the basis for reflection and critique. The
experience of a fragmentary, always incomplete, "damaged" happiness
points towards what is objectively possible and constitutes the basis of a
quasi-utopian vision. In contrast to common depictions of Adorno as a
rigidly anti-utopian thinker, the criticism of "damaged life" leads to a vision of a better condition in which it is possible "to be different without
fear" (Adorno 2003a, 116).

But for this impulse to exist, a "rest" of happiness necessarily needs to
be present even in the alienated society. In interviews, Adorno identified
this rest of happiness (in a rather biographical argumentation) with child-
hood memories, but it is also present in the promise of happiness promoted
by the culture industry, in family life and friendship. The absence of experience is therefore not absolute, but what is left to experience is always
damaged, disrupted by processes of commoditisation and undermined by
the general tendency of objectification, reaching even into the most intimate relations.

According to Adorno, the sphere of art constitutes one of the last re-
sorts of experience. The active engagement of the artist with the object of
artistic labour and the semi-autonomous status of art in relation to society
constitute a privileged refuge for experience, even though the products of
artistic labour are constantly threatened by commoditisation.

Unfortunately, Adorno did not elaborate much on the question, how the experience of non-experience can be translated into a political *praxis*. Adorno's description of culture industry and his concentration on the commoditisation of cultural products certainly led him to under-estimate the potential of individual re-appropriation of culture, a fact that might explain his pessimism concerning the possibility of an emancipatory political praxis. But despite their fierce criticism of culture industry, Adorno and Horkheimer frequently participated in radio shows, using the access to a large audience to popularise their critique. Adorno's verdict that "praxis, delayed for the foreseeable future, is no longer the court of appeals against self-satisfied speculation" (Adorno 2003b, 15) should therefore be understood in the context of Adorno's own engagement in what Habermas described as a project of "Kantian education for autonomy" (Habermas 1989, 393).

Although it is difficult to draw conclusions for a political praxis beyond this articulation of critique, it is nevertheless possible to describe some requirements for the praxis of non-identifying solidarity: The negative dialectical concept of solidarity based on a critique of alienation and objectification. It asks for the condition of possibility of autonomy in capitalist democracy. This includes a critique of the identificatory logic of instrumental reason, a materialist analysis of the structuring principles of society and a critical consideration of current forms of subjectivity. Negative solidarity bases on the suffering of the damaged individuals and *a shared experience of oppression*. Following the logic of non-identity, this experience does not lead to a unified political identity. But without suffering, there would be no incentive to critique. Moreover, negative solidarity is not only critical of society, but of identity as such. It is therefore put forward in a mode of *self-reflection* and it is reflexively aware of its own regime of political identifications and exclusions. This reflexivity refers, in a practical sense, also to the necessity to 'undo' identity. Finally, negative solidarity *aims at the autonomy of the individual,* but it is at the same time aware of the impossibility of autonomy in current society. A non-identical approach towards solidarity therefore also points to the fact that "freedom is solely to be grasped in determinate negation, in accordance with the concrete form of unfreedom" (Adorno 2003b, 230).

References

Académie Française. 1694. *Le dictionnaire de l'Académie Françoise, dédié au Roy*, Vol. 2, edited by Jean-Baptiste Coignard.

Adorno, Theodor W. 1970. *Erziehung zur Mündigkeit. Vorträge und Gespräche mit Hellmut Becker 1959-1969*. Fankfurt a.M.: Fischer Verlag.

—. 1979 [1959]. "Theorie der Halbbildung." In *Soziologische Schriften II, 91-121*. Fankfurt a.M.: Suhrkamp Verlag.

—. 2003a [1951]. *Minima Moralia*. Fankfurt a.M.: Suhrkamp Verlag.

—. 2003b [1966]. *Negative Dialektik. Jargon der Eigentlichkeit*. Fankfurt a.M.: Suhrkamp Verlag.

—. 2003c [1970]. *Ästhetische Theorie*. Fankfurt a.M.: Suhrkamp Verlag.

Adorno, Theodor W. and Horkheimer, Max. 2006 [1944]. *Dialektik der Aufklärung*. Fankfurt a.M.: Fischer Verlag.

Benhabib, Seyla. 1987. "The Generalized and the Concrete Other: The Kohlberg-Gilligan Controversy and Feminist Theory." In *Feminism as Critique*, edited by Seyla Benhabib and Drucilla Cornell, 77-95. Minneapolis: University of Minnesota Press.

Benjamin, Walter. 1972 [1939]. "Über einige Motive bei Beaudelaire." In *Walter Benjamin. Illuminationen. Ausgewählte Schriften*, edited by Siegfried Unseld, 185-229. Fankfurt a.M.: Suhrkamp Verlag.

Bonnet, Alberto R. 2009. "Antagonism and Difference: Negative Dialectics and Post-Structuralism in View of the Critique of Modern Capitalism." In *Negativity and Revolution*, edited by John Holloway, Fernando Matamoros and Sergio Tischler, 41-78. London: Pluto Press.

Comte, Auguste. 2002 [1842]. *Discours sur l'esprit positif. Suivi de cinq documents annexes*. Une édition électronique réalisée à partir du livre d'Auguste Comte, edited by Jean-Marie Temblay.

Durkheim, Emile. 1926 [1893]. *De la Division du Travail Social*. Paris: Librairie Félix Alcan.

Habermas, Jürgen. 1989. "Ein Brief." In *Kritische Theorie und Kultur*, edited by Rainer Erd, Dietrich Hoß, Otto Jacobi and Peter Noller, 391-394. Fankfurt a.M.: Suhrkamp Verlag.

—. 1995. *Die Normalität einer Berliner Republik*. Fankfurt a.M.: Suhrkamp Verlag.

—. 1996. *Die Einbeziehung des Anderen*. Fankfurt a.M.: Suhrkamp Verlag.

Hardt, Michael and Negri, Antonio. 2000. *Empire*. Cambridge, Massachusetts: Harvard University Press.

—. 2004. *Multitude: War and Democracy in the Age of Empire*. London: Penguin Books.

—. 2009. *Commonwealth*. Cambridge, Massachusetts: Harvard University Press.

Martínez, José Manuel. 2009. "Mimesis and Distance: Arts and the Social in Adorno's Thought." In *Negativity and Revolution,* ed. by John Holloway, Fernando Matamoros and Sergio Tischler, 228-240. London: Pluto Press.

Metz, Karl H. 1999. "Solidarity and History. Institutions and Social Concepts of Solidarity in 19th Century Western Europe." In *Solidarity,* edited by Kurt Bayertz, 191-207. Dordrecht: Kluwer Academic Publishers.

Munoz Dardé, Véronique. 1999. "Fraternity and Justice." In *Solidarity,* edited by Kurt Bayertz, 81-97. Dordrecht: Kluwer Academic Publishers.

Pensky, Max. 2008. *The Ends of Solidarity. Discourse Theory in Ethics and Politics.* New York: State University of New York Press.

Reitter, Karl. 2010. "Produktivität als Autonomie? Zum Abschluss der Trilogie Empire, Multitude, Commonwealth von Antonio Negri und Michael Hardt." *Grundrisse* 35:35-43.

Schieder, Wolfgang. 1972. "Brüderlichkeit." In *Geschichtliche Grundbegriffe. Historisches Lexikon zur politisch-sozialen Sprache in Deutschland Vol. 1,* edited by Günther Franz, 552-581. Stuttgart: Klett-Cotta Verlag.

Wildt, Andreas. 1999a. "Solidarity: Its History and Contemporary Definition." In *Solidarity,* edited by Kurt Bayertz, 209-220. Dordrecht: Kluwer Academic Publishers.

Zoll, Rainer. 2000. *Was ist Solidarität heute?* Fankfurt a.M.: Suhrkamp Verlag.

CHAPTER FOUR

SOLIDARITY THROUGH PRACTICE? MACINTYRE'S REVOLUTIONARY ARISTOTELIANISM: A MARXIST READING

PAUL REYNOLDS

In this chapter I want to explore solidarity within the context of a particular problem in Marxist theory. How is a collective commitment to a communist (or an alternative shaped and influenced by Marxist thinking) society achieved? Or to put it another way, how do Marxists ensure solidarity in and for communist societies? If a utopian conception of communist societies is to be avoided, solidarity must involve a continuous process of moral, social, and political re-making of the community in order to allow for emergent changes and differences, the persistence of democratic participation and politics, and the moral and political commitment to a society where class divisions are broken down and reconstituted by a collectivist political economy typified in the theory of communism. If this claim is accepted, then it is the character and mechanisms of the continuous process of re-making that are critical to understand both how a politics of change is promulgated and a politics of communism is sustained. In exploring this question, a central assumption will be that both Marxism—an approach to understanding the world through a materialist and dialectical conception of history—and the problem of remaking are fruitfully explored and centrally constituted through the concept of *practice*. It is through a focus on and understanding of social, cultural, political, and economic practices that solidarity is meaningfully produced and reproduced and this solidarity becomes critical in any form of revolutionary politics and the communist politics that comes after.

This focus on the relationship between practices and making and remaking solidarity is one that might be pursued through a number of different strands of social and philosophical thought, but this short discussion will focus on one thinker who has gained contemporary attention as a significant source of fertile ideas in understanding the scope and limits to a radical and moral community: Alisdair MacIntyre. MacIntyre's successive engagements with Marxism, Christianity, and more recently a rearticulation of Aristotelian virtue ethics, has produced what Knight (2007, 2011) has aptly termed "Revolutionary Aristotelianian." MacIntyre's pessimistic claims for communities bound by virtue are nevertheless useful in exploring the conditions, scope, and limits of practices to make and remake solidarity in contemporary societies. This Marxist reading of MacIntyre will seek to provide a critical basis for understanding the construction of solidarity through practice for a communist politics.

Solidarity and Politics

If a general sense of the different framings of solidarity in political discourse is useful, three distinct forms might be sketched. First, is the metaphysically constituted solidarity. This is a solidarity that is rooted in a common metaphysical system of beliefs that gives a community or society its cohesion. Classically, any society with strong ideological and institutional religious forces, especially where they come together historically in monarchies, might be regarded as being held together by the power of that metaphysicality—in the Judaeo-Christian world, the Christian God. This sort of metaphysical root to solidarity might be extended to teleological notions of how societies develop, such as the Hegelian *geist* that underpins the development of the democratic and constitutional state as a forward-looking political development, or a notion of nature that gives the community a particular form of teleology.

Second is the collectivist materialist constituted solidarity. This is signposted by Marx's radical rejection of metaphysical forces shaping politics and society, and his focus on a material and historical analysis, focused on political economy as shaping the material conditions in which societies develop. Here, solidarity is formed directly in relation to the material distribution of wealth and power. Appeals to metaphysics, or to an inherent "natural" character to substantive class inequality and dispossession in the social order are regarded as a political (hegemonic) attempt to secure solidarity as a means of maintaining the balance of wealth and power. Strategies for solidarity become an exercise of power and have to be retrieved through building a solidarity amongst the dispossessed (class solidarity) and theorising a radical alternative where solidarity is built by

common values and norms underpinned by common ownership and distributions of wealth and power. This collectivism is evident in other forms of
radicalism, such as forms of feminism and anti-racist/imperialist politics.

Third is the intersubjective constituted solidarity. This emerges with
identity politics and post-modern critiques of the "grand narratives" of
modernity (see indicatively Seidman 2013). Solidarity is not constituted
by a determinant relationship, whether metaphysic or material, but by the
moral and political agency of particular subjects, whether they represent
particular identities or intersectionalities of identity or interests. An intersubjectively constituted solidarity sees the nexus of social interrelations as
being diverse in the constituencies that form common associations, the
forms of association, the duration and occupation of space by these associations, and the different levels of subjective and common characteristics of
association that represent the relationship. They are represented best by
their fluidity, plasticity, and diversity in a continual state of contingent
remaking.

Marxists clearly take the position of rejecting the notion of metaphysically constituted solidarity in society. They expose these forms of
solidarity under capitalism as being hegemonic and class based strategies
for domination and the continued appropriation of profit and capital.
Equally, they reject intersubjectivity as a diffusion of radical politics into
relativistic, identitarian concerns that fail to see the persistence of class
power and the connections between different forms of class oppression
and exploitation as they are experienced in the form of interest and identity
politics.

Framing the question of collectivist commitment as solidarity exposes
a contradiction within the focus of Marxist theory, as the concept of solidarity is an *absent presence* in Marxist theory. The place where solidarity
would be used is occupied by the concept of class in two senses: as material analysis of society organised around the ownership and control of the
means of production, which conceives common class positions arising
from the social relations of production; and a more subjective political
articulation of class politics in seeking to subvert, corrode, overthrow, and
restructure these social relations through appeals to class politics. Solidarity is effectively a *description* of the way and extent to which political
subjects organise to uncover and wage revolutionary politics on the existing material social relations under capitalism based on common class
consciousness and commitment within particular contexts and conjunctures. It describes what is necessary for the class subject to realise their
revolutionary potential, and so a strategic goal and function of class politics, and a *characteristic* of classless society as it is theorised. Whilst there

is considerably more to say about subject-material relations as a dialectical relationship central to Marxist analyses of capitalist societies, revolutionary politics, and the transition of communism, this suffices to provide an explanation of the relative absence of solidarity as a *critical* concept in Marxist discourse. It is present in the goals, conduct, and strategic engagement with class politics. Other than part of rhetorical flourishes, the conceptual constituency of the idea of solidarity is subsumed into class theory and politics.

For Marxists, where solidarity is used in bourgeois theories, notably by Durkheim, it misrepresents and misdirects from the means and strategies by which capitalist societies organise cohesion through social organisation and ideological politics that diminish and obscure the centrality of class politics in constituting the subject around exploitative and alienating social relations of production. As such, even socialist routes of theories of solidarity are problematic because they tend to seek to maintain social cohesion and the functionality of some amended or reformed version of social organisation under capitalism, as opposed to recognising the need to forge a substantially different form of solidarity through class politics. Solidarity, in a Marxist account, becomes a *political* function rather than a *social* function, and the task of making and remaking solidarity is achieved through a heightened class consciousness and the organisation of social and material relations upon collectivist principles; a solidarity of the revolutionary to supplant the solidarity functions of social institutions in capitalist societies. For Marxists, there is no teleology or naturalised process by which solidarity evolves in society, and no necessary progress within the functionality of society—scientific, technological or otherwise—as "bourgeois theory" would tend to assert. Such ideological apparatus detracts from the terms of an alternative collectivist society and the balance of commitment to solidarity and expressions of diffusion, difference, or diversity such a society involves.

Conceptually, Marx's early works, notably the *Paris Manuscripts* (Marx 1964), provide sketches of a communist society in which work, leisure, and communal commitments are organised for the benefit of the collective, for all to share in, as a contrast to capitalism's system of estranged labour, private property and an economic system driven by profit. Whilst not explicit, Marx's drawing out of the possibilities of an alternative are predicated on a common, Marxist understanding of the failings of capitalism and a commitment to solidarity in a collectivist alternative. That this is a utopian position or one which counterpoints the real possibilities of socialist transformation through class agency in a developing capitalist economy, is a matter of dispute. As Geoghegan points out, the tendency

for Marx to be regarded as against utopianism is partly a product of criticisms of nineteenth century utopian socialism, and a strategic commitment
to class politics with a scientific approach to what could be envisaged as
emerging from class struggle in the mid-nineteenth century (Geoghegan
1987, 22-34).

Marx is far more explicit about the importance of solidarity in the
Communist Manifesto (Marx 1952), with its exhortation that workers of
the world unite under the banner of proletarian revolution. Yet thereafter,
solidarity becomes largely subsumed within the debates around class
struggle and class contradictions within capitalist economies. Subsequently, Marx's political writings, particularly on the class struggles in France
and later the Paris Commune, chart the attempts and failings of political
struggles to develop a class solidarity that followed the coda of the *Manifesto* (Marx 1971, 1974).

Solidarity, in both making class struggle and consciousness and envis-
aging post-capitalist alternatives, has been an enduring problem for
Marxists. It is present in the organisational question of the relationship
between party and class in Marxist politics (Lenin 1947, also see Lenin
1968 and Lih 2006). It is present in claims for an inherent organicism of
class politics or the necessity of political strategies that build collective
commitment (see Townsend 1996). It is present in the articulation of the
ideological politics by which class hegemony is deconstructed and counter-hegemony articulated (Gramsci 2011, also see Thomas 2009). It is
present in the possibilities for class strategies to mobilise mass protest and
revolutionary activity, and more pessimistic claims that the "structures of
practice" in capitalist societies are so enduring and all-pervasive that class
solidarity is impossible (Althusser 1977, 2001, Althusser and Balibar
1970, also see Elliott 2006). It is present in the possibilities of an enriched
communicative solidarity focused on discourse ethics and universal pragmatics (selectively Habermas 1985, 1998b)

The revolutionary politics of Marxist influenced parties and organisations have historically been ceded to more authoritarian attempts to
maintain solidarity by policing and disciplining strategies, as in the Soviet
Union and China. In Bolshevik Russia, the Leninist revolution initially
galvanised a wide constituency of support and solidarity amongst workers,
and was undermined chiefly by the mobilisation of international opposition that energised internal resistance, and the pessimism of the Bolshevik
leadership that could not move beyond hijacking state apparatus to transform them to incorporate worker's democracy (for an accessible study see
Haynes 2002).

In China, Mao's revolution sought to impress a distinctively Chinese communist solidarity by fundamentally restructuring social institutions and cultures, and was undermined by both the scale and authoritarian underpinning of those changes with estrangement from a larger global communist project, itself riven by authoritarian politics (indicatively Karl 2010, Chan 2003 and Draguhn and Goodman 2002). In Cuba, isolation encouraged a siege mentality and authoritarian politics in defence of a revolution largely isolated by the effectiveness of US hegemony (Trento 2001, Guevara and Castro 2009). The degenerations of revolutionary promise to Stalinism and Maoism can be partly expressed as changing strategies of solidarity from a solidarity made and remade within collectivist struggle to a solidarity made and sustained by the evolving of policing and political organisations that emphasise conformity and cohesion based on ideological and elite power. Solidarity becomes, as with the bourgeois conception, naturalised within the social vision produced within the existing ideological and political power structures and hierarchies in society.

Throughout twentieth century global politics, left solidarity has failed to adequately cohere a popular hegemony project before it has been undermined, whether from within or from without. Where there has been evidence of the inculcation of solidarity around left struggles and ideas, left organisations have been able to advance their political agendas and engage in governance, if not always with sustained success or without reinforcing the strategies for solidarity with a hegemonic project incorporating discipline and resistance to external interference. Examples of popular struggles exhibiting solidarity might be the Solidarity movement and its successes in Poland, the Sandinistas in Nicaragua, and Chavez's Venezuela. Marxists hold on to the promise of revolutionary change evidenced in particular periods of class and political struggles that have produced participatory revolutionary parties and movements and created moments for democracy and social justice in particular contexts and conjunctures, no matter how brief or subsequently normalised these become.

Particularly in the context of a neoliberal global enterprise that seeks primarily to privatise, atomise, and individualise social life, solidarity has become a critical concept by which radical responses are organised. Conservatives and neoliberals seek to construct forms of solidarity around an atomising and individuated commitment to the functionality of free economy, reinforced by a strong but limited liberal democratic state. They adopt a "realism" that both accepts and benefits from globalised economic relations and the limits of democratic politics, particularly in the scope and limits to transnational political regulation and economic organisation, and propagate a global geo-politics of "mature capitalist democracies," those states who "play by the rules," against the dangerous "other," and nation-alist, ethnic, and religious commitments. For centrist liberal democrat and social democrats, solidarity involves the making and remaking of a per-ceived balance of interests and identities within democratic politics and within the context of uneven development within global capitalism which requires national responses that secure economic solvency if not prosperi-ty. Within radical politics, solidarity presents a twofold problem: how is solidarity achieved within the context of the radical politics of intersec-tionality, difference, diversity, and deconstruction in identities and interests; and how is solidarity achieved as a counter-hegemony against the neoliberal project?

Solidarity for the left is, then, an elusive and complex political concept, with constitutive discourses of solidarity. If the left is said to consist of a range of political visions, from Marxist through anarchist to identitarian (feminist, anti-racist, disability and sexuality radicals) through to demo-crats and other forms of socialism, notions of solidarity are often variable in their spatial, temporal, and contextual characterisations. Often, there is a tension between the subject politics of struggling for change and what pol-itics are at the core of that particular left variant, so, for example, anarchists and Marxists can co-operate in supporting the global Occupy movement whilst having very different positions on its value, longevity, and eventual impacts (Jackson 2012; Wolff and Barsamian 2012). Like-wise, left movements are diverse in their analysis of cultural, political, and social pre-conditions for political engagement, forms of politics, cohering characteristics, and discursive constitutions. Solidarity is often, therefore, somewhat temporary and focused on what can be agreed on, such as im-mediate campaigns or protests.

Yet at the same time, solidarity is central to any attempt to theorise so-cial cohesion within a community or society. It is of particular concern to all variants of the left, whose agendas stand or fall on the extent to which radical political and ideological change can be inculcated into a society that coheres—and is hegemonically cohered—around particular values, recognitions and redistributions of power, wealth and ownership If left solidarity cannot be achieved, political struggle is diminished, the possibil-ity of effecting radical change reduced or the moment of radical or revolutionary change deferred, defeated or corrupted. Left politics are fun-damentally subverted by the need to defend its frailty within struggles in liberal democracies through the use of discipline, coercion, and the manu-facture of consent—the very tools of its enemies.

It is clear that in this discussion solidarity is not simply a describable *characteristic* of a particular society, which might have lesser or greater solidarity according to the character and functions of its social, cultural and political institutions, organisations, structures, processes, and group activity. Solidarity is both an *aim* of competing political interests who wish to create it around its own preferences for social and political structure, function and order, and a *feature* of the organisational, strategic, ideological, theoretical, and practical means by which that aim is achieved. Solidarity is not just a state of *being* in society, a quality of cohesion or communality in society at a given time: it is a process—consensual but principally conflictual in different moments—by which cohesion and communality are made and remade and societies or communities *become* what the dominant amalgam of interests regard as a sustainable and desirable settlement of interests within the content of a claimed—hegemonic— common cause. It is a feature of political mobilisation, the effectiveness of counter-hegemonic strategy, and the strength of movement to achieve change.

Moreover, solidarity is something that is normative, in that collective endeavour is something seen as desirable and intrinsically valuable to a society. Common factors in the different variants of left politics are a sense of collective welfare and political commitment, a greater distribution of both ownership and wealth of resources across society, a greater degree of participation and devolved power in governance and a sense that liberty, in a real sense, involves a recognition of the liberty of others and self-discipline and constraint in the liberty of all to achieve greater equality, justice, and quality of life. All of these factors point to the necessity of solidarity as a normative quality in society, where the value of solidarity is in the character and achievement of these factors and the sense of living beyond the self and recognising others, strangers, and differences.

Unless there is a supposition that societies cohere organically, without co-ordination or regardless of the exercise of unequal power in hierarchies within society, this political articulation of solidarity is central to the achievement of a society that exhibits social solidarity. It is therefore a political concept, suffused with power, the presence of opposition and/or alternative to any particular form or articulation it takes, and the challenge of strategizing and constantly remaking solidarity as both an aim and as part of the means to that aim.

Solidarity: Thinking with MacIntyre

Alisdair MacIntyre's contribution to a radical rethinking of the prospects for solidarity arise from his attempts to explore the possibility of placing virtue at the core of a progressive politics of social and cultural change in contemporary societies. More specifically, it is his pessimistic rejection of such a possibility, and his formulation of how communities at the margins might seek to be virtuous in the context of a degenerate capitalist late modernity, that offers some possibilities to thinking further about solidarity. MacIntyre (1985, 1988, 1998, 1999, 2006) develops his analysis from a standpoint of thinking rooted in both Marxism and Christianity, and a commitment to an Aristotelian notion of virtue and its centrality to a human life that has value and meaning.

In *After Virtue*, his most important work, MacIntyre (1985) proposes a damning analysis of the enlightenment project and moral agency and their impact on contemporary societies. The root of this analysis lies in the rejection of ancient (particularly Aristotelian) and early Christian and medieval moral presuppositions, which argued for a central teleology to human experience, whereby in the course of developing and flourishing humanity, there was a teleological end characterised by the virtues that humans necessarily progressed towards. What philosophy after the Renaissance, and particularly enlightenment philosophy, did was to erode that teleology and formulate morality in a scientific form. Detached from its culture and context and formulated in forms of logic and rationality, where subjectivity and the logic of process replace the virtues of both a clear notion of the character of human species and the cultural traditions within which morals and values are formed. For MacIntyre, this reduces ethics to a language game rather than providing meaningful and contextually enriched bases for understanding and aspiring to human good. Subjectivity gets in the way of a shared moral commitment to a common understanding of flourishing and human endeavour, and the absence of clear moral values for guidance leads to endless contestation or a celebration of the absence of moral certainties. Moral questions become questions engaged with by individuals who seek to make sense of their moral agency through their subjective response to the range of value positions placed in front of them, if they do not simply conform to dominant values in the absence of meaningful collective engagements with questions of moral values. The individuating function of the market, the capitalist valorisation of property, accumulation and wealth, and the promotion of sectional interests over common values all speak to struggles to establish moral agency on an individual basis in a society suffused with institutional and organisational processes that mitigate against moral agency as a collective enterprise.

MacIntyre sees the roots of moral conduct in three presuppositions. First, that they have to be collectively developed and not individually reasoned. Second, that there has to be a clear understanding of what moral conduct is and to what end it serves, from which MacIntyre is drawn to

Aristotelianism and the constitution of virtues. Finally, any notion of humanity has to account for people as they are and not as they might be ideally understood to be or aspired to be in terms of their development.

Central to this conception of moral conduct are two concepts: practices and traditions.[1] For MacIntyre (1985), drawing from Aristotle, moral conduct is always practiced. It is in the practising of the "craft" of moral conduct that moral conduct is learned. It does not come from recognising abstract principles and debating them within particular institutions such as deliberative governmental forums or academies. It is about practising moral conduct as a means of living that conduct and having it embodied as part of every activity within a community. Both the character of what is done and the way things are done are as, if not more, important than what is produced. It is practising that makes for a virtuous society, and so it is the quality of practices that are central to establishing virtue. For Aristotle:

> Virtue . . . we acquire, just as we acquire crafts, by having first activated them. For we learn a craft by producing the same product that we must produce when we have learned it . . . for actions in accord to the virtues to be done temperately or justly it does not suffice that they are they themselves have the right qualities. Rather, the agent must also be in the right state of mind when he does them. First, he must know (that he is doing virtuous actions); second, he must decide on them, and decide on them for themselves; and third, he must also do them with a firm and unchanging state. . . . It is right, then, to say that a person comes to be just from doing just actions and temperate from doing temperate actions; for no one has the least prospect of becoming good without failing to do them . . . The many, however, do not do these actions. They take refuge in arguments, thinking that they are doing philosophy, and that this is the way to become excellent people. They are like a sick person who listens attentively to the doctor, but acts on none of his instructions . . . . (1999, 19-22)

Practices are central to this Aristotelian conception of what is good, where the exercise of practical rationality and virtue in everyday practices are central to lives lived that flourish (*Eudiamonia*) in excellence (*arete*). Practices provide the means by which the performance of excellence is learned and evidenced, whether these practices are contemplative in philosophy or, for example associative in political engagement. Yet these

---

1. The accounts of practices and traditions here will not dwell on what MacIntyre distinguishes as practices, nor what the different traditions are. For the purpose of this chapter what is more important is an outline of how practices and traditions give form to MacIntyre's understanding of the possibility of virtue in community.

practices are not acquired or learned or accumulated randomly. MacIntyre recognises they develop within traditions:

> A tradition is an argument extended through time in which certain funda-mental agreements and disagreements are defined or redefined in terms of two kinds of conflict: with critics and enemies external to the tradition who reject all or at least key parts of those fundamental agreements, and those internal, interpretative debates through which the meaning and rationale of fundamental agreements come to be expressed and by who progress a tra-dition is constituted. (1988, 12)

Traditions provide the cultural and historical context through which moral conduct and the values and virtues that inform it are developed. They give the virtues and values to be learned and practiced a sense of tangibility in the context of community in which they are made. MacIntyre recognises how practices emerge from traditions in such a way as to pro-duce a narrative order to human life in this learning, which provides a meaningful sense of engaging with a conception of flourishing that emerg-es from tradition, its embodiment within practice and a subject-centred domain for practice that puts the subject at the centre of considerations of virtuous life, and not transcendental speculations.

Following from Aristotle, MacIntyre's virtue is a product of practices and working within and appreciating the cultural traditions within which the collective developed. It is precisely the learning and performing of practices that embodies and instantiates virtue within the community. As MacIntyre observes:

> Any coherent and complex form of socially established cooperative human activity through which goods internal to that form of activity are realised in the course of trying to achieve those standards of excellence which are ap-propriate to, and partially definitive of, that form of activity, with the result that human powers to achieve excellence, and human conceptions of the ends and goods involved, are systematically extended. (2007, 187)

What MacIntyre provides, then, is a sense of the way a moral commu-nity can be concretely constructed through a recognition of traditions and practices at the centre of how virtue is instantiated. It provides a vivid con-trast with a society where social practices under modernity are suborned to commodification as central to entering the cultural world, capitalism, and the reification of science and technological development and their as-sumed prospects for human enhancement. MacIntyre's response to the challenge of what he regards as a fundamentally amoral modern world was to claim that the means by which a more virtuous life might be encouraged were absent in modernity itself, but possible for communities on the margins of modernity. He saw these as small and cohesive communities that were able to engage in a degree of boundary-setting in respect of the values and processes that constituted modern societies.

Knight's (2011) seminal essay *Revolutionary Aristotelianism* emphasises the radical potential of MacIntyre's conception of virtue in practice by placing practices in contrast to institutions. It is when practices become instantiated beyond their performance and into institutions with managerial and bureaucratic processes that they become atrophied and barren in their morality. Hence it is not simply that a focus on practices appears to encourage associations that are most typical of marginal communities, communes for example, it is that the transformation of practices beyond their immediate instantiation, and into institutions, necessarily produces processes that are antithetical to practices continuing to be infused by virtue. Hence MacIntyre's conclusion that late modernity has little to offer as a basis for a re-moralisation of community and society. Yet Knight recognises that there is radical potential for this otherwise pessimistic conclusion:

> The bases of these certain forms of community are to be found no longer in locality, but rather in particular practices . . . the task for a politics of the Aristotelian tradition are to defend the rationality, ideals creativity, and co-operative care for common goods of practices against institutional corruption and managerial manipulation, and to uphold internal goods of excellence against external goods and claims of effectiveness. The present dominance of institutions over practices, and of bureaucratic technique and procedural rules over practical wisdom, is the embodiment of the dominance of abstract reason and will over tradition. . . . It is collective defence of the goods and rationalities against those of institutions that the bases for a politics in the Aristotelian tradition are now to be found. (2010, 32)

For MacIntyre, it is the everyday practice of virtuous behaviour, and its meaningfulness to the community, its practice within the community and its careful engagement with tradition that literally embody virtue. Rather than a language game or an ideal or aspiration, virtue is practiced and reflected on. This practice and reflection is achieved as part of being in the community. Whilst this practice may take a variety of forms, MacIntyre thinks it important that this practice is understood as applying practical rationality (*phronesis*) and involves a contemplative moment whereby the practices of the community involve a conscious engagement with questions of moral values and how practices conform to what the community believes is the point of being in the community and living a good life.

This is a not a stagnant community, with a singular sense of having one tradition of moral values and one articulation of virtue, although one may take primacy. There is a plurality of traditions both within communities and between different communities. Likewise, this is not a simple appeal to a form of communitarianism such as that of Etzioni (1993, 1996), as MacIntyre is quite specific about how community is formed around the practice of virtues rather than a particular geographical population, resource of social capital, or particular interests and identities. Instead, in MacIntyre, there is a sense that the question of how the community works to promote virtuous lives is more important than its status as a viable civil space between state political management and individuated market relations.

What MacIntyre offers to thinkers about solidarity is the possibility of theorising shared moral and political commitment and the building of common institutional and organisational bonds to enable social cohesion in a way that need not limit diversity. For MacIntyre, provided there is a clear understanding that a virtuous life can be lived in the community, it is possible for diverse interests and identities to co-exist. However, in applying MacIntyre to the particular problem of solidarity in a diverse society, it should be recognised that he has largely explored such issues within philosophical discourse rather than substantively worked through political articulations. Nevertheless, his conception of virtuous communities constituted through practice can be usefully extended into a discussion of solidarity, providing foundations for shared moral and political cohesion.

In making solidarity, the community has a shared sense of the value of traditions, and the value of rival traditions in providing a common basis in how they contribute to what might be regarded as a good and meaningful life. MacIntyre draws a line between tolerance and intolerance of difference, which he anticipates as occurring both within groups and between groups that hold different positions within different traditions. He sees the impetus to find at least common frames of reference or departure points for debate important in the building of tolerance within a cohesive community. It is within the dialogue between different positions that MacIntyre sees disagreement and conflict as important:

> It is an important part through disagreement and conflict that the common life of such groups is enriched. For it is only through development and conflict, only through aiming at conclusions that emerge from being tested by the most powerful counter-arguments available, that such groups are able to embody in their shared lives the rational pursuit and achievement of the relevant goods. Therefore when we evaluate the argumentative contributions to some on-going debate within a group in whose life we participate, we should do so with an eye to how far they do or do not contribute to achieving the goods of conflict. So what is to be treated as intolerant is anything the toleration of which would tend to frustrate or prevent the

achievement of those goods. Particular practices of or proposals for the practice of toleration can only be adequately evaluated from within the context of conflicts. (2006b, 207)

For MacIntyre, the recognition that different traditions have value both in the plurality they produce within a community and the terms of debate they make in conflict and disagreement, requires a community to have a commitment to plurality. Whilst this will have limits in conflicts and disagreements over foundational values and their articulation in social space, there is a foundational value of recognising the value of plurality and in seeing the co-existence of traditions and their tensions and contradictions as providing fertile ground for a constant critical gaze that allows for momentum in considering change and periodic development for the incremental remaking of the community by democratic processes.

This sense of virtue and commitment to flourishing is constituted in social practices. It comes not from a set of abstract values and rules that set a code for what is within and without the boundaries of the community. It is embodied in the practices that utilise practical rationality of everyday life for the enriching of that community.[2] These might include a civic commitment to serve in structures of governance of civil decision-making, or a commitment to charitable enterprise that enriches other's lives, or a commitment to excellence in practising the relationships and forms of creative enterprise that ensure the community flourishes. What is critical is that solidarity is practiced. It is a feature of the practices that are engaged in, which exhibit *arete* and *phronesis,* that they bind the community together so that solidarity is a condition of practice, and this engagement in practice and the exercise of practical reason integral to it is never an individual act. The argument can be extended to claim that practices underpinned by the critical rational enquiry to maintain their virtue cannot achieve the goals they set themselves unless they are seen as shared, interactive, engaged with others. It is that practice, the empathy and mutuality they produce, that reinforces the commitment to toleration and appreciation of the critical value of plural traditions in making a feasible and viable community. As MacIntyre observes:

> What social and political forms are required to achieve the common good of those who participate in the relevant kinds of relationship of giving and receiving . . . the moral and political relationships that are required for the

---

2. Embodiment here refers to a recognition that practices involve regularised forms of practice and does not relate to Connolly's (1982) broader argument about biological embodiment and how *telos* is theorised.

achievement of that common good involve commitments that are in some respects conditional not only to a certain range of goods, but also to those particular others together with whom we attempt to achieve that common good. (1999, 156)

A central feature of such a community and its solidarity would be its resistance to and counterbalance of the regressive tendencies of institutions and their atrophying effects on the value created by practices. It is the extent to which organisations and processes central to the community can avoid being bureaucratised and managerialised, and/or counter-balanced by the permeation of practices into how these processes function that is critical to any sense of a community with solidarity that do not lose their virtue.

There are invariably criticisms that could be made of MacIntyre's approach to a virtuous community and its articulation with respect to solidarity. Such communities sit at the periphery of capitalist societies and do not challenge the wider contexts of the source of pessimism for virtue—the modern capitalist economy. Whilst MacIntyre's concern is to sketch out the condition of possibility for a virtuous community, the permeability of that community by capitalist values and transactions exacerbates the potential tensions in and problems of such a community. These include the terms of incommensurability in competing traditions within the community, the problems of distributing power to ensure the democratic terms and commitment of such a community, the impracticalities of turning away from some forms of institutions in all but the smallest communities, and the possibility that MacIntyre is positing a somewhat elitist and exclusive form of community in respect of the resources, education, and collegiality of the community. Yet MacIntyre does provide a distinctive approach to thinking community cohesion that is valuable in thinking about solidarity.

MacIntyre, Marxism and Solidarity: Some Reflections

MacIntyre's approach to a virtuous community, and the promise this allows for a conceptualisation of community and society that underlines the value of solidarity, is not without criticism. As Blackledge and Davidson (2008) observe, part of the power of MacIntyre's critique is that it embeds the enterprise of virtue within concrete history, if his withering critique of the amorality of capitalism lacks a viable political alternative for resistance to it outside the marginal communities. Callinicos (2011) observes that the possibilities for revolutionary challenges to capitalism in part arise from the enlightenment discourses that MacIntyre rejects, that

MacIntyre struggles to move beyond the inherent inequalities that an Aristotelian notion of virtue seems to produce, and that MacIntyre's politics are limited to the local. MacIntyre (2011) counters this claim by noting that revolutionary politics start with participation in practices for the common good, and that two conditions of such a politics that elude Leninist alternatives are the free flow of information and the capacity for questioning across centre-periphery relations within organisations.

Nevertheless, for Marxists whose vision is a politics that is founded on a conception of solidarity in both the strategic development of a viable political opposition that has mass appeal in the struggle for alternatives, and a society that is founded on mutuality, collectivism and solidarity, MacIntyre does have much to offer. The integration of solidarity through practice, and through the necessity of sociality and collectivism in practice, provides a central grounding for radical politics. Radical politics becomes a critical engagement of the collective in producing a politics from their practices, which draws its authenticity from within their practices, and is constituted by practice. That conception of politics is a counterweight to the idea that politics requires hierarchical organisational structures and bureaucratic/managerial processes to be effective, and requires such functions to be constituted within practices that retain democratic discourse, the free flow of critical thinking, and the primacy of revolutionary politics over machinery of administration or governance. In thinking of the collective pooling of resources in local party organisation, where paying subscriptions, taking part in activities for the communication of ideas, and working on campaigns and protests to both propagate a politics and build a movement based on alternative values, the task for the left is to have a co-ordination and organisation of such local politics within larger contexts without falling into the traps of bureaucratic/managerial politics. The party machinery, and the political-administrative structures theorised in a post-revolutionary scenario always have to be subordinate to and in service of the community itself, and the political mechanisms by which practices, critical reasoning and collective endeavour are enabled.

MacIntyre also provides a caution against the separation of the work of theorising both critiques of capitalism, the terms of strategies of opposition, and the possibilities of alternatives and the practice of politics. The propagation of theory within the academy or particular factions of revolutionary organisations gives rise to the production of barren abstracted articulations of theory that are divorced from the actual practices of making politics and change, and by their form and language often exclusive of the very people they should wish to engage. Again, MacIntyre provides a caution that even in the present context of theoretical work produced largely in and around the academy, urgent consideration should always be given to how these ideas are instantiated in a participative politics and in practices that circulate, share and encourage critical thinking as a collective activity.

Finally, MacIntyre's notion of tradition mitigates against closure from debates both across traditions, encouraging debate with those of other radical persuasions and with those of opposing traditions, and also debate within the traditions of radical thinking, not least the different and nuanced readings of Marx and propagations of Marxism. It allows for the possibility of making political progress through collective and participative politics that is not debilitated by sectarianism yet not afraid to encourage real debate and allow for the possibility of refining and amending positions in the moments of political struggle and protest. This inclusiveness might be limited given that radical political struggle does involve the reallocation of resources and the reorganisation of social structures and institutions, but it nevertheless speaks to the possibilities of a politics of struggle that can advance the interests and virtues of collectivist enterprise—greater equality, recognition of differences, recognition of mutual needs and desires and social justice—whilst not being undermined by internal debates as to the exact terms of such enterprise and the struggles that make them.

Such a reading requires a longer, more detailed theoretical reflection and needs to combine a wider theoretical reading with a consideration of historical and contemporary politics and struggles. Here, there is simply a sketch of the possibilities MacIntyre's philosophy offers to a twenty-first century politics that places solidarity and difference, in balance, at the centre of its project. It is perhaps in the spirit of the essential collectivism of practice that this sketch and suggestion is nevertheless offered for consideration by the constituency of readers of this collection, to object to, criticise and engage with in the interests of building more effective argument.

References

Althusser, Louis. 1977a. *For Marx.* London: New Left Books.
—. 1977b. *Lenin and Philosophy and Other Essays.* New York: Monthly Review Press.
Althusser, Louis and Etienee Balibar. 1970. *Reading Capital.* London: New Left Books.
Aristotle. 1999. *Nicomachean Ethics,* 2nd ed. Translated by Terence Irwin. Cambridge: Hackett Publishing.

Blackledge, Paul and Kelvin Knight, editors. 2011. *Virtue and Politics: Alisdair MacIntyre's Revolutionary Aristotelianism.* Indiana: University of Notre Dame Press.

Callinicos, Alex. 2011. "Two Cheers For Enlightenment Universalism: Or, Why It's Hard To Be An Aristotelian Revolutionary." In *Virtue and Politics: Alisdair MacIntyre's Revolutionary Aristotelianism,* edited by Paul Blackledge and Kelvin Knight, 54-78. Indiana: University of Notre Dame Press.

Chan, Adrian. 2003. *Chinese Marxism.* London:Continuum.

Connolly, William E. 1982. "After Virtue." *Political Theory* 10(2):315-319.

Draguhn, Werner and David SG Goodman, editors. 2002. *China's Communist Revolutions: Fifty Years of the People's Republic of China.* London: Routledge Curzon.

Elliott, Gregory. 2006. *Althusser: The Detour of Theory.* Leiden: Brill.

Etzioni, Amitai. 1993. *The Spirit of Community.* London: Fontana.

—. 1996. *The New Golden Rule: Community and Morality in a Democratic Society.* London: Basic Books.

Geoghegan, Vincent. 1987. *Utopianism and Marxism.* London: Methuen and Co.

Gramsci, Antonio. 2011. *Prison Notebooks.* Edited by Joseph Buttigieg. New York: Columbia University Press.

Guevara, Che and Fidel Castro. 2009. *Socialism and Man in Cuba.* Atlanta: Pathfinder Press.

Habermas, Jurgen. 1985. *The Philosophical Discourses of Modernity.* Cambridge: Polity Press.

—. 1998. *On the Pragmatics of Communication.* Cambridge: Polity Press.

Haynes, Mike. 2002. *Russia: Class and Power 1917-2000.* London: Bookmarks.

Jackson, Ross. 2012. *Occupy World Street: A Global Roadmap for Political and Economic Reform.* Dartington: Green Books.

Karl, Rebecca. 2010. *Mao Zedong and China in the Twentieth-century World: A Concise History.* Durham: Duke University Press.

Knight, Kelvin. 2007. *Aristotelian Philosophy: Ethics and Politics From Aristotle to MacIntyre.* Cambridge: Polity.

—. 2011. "Revolutionary Aristotelianism." In *Virtue and Politics: Alisdair MacIntyre's Revolutionary Aristotelianism,* edited by Paul Blackledge and Kelvin Knight, 20-34. Indiana: University of Notre Dame Press.

Lenin, V I. 1947. *What Is To Be Done?* Moscow: Progress Press.

—. 1968. *Selected Works.* Moscow: Progress Press.

Lih, Lars. 2006. *Lenin Rediscovered: What Is To Be Done in Context.* Leiden: Brill.

MacIntyre, Alisdair. 1985. *After Virtue,* 2nd edition. London: Gerald Duckworth.

—. 1988. *Whose Justice, Whose Rationality?* Indiana: University of Notre Dame Press.

—. 1998. "Politics, Philosophy and the Common Good." In *The MacIntyre: Reader,* edited by Kelvin Knight, 235-252. Cambridge: Polity Press.

—. 1999. *Dependent Rational Animals: Why Human Beings Need the Virtues.* London: Gerald Duckworth.

—. 2006. "Three Perspectives on Marxism: 1953, 1968, 1995." In *Alisdair MacIntyre: Ethics and Politics Selected Essays Volume 2,* 145-158. Cambridge: Cambridge University Press.

—. 2006. "Toleration and the Goods of Conflict." In *Alisdair MacIntyre: Ethics and Politics Selected Essays Volume 2,* 205-223. Cambridge: Cambridge University Press.

—. 2011. "Where We Were, Where We Are, Where We Need To Be." In *Virtue and Politics: Alisdair MacIntyre's Revolutionary Aristotelianism,* edited by Paul Blackledge and Kelvin Knight, 307-334.

Marx, Karl. 1964. *The Economic and Philosophic Manuscripts of 1844.* New York: International Publishers.

—. 1973. *Surveys from Exile: Political Writings Volume 2.* Edited and introduced by David Fernbach. Harmondsworth: Penguin.

—. 1974. *The First International and After: Political Writings Volume 3.* Edited and introduced by David Fernbach. Harmondsworth: Penguin.

Marx, Karl and Fredrich Engels. 1952. *Manifesto of the Communist Party.* Moscow: Progress Publishers.

Seidman, Steven. 2013. *Contested Knowledge: Social Theory Today.* Oxford: Wiley-Blackwell.

Thomas, Peter D. 2009. *The Gramscian Moment: Philosophy, Hegemony and Marxism.* Leiden: Brill.

Townsend, Jules. 1996. *The Politics of Marxism: The Critical Debates.* London: Leicester University Press.

Trento, Angelo. 2001. *Castro and Cuba: From the Revolution to the Present.* Northampton: Interlink Books.

Wolff, Richard and David Barsamian. 2012. *Occupy the Economy: Challenging Capitalism.* San Francisco: City Lights.

CHAPTER FIVE

THE SOCIAL FUNCTION OF POSTCOLONIAL LITERARY THEORIES

ZUZANA KLÍMOVÁ

At its inception in the 1950s the first theoretical concepts on cultural colonialism were openly political in their appeal. Their aim was to achieve changes in political structures as well as other socio-cultural paradigms of the time. Literature was one of the ways to demonstrate the intellectual qualities of newly emerging states, and also a medium to express their identities and counterbalance the dominant voices of the (former) colonisers. What started as new national literatures, spread with the decolonisation process into most communities with common (post)colonial experiences. With this widening scope of appeal the solidarity associated with postcolonialism[1] abandoned its basic form of national community with the experience of the colonised in favour of a "Third World" community. Further evolution of postcolonialism began to employ ideas of hybridity, reciprocity and interdependence which later led to inclusion of "the West" into the concept of the postcolonial. Postcoloniality gradually became to be perceived as a global phenomenon. According to Arif Dirlik, it is authentic globalisation that is the main aim of the postcolonial—"to achieve an authentic globalisation of cultural discourses by the extension globally

---

1. I am using the term "postcolonial" retrospectively in this paper. Even though the term itself is much younger, I prefer it to other earlier names such as "Third World," because they are restrictive in their appeal and do not allow the inclusion of both the colonised as well as the coloniser which is a tendency in more recent developments in postcolonial theory. As the term "Third World" is still frequently used, it will appear in the text when referring to particular approaches and concepts originally using this term, or when the term is aimed to differentiate geographically the artistic or academic work and/or its representatives (who can and often do share Western cultural traditions) as opposed to those of Western cultural as well as geographical origin.

of intellectual concerns and orientations originating at the central sites of Euro-American cultural criticism and by the introduction into the latter of voices and subjectivities from the margins of earlier political and ideological colonialism that now demand a hearing of those very sites at the center" (Dirlik 1994, 329).

The disadvantage of such development of postcolonial theory on the verge of the millennium is that it became too abstract, reducing the impact of its ideas to the theoretical sphere of academia. Helen Scott describes this problem partly as the influence of postmodern ideas which were also adopted into postcolonial studies and which she sees as inadequate, because its "celebration of multiplicity [. . .] can lead to reductive reading of texts as linguistic, discursive allegories" and depoliticizing of the field of study as it pulls away from concrete histories and specific artistic movements and works which leads to mono-focused questions of "discourse, representation, language and identity" (Scott 2006). Postmodernism is simply too dogmatic, too universal with its "cult of non-determinacy" (Ahmad 1987, 23-24), to be able to fulfil the demands of postcolonial studies to understand history or explain social forces (Scott 2006). But even these demands, as described by Scott, lack the focus on practical effects and show the "scholastic reflection" of postcolonialism Gilroy criticizes for turning away from anti-racist and anti-colonial politics, replacing them by "polite academic analysis of race and (post)colonialism" (Gilroy in Alessandrini 2011a, 66). The understanding of postcolonial global interdependency brought closer the possibility of a globally accessible solidarity, but it also became rather superficial and distanced from its practical application. The beginning of the twenty-first century indicates the emergence of possible future approaches challenging the existing generalising tendencies with a return towards the balance of the aesthetic-political within postcolonial studies which should manage to preserve the more theoretical and artistic aspects as well as its practical application on socio-political level. This equilibrium is necessary for the development of an ethnically transgressive but involved solidarity among various groups world-wide.

To accomplish such a development I believe it is important for the newly emerging approaches of postcolonial studies to stress the interconnectedness of the aesthetic and the social in literature. As Rita Felski notes, a purely aesthetic perception does not exist, as "aesthetic pleasure is never unmediated or intrinsic [but always] shaped by dispositions transmitted through education and culture" (Felski 2008, 15). However, even though we cannot avoid the influence of acquired beliefs and assumptions, it does not make us the passive subjects of our upbringing. Felski is very clear about her belief in the human capacity for learning to question acquired beliefs, as well as the whole system which provides them (Felski 2008, 17). In his *Aesthetics and Subjectivity*, Andrew Bowie remarks on the changing ontological and social status of the work of art in time, and stresses the ability of art and aesthetic experience "to provoke philosophical reorientation" by "revealing limits," "suggesting new ways of questioning," "provoking new kinds of reading," "revealing new understandings of the background knowledge," and above all by "enabling a wider picture to be grasped that is being obscured by dominant and specialised theories" (Bowie 2003, 331). The necessity of critical consciousness is also expressed by Said who sees a close link between solidarity and criticism (Said in Alessandrini 2011b). The aesthetic approach to literature, shunning discussion of its possible impact on a social level, is simplistic and virtually places art solely into the personal experience, separating it from the public sphere. Similarly, were we to forget the aesthetic function of art, it would shrink literature (or art in general) to the instance of ideology (an unhappy example of a biased and reductionist interpretation can be seen, for instance, in some of the religiously or ideologically focused receptions of Rushdie's *The Satanic Verses*). Such treatment of works of art might support some sorts of solidarity, but they would be doomed to short life and have a very limited impact.

Postcolonial literary criticism was established to stress the social function and revolutionary potential of literary works. Nevertheless, there have appeared significant changes in approaches of postcolonial studies since the 1960s, which is approximately the time when many formerly colonised countries gained their political independence, but also the time of establishing the Theory[2] which "revitalised the study of literature after the Second World War" (Cunningham 2002, 38). I will stretch the scope of this paper also to the 1950s, because of the works of Aimé Césaire and Frantz Fanon, who are the pioneers and predecessors of established postcolonial studies, and who dealt in their works with questions of solidarity as a connecting element of the postcolonial community. The problem for the concept of solidarity and its pursuit is affected by the fact that postcolonial studies do not possess a homogenous theory. They are rather a set of various approaches, applied to particular conditions or experience that

---

2. Cunningham uses Theory with the capital T to talk about the modern kind of theory dominating the academia since the 1960s, characterized by its richness of approaches and multidisciplinarity, re-opening some areas of literary impact—such as politics and morality, but also its "obsessive linguisticity" (Cunningham 2002, 19).

are understood as "postcolonial" by its users.[3] The understanding of solidarity and the creation of community(ies) joined by these feelings of
solidarity can therefore vary significantly, depending on the particular
approach applied. Were we to identify some unifying element, apart from
the particular experience which is identified with postcolonialism (although such experience is not always easily described or even recognised),
we could talk about a prevailing general aim of postcolonial theory—the
emergence of a politically as well as a culturally and personally free sub-
ject/community. I believe this is the primary purpose that brought about
the rise of theoretical re-thinking and transformations in the post-World
War II world and gave birth to what we now call postcolonial studies.
With the changing focus of the theory came also the changing concepts of
solidarity, which reflected topical issues of particular stages of postcolonial development, ranging from oppositional (negative) solidarity of
nationalism and anti-colonialism towards more universalising transgressive notions of solidarity as a potentially global phenomenon.

In spite of its original aim, it is problematic for postcolonial theory,
which is basically a creation of literary studies (Ashcroft, Griffiths and
Tiffin 1989, 199), to keep its socially active role and involvement in politics. Within the field of humanities, as Shankar noted in 1994, intentions
are still a taboo, because "modes of legitimation operative for academic
discourse do not permit reference to intention" (Shankar 1994, 480). The
problem, as far as I am concerned, lies in a stereotypical association of
aims/intentions with ideologies that have been avoided by literary criticism wishing to elevate the aesthetic essence of art, thus proving its
sovereignty and freedom from political ideologies. In postcolonial studies,
however, such detachment from any intention would go against the very
foundations of postcolonial studies that emerged as a reaction to particular
historical events (involving struggles for political independence) and that
took it as their innermost duty to challenge theoretical Eurocentric constructs, which were understood as oppressive and exploitative not only on
the theoretical, but also more practical socio-cultural level. Yet the tendency of apolitical literary criticism significantly influenced postcolonial
theory and its understanding of solidarity. After the initial radical and

---

3. Robert Young describes postcolonialism as "a product of human experience [,]
the result of the different experiences of cultural and national origins" (Young
2008, 2). A different view is present in Dirlik's work. He identifies three uses that
coexist simultaneously within postcolonial studies—"the postcolonial" as used for
description of conditions in formerly colonised societies; then as a global condition
after the period of colonialism; and thirdly as a discourse on the before named
conditions (Dirlik 1994, 332).

openly politically active phases, with their evolution into a fully-fledged academically recognised theory, the focus of postcolonial studies turned towards rather descriptive accounts of linguistic and stylistic displays of the oppressive power relations applicable globally. Ella Shohat notes, that this is the greatest paradox of the postcolonial theory—that while stressing its opposition to Eurocentric and universalising metanarratives, and insisting on "historicity and difference," postcoloniality often "mimics in its deployment the ahistorical and universalising tendencies in colonialist thinking" (Shohat in Dirlik 1994, 334). In this way, postcolonial theory moves in a vicious circle in its attempts to counter colonial practices while often reinforcing them in some other form, or by constant generalisation and abstraction which depoliticises the topic so that the original aim of the social transformation vanishes.

I see part of the constant dissatisfaction with the results of various approaches of postcolonial theory in the aim itself. Independence and freedom are necessarily defined as independence/freedom from someone/something, reinforcing the feelings of difference and separation which practitioners of postcolonial studies want to fight against. This kind of freedom is supported by the feeling of solidarity which is formed among the members of the community by identification through segregation. That is by defining itself in terms of one's difference or the so called "Otherness." Emile Durkheim uses the term "negative solidarity" which is understood as being created only to prevent or repair damage. It is passive and does not imply co-operation of different parts of society (Durkheim 1893, 74). A somewhat similar idea, with a label more fitting with my understanding of the developments in postcolonial theory, comes from James Woodburn. He talks about "oppositional solidarity" because it develops "in opposition to domination by outsiders" (Woodburn 2005, 19).

Oppositional solidarity marks the national anti-colonial theoretical approaches as well as works of art informed by these ideas. Their revolutionary stance and attempt to establish their identity as independent of the coloniser was extremely important despite its temporal appeal. They grew out of direct political struggles for national independence, focused on changes in the socio-political sphere, and made it possible to bring to attention topics that later became vital for postcolonial studies. Because of the necessary limitations of oppositional solidarity promoted by national anti-colonialism, it soon became clear that there was a possibility of solidarity to arise also among groups which have suffered a similar fate under colonial rule and which now demanded to be recognised. Its key feature was still the unity based on the opposition (especially non-white, non-Western) and questions that were being dealt with revolved around notions of mimicry, enthusiastic nationalism, and politically involved, often violent, anti-colonialism. Yet the appeal of the approaches became much wider and involved large numbers of groups that were trying to unite to fight their marginalisation by the dominant colonising power.

Two important figures that stood at the roots of what later became postcolonial theory are Aimé Césaire and Frantz Fanon—both significant pre-independence thinkers of the 1950s who were actively participating in the struggles for political, but already also cultural independence of colonised territories and who were already aware of the dangers and necessary failures of mimicry as well as fundamental nationalism. As Dollimore says, the greatest limit of nationalistic literatures lay especially in its high risk of "re-enacting the very exploitation which it is resisting" (Dollimore 1985, 85). Césaire as well as Fanon opposed solidarity created solely around the idea of nationality. Their West Indian background was vital for this understanding of the concept of wider solidarity. Although their race-based solidarity (still clearly oppositional) was now overcome, it represents a significant step in the process towards possible unstinting solidarity,[4] which is trying to achieve the feeling of unity based on similarities rather than differences, and requires active cooperation of the participants in their attempts, as Richard Rorty stresses, to expand their sense of "we" as much as possible (Rorty 1989, 192).

Aimé Césaire's vital text *Discourse on Colonialism* anticipated postcolonial studies by its critique of colonial discourse and material and the spiritual havoc created by colonialism (Kelley 2000, 7-8). Césaire's and Fanon's work, together with those of W.E.B. Du Bois and Padmore, stands for the wave of anti-colonial literature of the post-war period reflecting the revolutionary mood of the time and taking inspiration from theoretical movements which were shaking the traditional concepts of Western thought. Césaire was deeply influenced by the surrealist movement and Marxist theories. He revised and introduced into them some important questions about colonialism, fascism and revolution. Another significant impact on Césaire was caused by the Négritude movement, its founder Léopold Sédar Senghor, and Modernism's appreciation of pre-colonial African tradition (Kelley 2000). Césaire admits that it was the Negro Renaissance movement in the United States that made him "conscious of the solidarity of the black world" transgressing geographical borders. Négritude meant for him a form of solidarity (Césaire in Depestre 1967, 87-89). In contrast to other early anti-colonial thinkers, he was

---

4. Term used by Alessandrini when talking about Said's legacy (Alessandrini 2011b).

aware of the impossibility of a complete return to "ante-European past" and he saw "the importance of Europe in the history of human thought" (Césaire 1972, 7). His considerably complex vision and commitment to "non-national colonial emancipation" (Wilder 2009) places Césaire at the beginning of postcolonial studies as a fully-fledged academic discipline and also at the first steps from the separatist oppositional solidarity.

Fanon's 1961 publication *The Wretched of the Earth,* and the earlier *Black Skin, White Masks* (1952), bear marks typical of the beginnings of the decolonisation period with its revolutionary and often violent mood. Fanon himself took part in the Algerian liberation movement in 1954 and became a supporter of Pan-African unity (Hawley 2001). Fanon, like Césaire, was cautious about nativism and nationalism (vehemently advertised at the early stages by Senghor, Cabral, and Ngugi wa Thiong'o). Fanon saw the danger of "nationalism's exoticised worship of native culture and a blind discarding of Western ways" (Fanon 1965 in Hawley 2001, 321). Later on, these views were supported by Edward Said and Wole Soyinka, who were concerned about the possible outcomes of nativism, pan-Africanism and Islamic fundamentalism (Hawley 2001, 321).

The radical tone of Fanon (as well as Césaire) was a response to the political and social turmoil of the era. It was a time with a high potential of social transformation[5] calling for the establishment of solidarity among people who felt subjugated by the colonialism. Anthony C. Alessandrini emphasises the importance of Fanon's singularity as a Martinican intellectual which allowed him, as well as Césaire, to develop their specific feelings of non-national solidarity (Alessandrini 2011a, 56). Moreover, Fanon was in favour of active support, because he understood "commitment to the struggle [as] a process of solidarity" (Alessandrini 2011a, 62). Edouard Glissant sees typically West Indian postcolonial feelings of ambiguity, discontinuity and creolisation as vital for developing non-national solidarity. Examples of other West Indian intellectuals involved worldwide in decolonisation support his view (Garvey in the USA, Padmore in Ghana) and explain the importance of an early "orthodox" postcolonialism[6] (especially its hybrid West Indian variant) in the transgression towards more unstinting solidarity (Alessandrini 2011a, 63-66). Although Césaire's and Fanon's solidarity was still ethnic or race-based in its opposition to white Western hegemony, it was already more permeable,

---

5. Fanon's work is especially reflective of the radical mood of the 1950s, because of his early death in 1961, which did not allow him to transform and develop his ideas further under the changing circumstances of the following decades.
6. By this I mean postcolonialism coming from the formerly colonised territory, not the newer reciprocal global concept.

forming a background for solidarity based on morality and social justice. Despite the limiting radicalism and racial/ethnical focus, Césaire's and Fanon's thoughts bestirred action and accompanying theoretical debate, necessary for the emergence of postcolonialism. Their work could not yet overcome the boundaries of difference-based solidarity, but it pointed out the deteriorating effects colonialism and imperialism have on such ideas.[7]

With regard to postcolonialism, the 1970s are notable for their transitory character, with strong inclinations towards anti-colonial ideas introduced by Fanon and Césaire, but also emerging dissatisfaction in the already independent countries and disillusionment stemming from the continuing division of power along economic and political as well as cultural lines. Raphael Dalleo talks about the 1970s in the West Indies as a passage from colonialism towards postcolonialism with the context that was no longer strictly anti-colonial and yet not yet fully postcolonial (Dalleo 2011). There were still many countries struggling to gain political independence and directly anti-colonial movements continued to be active (Shohat 1992, 100-103). On the other hand, countries whose expectations were not met by acquisition of political independence moved along what Kim Robinson-Walcott describes as an "ideological trajectory from activism to apathy" in which "an ideological vacuum has been created" (Robinson-Walcott 2008, 129). One of the emerging theoretical concepts reflecting this situation was the idea of neo-colonialism (Gikandi 2006). Multiculturalism, on the other hand, was a more academic-oriented approach that appeared in Western universities and was based on the Western approach to the socio-political situation worldwide.[8] Kerrigan sees multiculturalism as basically a result of the efforts of white settler nations and their states' commitment to equality, which tends somewhat unfortunately to focus on accommodation of different groups rather than their integration (Kerrigan 2012, 17). This theoretical interest in questions of colonisation and power structures, together with ideas introduced by post-structuralism and post-modernism led to the further development of postcolonial theory that settled within Western academia during the following two decades especially due to another dominant figure—Edward Said.

---

7. In many instances, the question of personal identity as well as that of the nation, which is formed by the feeling of solidarity among its members, was almost nonexistent. That is why formation of a postcolonial nation has often gained prominence over more cross-cultural notions of solidarity.
8. Henry Schwarz and Sangeeta Ray comment on the development of postcolonial theory (especially its stages during the 1980s and 1990s) as representing predominantly a "First World academic discourse" (Schwarz 2008, 114).

Edward Said[9] develops Fanon's and Césaire's concepts and moves them from revolutionary centres to academia. His seminal work, *Orientalism* (1978), which benefited greatly from the ideas of the 1950s and 1960s and their gradual transformation throughout the 1970s, represents a thorough theoretical analysis fulfilling requirements of wider academic acceptance establishing the discipline of postcolonial studies proper. To become acknowledged academically, postcolonial theory had to abandon the ideologically extreme position of its radical "preparatory stages," and move away from nationalism and anti-colonialist counter-discourse based on the negation of Western discourse.[10] As Helen Scott notes, the 1970s were the time of crisis in global capitalism and spreading globalisation which revealed continuing ways of colonisation. Moreover, the failure of national liberation to bring equality led to general disillusionment and distrust of nationalism, as many people attributed its failure to its Eurocentrism (Scott 2006). Said refuses a "fetishized national solidarity," which he discusses later in *Culture and Imperialism*, and instead "re-situates the struggle for decolonisation within the global context of the contemporary world system" (Graves 1998).

Orientalism's main concern becomes the examination of the Western discursive creation of the Orient and its stereotypical vision of otherness which supported and justified Western colonial policy. Analysing the connection between literary texts and power structure, Said brought literary studies into the central position within postcolonial theory. He strove to explain the relationship between power and knowledge (politics and scholarship), concepts he took over from Michel Foucault and Antonio Gramsci. In this way, he stresses the social function of literature. But it is not the work of art from the formerly colonised countries that is of vital importance to him. He chooses to re-read the texts coming from the West on which he demonstrates the discursive strategies creating the image of the Other—the Orient. Thus Said is the first postcolonial intellectual to significantly move appeal for solidarity away from the enclosed national anti-colonial or "Third World" community towards the coloniser.

It was from the 1970s that postcolonial critics began with "the deconstruction of the ethnocentric assumptions in Western knowledge" (Ngugi wa Thiong'o talks about "decolonising the mind") (Young 2008, 4). The social transformation which Said called for would be coming through interpretative strategies and from the Western critical reader whose

---

9. Said is a typical representative of the postcolonial intellectual: a Palestinian American academic, political activist, and literary critic with Western-based education.
10. Discussed by Bowie 2003.

understanding of paradigms is being challenged, and who should develop
solidarity based on the feeling of justice (e.g. Said's belief in the justice of
the Palestinian cause and its open support[11]), surpassing the localised national solidarities which Said opposes. Yet this approach (presented in
Orientalism but later becoming more self-critical and balanced in its focus) is still somewhat reductionist, in that Said focuses on the West and its
production of Otherness as well as its committing injustice in a world of
unequal distribution of power.[12] Because of this, Templeton argues, Said's
concept of Orient and Occident preserves the strong binary opposition of
the earlier national anti-colonialism despite its considerable complexity
(Templeton 2007). Despite its flaws, the early work of Said already shows
one of his great legacies, reflecting the mood of the time regarding the
gradual change in political and social structures from the 60s onwards—
the "Saidian impatience to act" (Alessandrini 2011b) which still speaks in
favour of the active participation of individuals in practical change, rather
than institutionalisation and generalisation of the field usually associated
with Said himself and especially his followers in the 1990s. Moreover,
throughout his later work, he makes a significant point by recognising a
vital link between solidarity and criticism which are the main "interactive
forces in the larger process of political engagement" (Keach 2003). The
link between solidarity and criticism which Said proposes is extremely
important for the future understanding and creation of solidarity through
postcolonial literature and theory, because it is capable of balancing the
influences and points of view of the various groups concerned as well as
the preservation of the personal responsibility of the individual whose feelings of justice, dignity and/or solidarity are being challenged. It refuses to
accept unquestioningly solidarity with any particular group. In the essay
"Secular Criticism," Said says that, "even in the very midst of battle in
which one is unmistakably on one side against another, there should be
criticism, because there must be critical consciousness if there are to be
issues, problems, values, even lives to be fought for." Solidarity cannot
come before criticism (Said in Alessandrini 2011b). Said strives for an
unstinting solidarity which can be triggered by revealing injustice of the
dominant system. Although it is aimed at and created basically for that
very system (for which Said's work is often criticised) it nevertheless offers vital ideas which are still applicable in a contemporary situation
provided that we focus not only on the re-education of the (former) coloniser, but all groups involved in the process of the formation of solidarity,

---

11. Discussed by Said in 2003 in "Dignity, Solidarity and the Penal Colony."
12. Said is criticised for this Western-oriented approach, for example, by Ibn
Warraq and Neil Templeton.

creating thus a more complex net of reciprocal inter-communal solidarities (something Said himself later calls for when calling for worldwide solidarity of a just cause of protecting human dignity, but also for the respect of this cause on the part of the victim[13]).

The problematic effect of the gradual institutionalisation of postcolonial theory and the dominance of deconstructive methods, which took over the field after the introduction of Said's persuasive ideas about the creation of the Other from a position of power, was greater vagueness of concepts and doubts about who is really being re(-)presented by them and by whom. After the exposure of hegemonic tendencies of nationalism, and under the influence of post-structuralism's deconstructive techniques, "scholarly discussions of imperialism shifted dramatically from material to representational phenomena" (Wolfe 1997, 406) and although the focus on the social question of postcolonial world dominated, the political aspect retreated into the background of academic discussion and with it the issue of what Gilroy calls practical solidarity. With diversification of the field it became much more difficult to define which group is being targeted, and because of that the idea of solidarity became also more vague and general, in order to accommodate all the different communities which various approaches within postcolonial theory focused on. After nationalism has been discarded for mimicking colonial hegemony, and Said's tendency towards Western-based solidarity became challenged because of its reductionism, some postcolonial theorists opted to focus on more particular representations of postcolonialism, while others tried to combine the early notion or race-based solidarity with Said's appeal to the West and introduce reciprocal interactions between all the groups in question, potentially leading to a mutual feeling of unity regardless of the continuing inequality of distribution of power and ethnic differences. These tendencies are typical for scholars since the 1980s and their exploration of the new discipline, gradually leading to the maturation and institutionalisation of postcolonial studies in the 90s, and to a "codification of a field" by works by Anita Loomba, Bart Moore-Gilbert, Leela Gandhi and others who already opened the question of what shall come after postcolonialism (Hawley 2001, 361). Once institutionalised, postcolonial studies moved away from the political implications of the theory and its historical perspective towards more complex, but also more universalising, concepts. This inevitably led to a reduction of attention paid to attempts to make practical differences including the creation and acquisition of the feeling of inter- as

---

13. Said in 2003 in a video recording of "On Dignity and Solidarity: Scholar, Activist, Palestinian, Edward Said Speaks Out in One of His Last Major Addresses."

well as intra-community solidarity.[14] Yet these questions were tackled on the theoretical level, and thanks to the diversification of the aims of post-colonial intellectuals, new relationships between groups were introduced into the discussion. By questioning all the earlier approaches, the idea of solidarity could transgress the national and racial boundaries of anti-colonialism and pan-Africanism as well as the strong focus on the Western appeal introduced in *Orientalism*.

The field split in the mood of postmodern celebration of multiplicity into approaches analysing the postcolonial intellectual identity of "the subaltern" and his representation (the main concerns of Gayatri Chakravorty Spivak), colonisation and gender, mimicry, hybridity (crucial topics of Homi Bhabha's work) and many more. Despite the limitations of deconstruction, Valentine Cunningham sees the merit of this approach, especially in its achievement to make "readers all at once uneasy about easy meanings, and relaxed about polyphony, multiplicity, and meaning over-spill" (Cunningham 2002, 39) which is necessary in order to accept the diversity of the world in the twenty-first century. Making diversity an accepted norm can help to finally overcome the solidarity boundaries of race or religion, whose influence is still strong in some areas, in favour of solidarity transgressing these more constricted interpretations of commonality and focus more on dignity and justice (called for by Said) as goals to be achieved between groups who understand and are sympathetic to instances of suffering and humiliation (key characteristics of the grounds for solidarity presented by Rorty) regardless of the affiliation of the community concerned.

A postcolonial intellectual who has helped to widen the scope of solidarity in this way is Homi Bhabha. In his observations on colonial mimicry and hybridity he continues to draw on Said's ideas, but goes beyond "notions of colonial discourse as a unilateral projection to open up the reciprocal complexities of the colonial encounter" (Bhabha in Wolfe 1997, 415). Like Spivak, Bhabha uses Derrida, Foucault, Freud, Lacan, or Marx as his sources. However, his main concerns differ from those of Spivak. His work tries to move beyond Said's *Orientalism* and Fanon's *The Wretched of the Earth* by revising "nationalist and nativist pedagogies that set up the relation of Third World and the First World in a binary structure of opposition" (Bhabha in Hawley 2001, 60). Bhabha criticises the homogeneity of Said's colonial discourse (Hawley 2001, 102) which is, according to him, too close to universalising Enlightenment thought.

---

14. Solidarity within smaller groups (such as nations or ethnic groups) as well as reciprocal solidarity between those different groups based on other characteristics than race, ethnicity or nationality.

We can see a great turn in the orientation here, since Bhabha tries to bring postcolonial non-Western society and its perception of the postcolonial experience back into the centre of attention. But most of all, he turns our attention to the reciprocity of the relationships between all the spheres of the colonised-coloniser continuum. With this transformation of the paradigm, postcolonialism can describe not only the experience of those formerly colonised, but a complex experience of all those involved in the process of colonisation. Such a point of view comes closest to enabling the creation of truly unstinting solidarity as it is trying to encompass the complexity of possible relationships that come to form what became understood as the twenty-first century postcolonial society.

As indicated before, based on Said's and Bhabha's understandings of hybridity, and notions such as multiculturalism or globalisation, the literary criticism of postcolonial texts and postcolonial studies in general, take on a kind of hybrid form themselves. Although there are important names representing different approaches, they are not as prominent as the figures of Césaire, Fanon, Said, Spivak and Bhabha. Since the 1990s, we can encounter a rich amalgam of ideas reaching into many fields, exploring further issues of the position and role of the postcolonial intellectual and pedagogical implications (Shankar's need to revise curricula in history and literature classes), limitations of theories used before for postcolonial criticism (Marxism, poststructuralism, postmodernism, dependency theory, theory of globalisation), the insufficiency of existing terminology and its interpretation (postcolonial, Third World, multicultural), neo-colonialism, the role of the individual author/reader in resistance to dominant forms, the return to more politically active reading and writing through a return to rhetoric, but also newly emerging fields drawing upon experience of postcolonial studies such as whiteness studies (Sara Ahmed) or ecocriticism (Greg Garrard). There are even voices calling for the abandonment of postcolonial theory altogether, because of its ongoing generalisation and globalisation (McClintock), and because of its supposed exhaustion, or its inadequacy in a world that is still full of colonial structures.[15]

Despite these rather pessimistic propositions about the current state of postcolonial studies and its future, artistic production, which we would describe as postcolonial, is still kept in the focus of many intellectuals who struggle with the complexity of the field of postcolonial studies which has become increasingly difficult to handle. Redirecting the aim of the field towards the possibility of unstinting solidarity achieved by imagination could help to guide postcolonial theory on a new (or maybe rather

---

15. Difficulties discussed for example in McClintok and Hawley.

rediscovered) trail of thought, because although the idea of solidarity has always been present in some way in the concept of the postcolonial, it has not been realised to its full potential. The main point is to acknowledge and use the potential of postcolonial literature not only to describe/distribute the idea of solidarity, but significantly and directly contribute to its creation through its informational value but also its emotional effect on the audience. The possible return to more socio-politically involved texts and their interpretations is also reflected in some recent approaches following the ideas of rhetoric, integrating again the aesthetic as well as social function of art emphasising not independence of the subject (leading to oppositional solidarity) but inter-communal unstinting solidarity (not restricted to racial, ethnical or national identity). Focus on the concept of solidarity as such could help to overcome the continuing binarism of approaches, with its consequential prolongation of the feeling of separation and inequality.

After many shifts in the focus of postcolonial theory we have come to a point where it is clear that some kind of dependence is always present between the parts of a global world. As I have indicated before, independence as the aim of postcolonial studies can be substituted by the desire to create a feeling of solidarity based on the developing feeling of justice engaging people's morals. Rorty points out the crucial role of literature in this process (especially focusing on the novel), thanks to its ability to teach us to see "more traditional differences (of tribe, religion, race, customs, and the like) as unimportant when compared with similarities with respect to pain and humiliation" thus widening our sense of "we" as much as possible (Rorty 1989, 192). Such form of solidarity is capable of accepting diversity in the complex structures of the global world and is therefore really capable of transgressing the old power dichotomies postcolonial theory has been trying to erase.

Postcolonial theory as a literary-based approach has a great, still unexploited potential presented by the combination of the aesthetic and socio-political aspects of experience present in a literary work to develop various feelings of solidarity. The reason, and why this chapter focuses on the role of postcolonial literary criticism, is its close connection to questions of social transformation and its emphasis on the political aspects of art and the important position of solidarity as one of its concepts; phenomena largely neglected in recent postcolonial theory. Literature reflects social changes and is itself capable of initiating them. Postcolonial theory, which tried to challenge and change social structures (especially those power-based), found a powerful instrument in literature, which is suitable for non-violent action working through an individual reader's/writer's conscience through which it has been striving to change some basic stereotypical structures of perception (ranging from the early examples of works such as those of Olaudah Equiano or Harriet Beecher Stowe, typical post-war (post-independence) representatives like George Lamming and Chinua Achebe, to more recent work of Salman Rushdie or Hanif Kureishi). Postcolonial thinkers supplemented imaginative literature with their new approaches and topics, thus creating and teaching new ways of reading that would guide the individual reader to a greater variability of the understanding of texts and through them perception of the world.

Nevertheless, the socio-political orientation of postcolonial studies collides with its desire to fit into the field of the humanities which has tendencies towards generalisation and theorisation rather than striving for direct impact on society. After the focus on the aesthetic value of art and its sublimity, dominant until the early twentieth century, it was postcolonial theory (together with Marxism and feminism) that brought the socio-political aspect of art back into consideration, and the aesthetic receded into the background. Paradoxically, the focus on the socio-political sphere has long been a limitation on the development of postcolonial literary criticism. Lalita Pandit in her essay "Introduction: Local, Global, Postcolonial" says that it wanted to undo the previous Eurocentric aesthetically-oriented critical tradition so much, that it led to a "general distrust of already established criteria" resulting in a focus on counter-discourse and its ability to reveal and transgress power-structures imposed by Western theories. This gradually caused postcolonial theory to reach "an impasse where discussion of the aesthetic merits of postcolonial literature are almost forbidden" (Pandit 1993, 6). On the other hand, she feels in 1993 that a time is approaching when "postcolonial theorists will no longer consider it necessary to dogmatically separate the aesthetic from the political" (Pandit 1993, 6).[16] The late twentieth and early twenty-first century theoretical developments suggest that there are emerging attempts to reconnect and balance the aesthetic and the socio-political within the study of postcolonial literature. One of them is the aforementioned return to ideas of rhetoric supporting the reading of intention in literature while still calling for aesthetic refinement. Raka Shome talks about adding the postcolonial perspective to the new revisions of rhetoric (including reassessed criteria, assumptions and methods) as a still new, but extremely important development (Shome 1996, 40).[17]

---

16. Also called for by Richard Rorty.
17. Shome is interested in rhetoric studies as her main field of research, but even the idea of including postcolonial perspective into this field (not vice versa) is extremely important within the context discussed in this text.

This development is vital if postcolonial literary criticism wants to ex-
ploit fully the potential that postcolonial literature offers. The advantage of
literary work as a source of potential transformative impulses is exactly
the combination of the feeling of justice and moral conscience aroused by
the events described and its historical circumstances, but also by the emotional message supported by the form and style of the work with which the
audience is able to identify, and later actively fight against the pain and
humiliation conveyed by the text.[18] The aesthetic impact of the work is
taking place mostly on the personal subjective level of perception and interpretation. This is very important, as it allows the audience to view what
they see as a freedom of choice and a personal responsibility for their
moral commitments, the possibility of individual critical evaluation in
opposition to imposition of norms formulated by a dominant power structure. I believe that aesthetic pleasure, in fact, supports and strengthens the
participative emotion aroused by literary work leading towards the greater
human liberty that Rorty speaks about (Rorty 1989, 147).[19] Without the
theoretically acknowledged balance between the aesthetic and socio-
political levels of postcolonial literature, postcolonial literary production
threatens to become only a temporary academic interest, based on the time
and place of its origin, placing postcolonial literature at the same level
with the short-term influences of political manifestos. It is the complex
and mutable[20] works of art (not only postcolonial literature) that are capable of reflecting their specific spatio-temporal location of creation, but also
endure and enrich future interpretations of works of art through the more
generally perceptible experience they convey. By joining the socio-
political and aesthetic levels of postcolonial literature, postcolonial theory
can widen the scope of solidarity it can deal with and also convey this solidarity more effectively.

Creation of unstinting solidarity (or rather its pursuit)[21] in the culturally
hybrid global world needs individuals accepting their personal responsibility for their actions in the social context(s). In addition, it is exactly the
work of fiction, Felski says, that often leads us to the intensive self-
scrutiny (Felski 2008, 24) necessary for the possible change of our stereo-

---

18. Two important feelings discussed by Rorty in connection with the process of
learning solidarity.
19. Rorty describes the two effects as non-competitive but rather distinct. I want to
stress their compatibility and mutual support.
20. Mutability is one of the characteristics Harold Bloom identifies as leading to
canonicity of works of art and through it to their long-term influence.
21. I agree with Rorty that essential and ahistorical "human solidarity" is
impossible, yet worth fighting for (Rorty 1989, 189).

typical points of view and value systems. Personal "inner" experience therefore serves here as the impulse for subsequent questioning of acquired paradigms and possible redefinition of our attitudes, thus joining yet again the personal with the public. By offering unfamiliar points of view, imaginative literature leads the reader to a possible reinterpretation of his or her culturally-acquired perceptions. Solidarity is one of the most important concepts that can be challenged in this way. Rorty is sure that greater solidarity can be achieved through imaginative literature through its "detailed description of what unfamiliar people are like and of redescription of what we ourselves are like." It is created by increasing our sensitivity to pain and humiliation experienced by other, "unfamiliar sorts of people." "Such increased sensitivity," Rorty says, "makes it more difficult to marginalise people different from ourselves" (Rorty 1989, xvi). The aesthetic aspect of literary work can significantly support this increasing of sensitivity of individuals as it helps to trigger the emotional involvement of the reader in otherwise rather unfamiliar situations or contexts that may be described by the text.

I believe this kind of solidarity and its creation is suitable and desirable for the twenty-first century trans-cultural world, whose communities are faced with great diversity in all spheres of life. It will become increasingly important to work on the feeling of solidarity to enable various groups not only to tolerate but also to accept difference as a principal characteristic of a global society. Purely aesthetic, or other solely theoretical approaches to literature, are capable of arousing only intellectual forms of solidarity without its transposition into the real world. On the other hand, politically-based solidarity necessarily leads to some form of separation as it evolves around claims of sovereignty (or opposition to such claims). The balanced combination can make it possible to come closer to inter-subjective unstinting solidarity which is accessible through literary creation and its interpretation. There is also one of the significant points Alessandrini makes—and that is the creation of positive vision by criticism not as the affirmation of the present, but rather of a vision of a possible future (Alessandrini 2012). In this way it would be easier to abandon the focus on pessimistic visions of continuing inequality and methods to oppose them (reinforcing the binary structures of coloniser-colonised), and rather work towards the future improvement of relationships and increasing the scope of inter-communal solidarity that can transform systems of beliefs and values that are at the heart of the inequalities world societies are facing. Whether this goal will be reached by postcolonial theory depends on its future evolution. Contemporary calls for revision of the principles of rhetoric as well as other individual approaches trying to join the aesthetic and the political (as suggested for example by Raka Shome, Peter Childs or Anthony Alessandrini) seem to be appropriate steps towards this goal.

References

Alessandrini, Anthony C. 2011a. "Fanon Now: Singularity and Solidarity." *Journal of Pan-African Studies* 4.7:52-74.
—. 2011b. "Missing Edward Said." *Jadaliyya*, Arab Studies Institute. Accessed February 25, 2013.
http://www.jadaliyya.com/pages/index/2759/missing-edward-said.
—. 2012. "Singularity and Solidarity: Postcolonial Criticism after the Arab Spring." *The Postcolonial Studies Group*. Accessed May 12, 2013.
http://opencuny.org/psg/2012/04/april-19-singularity-and-solidarity-postcolonial-criticism-after-the-arab-spring/.
Ahmad, Aijaz. 1987. "Jameson's Rhetoric of Otherness and the 'National Allegory'." *Social Text* 17:3-25.
Ashcroft, Bill, Gareth Griffiths and Helen Tiffin. 2002. *The Empire Writes Back*, 2nd ed. London: Routledge.
Bowie, Andrew. 1997. *From Romanticism to Critical Theory: The Philosophy of German Literary Theory*. London: Routledge.
—. 2003. *Aesthetics and Subjectivity: From Kant to Nietzsche*, 2nd ed. Manchester United UP.
Césaire, Aimé. 1972. *Discourse on Colonialism*. Translated by Joan Pinkham. New York: Monthly Review Press.
Cunningham, Valentine. 2002. *Reading After Theory*. Oxford: Blackwell.
Dalleo, Raphael. 2013. "Performing Postcoloniality in the Jamaican Seventies." *Postcolonial Text*. 6.1. Accessed June 20, 2013.
http://postcolonial.org/index.php/pct/article/viewArticle/1213.
Depestre, René. 1967. "An Interview With Aimé Césaire". In *Discourse on Colonialism*, by Aimé Césaire, 79-94. New York: Monthly Review Press.
Dirlik, Arif. 1994. "The Postcolonial Aura: Third World Criticism in the Age of Global Capitalism." *Critical Inquiry* 20.2:328-356.
Dollimore, Jonathan. 1985. "Transgression and Surveillance in Measure for Measure." In *Political Shakespeare: New Essays in Cultural Materialism*. Manchester: Manchester UP.
Durkheim, Emile. 1893. *The Division of Labor in Society*. Translated by George Simpson. 1964. New York: Free Press.
Felski, Rita. 2008. *Uses of Literature*. Oxford: Blackwell.
Gikandi, Simon. 2006. "Postcolonialism's Ethical (Re)Turn: An Interview with Simon Gikandi by David Jefferes." *Postcolonial Text* 2.1. Ac-

cessed June 20, 2013. http://www.postcolonial.org/index.php/pct/article/viewArticle/464/845.

Graves, Benjamin. 1998. "Bruce Robbinson on Edward W. Said's 'Voyage In'." Postcolonialweb.org, Accessed December 10, 2012. http://www.postcolonialweb.org/poldiscourse/said/said4.html.

Hawley, John C. ed. 2001. *Encyclopedia of Postcolonial Studies*. Westport: Greenwood Press.

Keach, Bill. 2003. "A Burning Opposition to Imperialist Brutality." *International Socialist Review* 32. Accessed December 10, 2012. http://www.isreview.org/issues/32/said.shtml.

Kelley, Robin D.G. 2000. "A Poetics of Anticolonialism." Introduction to *Discourse on Colonialism*, by Aimé Césaire, 8-28. New York: Monthly Review Press.

Kerrigan, Dylan. 2012. "Culture Contact: Trinidad 'Pre-History,' Historical Representation and Multiculturalism." *Journal of the Department of Behavioural Science*, 1:15-33.

Pandit, Lalita. 1993. "Introduction: Local, Global, Postcolonial." *College Literature*. 20.1:1-6.

Robinson-Walcott, Kim. 2008. "Legitimate Resistance: A Survival Story – the Crisis of Political Ideology and the Quest for Resolution in Some Recent Jamaican Novels." *Lucayos* 1:128-38.

Rorty, Richard. 1989. *Contingency, Irony and Solidarity*. Cambridge: Cambridge University Press.

Said, Edward. 2003a. "On Dignity and Solidarity: Scholar, Activist, Palestinian, Edward Said Speaks Out in One of His Last Major Addresses." *Democracy Now!* Accessed February 24, 2013. http://www.democracynow.org/2003/10/20/on_dignity_and_solidarity_scholar_activist.

—. 2003b. "Dignity, Solidarity and the Penal Colony". *Counterpunch*. Accessed December 10, 2012. http://www.unz.org/Pub/CounterpunchWeb-2003sep-00185.

Schwarz, Henry and Sangeeta Ray. eds. 2000. *A Companion to Postcolonial Studies*. Oxford: Bleckwell.

Scott, Helen. 2006. "Reading the Text in its Worldly Situation: Marxism, Imperialism, and Contemporary Caribbean Women's Literature." *Postcolonial Text*, 2.1. *Postcolonial.org*, Accessed March 20, 2012. http://postcolonial.org/index.php/pct/article/view/491/174.

Shankar, S. 1994. "The Thumb of Ekalavya: Postcolonial Studies and the 'Third World'Scholar in a Neocolonial World." *World Literature Today*, 68.3:479-87.

Shohat, Ella. 1992. "Notes on the 'Post-Colonial.'" *Social Text* 31/32:99-113.

Shome, Raka. 1996. "Postcolonial Interventions in the Rhetorical Canon: An 'Other' View." *Communication Theory* 40-59. *Academia.edu.* Accessed June 12, 2013. http://www.academia.edu/501975/Postcolonial_ interventions_in_the_rhetorical_canon_An_other_view.

Spivak, GayatriChakravorty. 1994. "Can the Subaltern Speak?" *Colonial Discourse and Post-Colonial Theory,* edited by Williams and Chrisman, 66-100. New York: Columbia UP.

Templeton, Neil. 2007. "Orientalism: A Critique." *The Imperial Archive.* Accessed June 20, 2012. http://www.qub.ac.uk/schools/SchoolofEnglish/imperial/transnational/ Orientalism-critique.html.

Wilder, Gary. 2012. "Untimely Vision: AiméCésaire, Decolonization, Utopia." *Public Culture* 21.1. Accessed December 9, 2012. http://publicculture.dukejournals.org/content/21/1/101.abstract.

Woodburn, James. 2005. "Egalitarian Societies Revisited." *Property and Equality: Ritualization, Sharing, Egalitarianism: Volume I,* edited by Widlok and Gossa Tadesse, 18-31. Berghahn Books.

Young, Robert J.C. 2008. "What is the Postcolonial?: Anglican Identities and the Postcolonial." Talk presented at the Lamberth Conference, July 21.

SOCIAL FUNCTION

CHAPTER SIX

SOCIAL COHESION IN ISRAEL: DIFFERENCES BETWEEN MIGRANTS AND MINORITIES

SIBYLLE HEILBRUNN, LIEMA DAVIDOVICH AND LEAH ACHDUT

The purpose of this chapter is to investigate social cohesion in Israel. The theoretical model underlying this study is based upon works of Jenson (1998), Bernard (1999), Berger-Schmitt (1999), and Chan *et al.* (2006) and postulates that social cohesion is collective and multidimensional, encompassing the economic, political, and socio-cultural spheres. Israel is a society with a high level of diversity, composed of a variety of groups, including migrant as well as minority populations.

This chapter begins by giving an overview of the dominant discourse on social cohesion with a focus on its link with diversity. The second part explains the complexity of the Israeli context, followed by the presentation of the three particular groups investigated in the current study, namely immigrants from the former Soviet Union (FSU), immigrants from Ethiopia, and the Palestinian Arab minority. We then proceed to investigate the three groups in terms of economic, political, and socio-cultural domains of social cohesion.

The dominant discourse on social cohesion is about "living together" and the development of common values, shared symbols, and shared ceremonies, in short, common denominators. Following a first approach leaning on Durkheim's traditional concept of collective conscience, a society cannot continue to exist without a widespread body of norms accepted by the majority of its members, especially when they are expected to make sacrifices for the common good (Soroka *et al.* 2004). The lack of a common sense of national identity is considered the main reason for the unwillingness of national majorities to include "others" within a system of fair redistribution of society's resources. A second approach argues that extensive engagement and participation of society's members are crucial for social integration. The central question here concerns the way people live together rather than who they are. In diverse heterogeneous democratic societies, social cohesion cannot be acquired via common norms and values, but rather there is a need for a general consensus on the institutions and procedures of liberal democracy through which tensions can be mediated and conflicts adjudicated (Berger 1998). Thus, active engagement of diverse groups in society is crucial for social cohesion. A third approach focuses on social capital, represented by social networks and norms of trust (Osberg 2003). Interpersonal trust is assumed to foster cooperation among people and to facilitate collective action with powerful implications for economic, cultural and political life (Putnam 1995, 2000, 2004; Uslaner 2002). These and other attempts to define social cohesion have resulted in a multiplicity of understandings, summarised by Beauvais and Jensen (2002) as common values and a civic culture, social order and social control, social solidarity and reductions in wealth disparities, social networks and social capital, and territorial belonging/place attachment and identity. The authors further maintain that the definition used for social cohesion impacts the determination of variable constitution as well as recommended policies. Thus various patterns of causation emerge, with social cohesion being either cause or consequence in the respective studies. Social cohesion can be understood as impacting economic performance and wellbeing, health and participation rates and legitimacy of democratic institutions. Studies based on social cohesion as an independent variable concentrate on what it does to society focusing on social capital and networks. Putnam and others assume that social cohesion increases wellbeing, although most studies find covariance rather than causality between the variables. Along the same lines, there is an assumption that political, social, and economic participation increases social cohesion or at least interacts with it, thus relating to social cohesion as a dependent variable. Summarising the debate of causality of social cohesion we conclude with Beauvais and Jensen (2002) that social cohesion is not a unidirectional but rather an interactive, multidimensional phenomenon.

Globalisation, the growth in international migration and the subsequent demographic changes are encouraging increasing interest in the link between diversity and social cohesion, since they are considered factors influencing social cohesion and social solidarities. The underlying concern and assumption is that social exclusion of individuals and groups can become a major threat to economic prosperity and social cohesion for society as a whole. Therefore presumably processes of globalisation, migration and modernisation comprise a challenge to social cohesion, integration, justice and solidarity because societies are becoming increasingly diverse. Anhut and Heitmeyer (2005) maintain that social disintegration and de-solidarisation might be the result.

An overview of empirical studies reveals rather mixed findings as to the effects of ethnic diversity on dimensions of social cohesion. Putnam (2007) argues that ethnic diversity leads to declining solidarity and re-duced levels of trust, thus diversity is a factor potentially undermining social cohesion. Also, Alesina and La Ferrara (2002) maintain that in most of the current literature there is an assumption that diversity and social cohesion are negatively related. In other words, people would be less dis-posed to develop solidarity with all members of society the more diverse a society or community is. Studies conducted in the United States revealed that in diverse societies it is more difficult to foster generalised trust which is usually a reliable indicator of social cohesion. Some studies indicate that generalised trust tends to be lower in ethnically fractionalised communities or in geographic areas with large ethnic and/or racial minorities (Alesia and La Ferrara 2000; Costa and Kahn 2003; Gijberts *et al.* 2011). Studies conducted in western European countries show controversial findings, some supporting Putnam's thesis (Gesthuizen *et al.* 2008; Tolsma *et al.* 2009), whereas others find little empirical evidence to support the claim that ethnic diversity negatively affects cohesion (Li *et al.* 2005; Letki 2008; Gijberts *et al.* 2011). Cross-national comparisons assessing diversity as a national characteristic tend to reject the Putnam claim (cf. Gesthuizen, *et al.* 2008; Hooghe *et al.* 2009; Gijberts *et al.* 2011). While the empirical studies do not provide conclusive evidence as to the question whether and to what extent diversity undermines social cohesion, some research elabo-rates on the shortcomings of the discourse in itself.

Cheong *et al.* (2007) provide an excellent overview summarising the main arguments of the social diversity – social cohesion discourse critical-ly. They start with the key challenge which is to "strike a balance between cultural autonomy and social solidarity, so that the former does not lapse into separatist and essentialised identities and so that the latter does not slide into minority cultural assimilation and Western conformity" (Amin 2002, 974). They further point to the importance of stressing the multidi-mensionality of concepts of "belonging" and "social cohesion" (Yuval-Davis *et al.* 2005), rather than assuming a mono-culturalist concept of so-cial cohesion denying and negating the fact that identities are context dependent, complex and related to various intersections of nation-state, ethnicity, religion and culture. This assumption may lead to a path where social cohesion develops via social alienation of "others" who have not adopted the dominant language and culture of the mainstream. Ben-Tovim

(2002) goes further and rejects the idea that social cohesion can be achieved via a social capital building approach. He stresses that institutionalised practices and structures of racism have created inequalities in opportunities and outcomes of opportunities for minorities in the first place (Ben-Tovim 2002, 46).

While taking into consideration the potential ideological shortcomings of the diversity-cohesion discourse, we want to point to a number of challenges associated with the incorporation of people from different cultures within a society: reconciliation of diversity with common feelings of membership; tackling the connection between economic disadvantage and cultural exclusion of minorities; promoting mutual understanding between groups; and enabling greater public participation of all groups in society.

The theoretical model that best captures these challenges is based on works of Jenson (1998), Bernard (1999), Berger-Schmitt (1999) and Chan *et al.* (2006). It assumes that social cohesion is collective rather than individual and multidimensional including activity spheres (economic, political and socio-cultural) and formal relations and behaviors. The components of the economic domain concern inclusion versus exclusion, addressing the question of who is included or excluded from the economy, and equality versus inequality assuming that equality is an essential part of social cohesion. We named this dimension with the term "having part" of society. The components of the political domain concern legitimacy versus illegitimacy, addressing the question of how adequately institutions such as the government and political parties represent the people and are perceived as legitimate, and participation versus passivity which focuses on peoples' political participation. We named this dimension with the term "taking part" in society. The components of the socio-cultural domain concern recognition versus rejection, addressing tolerance for diversity, and belonging versus isolation, addressing the issue of existence or absence of shared values and a sense of identity. We named this dimension with the term "being part" of society.

In the remaining part of this chapter, we investigate the three domains of social cohesion in Israel focusing upon three population groups: immigrants from the former Soviet Union (FSU), immigrants from Ethiopia, and Israeli Palestinian Arabs, constituting a national minority in Israel.

The Israeli Context

Israel is characterised by its many cultures and ethnic and national groups. The Israeli case, whether defined as a Jewish state, a state of all its citizens or something in between, can be seen in context of a broader discussion on relations between subgroups and states and nation and emerging meanings of citizenship in heterogeneous countries (Migdal, 2006). The immigration of Jews to Israel is one of the formative events of this country's society. The Jewish people consider Israel to be their homeland, and thus under Israeli law, every Jew has the right to immigrate to Israel. As a result, Israeli society views Jewish immigration as a "returning diaspora" and not as an economic migration (Semyonov and Lewin-Epstein 2003). Israel is a democratic Jewish state, often described in terms of ethnocratic multiculturalism (Al-Haj 2004) or as an ethno-nationalist country since, following the Law of Return, Jews entering the country have extensive rights and receive social acceptance (Bartam 2010). Smooha (2004) maintains that Israel is an ethnic democracy or tri-cultural society without a multiculturalist ethos. He further states that the predominant culture is a rather secular Jewish one alongside Arab and ultra-Orthodox minority cultures. In the Israeli case, nationality is the main key to participation in various social domains. Jewishness is the main sociopolitical indicator dividing Arabs and Jews; whereas phenotypical and ethnic indicators are meaningful within the Jewish segment of society (Mizrachi and Herzog 2012, 419). Although there is a reality of multiplicity of cultures, subcultures and sectors, Israel is not a multicultural democracy in the classical sense (Kimmerling 1998). As Smooha (2004) explains, normatively Zionism is not concerned with multiculturalism. He maintains that when culture overlaps with class, cultural diversity inevitably turns into cultural hierarchy. Therefore separate cultures such as the Ethiopian (even though Jewish) or the Arab Muslim culture might be a hindrance to social mobility. For Arabs and ultra-Orthodox, the state provides institutions to promote separate life. "Arab culture is well protected but not respected by Jewish majority" (Smooha 2004, 49) and the ultra-Orthodox minority is not satisfied with its cultural autonomy and "attempts to impose its *halakhic* culture on the entire country" (Smooha 2004, 49).

Israel has a strong economy. Israel's 2009 economic performance, in the face of a global meltdown, suggests impressive growth in 2010. Israel's GDP grew in 2009 by 0.5%, compared to an average 3.5% decline in OECD countries. At the same time Israel's level of economic inequality is one of the highest among developed countries. In 2011, Israel was ranked fifth in unequal income distribution among thirty-four OECD countries with the US ranking fourth and Chile ranking first (OECD Data 2011). Israel's level of economic inequality is 22% higher than the average for OECD countries. One in four residents of Israel lives below the poverty line (1.7 million altogether), which is more than twice the average of

Western countries. Israel also has one of the highest migrant stock proportions of the world. Thus Israel is a society with many facets encompassing very diverse groups, with a strong economy on the one hand but vast inequalities on the other. In order to discuss the issue of the economic, political and socio-cultural domains of social cohesion in Israel, we chose to focus upon three groups, representing three types of populations in Israel, with probably the only similarity between them being the fact that they belong to the "others," namely they are not part of the dominant mainstream, even though for different reasons.

Since the mid-1980s, Israel has received immigrants from two major Jewish diasporas—the former Soviet Union (FSU) and Ethiopia. Each of these immigrant groups is characterised by unique ideological, cultural, social and economic attributes. Immigrants from the former Soviet Union comprise about 20% of the Jewish population in Israel today. The massive wave of these immigrants that arrived in Israel between 1989 and 2000 shaped a new dynamic and pluralistic social reality. The main features of this group include rich human assets, a greater motivation to leave the Soviet Union than to settle in Israel, and a desire to preserve their Russian cultural uniqueness while integrating into Israeli society. The Ethiopian immigrants arrived in three waves: the first wave arrived in mid-80s, the second wave in the beginning of the 90s, and the third wave continues until today. Since 1980, about 100,000 immigrants have arrived in Israel from Ethiopia. In several parameters, the Ethiopian immigration is highly different in character to the immigration from the former Soviet Union (HaCohen 2002; Peres and Ben-Rafael 2006). First, the FSU immigrants represent a large population of over one million individuals, while the Ethiopians are a relatively small group of 140,000 (1.4% of the Israeli population). Second, the overwhelming majority of FSU immigrants are secular, while the Ethiopian Jews are mostly religious. Third, the FSU immigrant population contains a high number of educated and professional individuals (higher than the percentage in the general population of Israel) (Remennick 2004; Peres and Ben-Rafael 2006); by contrast, the Ethiopian immigrants have a very low average level of education, as in their origin country 90% of the adult population is illiterate (Lazin 2002). This group constitutes a new phenomenon of black Jews in the Israeli context. Some research has been done on racially based discrimination of members of the Ethiopian community (Mizrachi and Herzog 2012; Ben-Eliezer 2004). Mizrachi and Herzog (2012) state that although belonging as Jews to the dominant majority in Israel, their phenotype (being black Jews) stigmatises and serves as a basis for discrimination.

However, disregarding their socio-economic disparities, in Israel both immigrant groups are minority "out-groups" in relation to the veteran Jewish majority population (the "in-group"). The differences between the groups, namely their size, socio-economic status, degree of religiosity, and level of education, lead us to expect substantial variance as to their integration and features of social cohesion.

Palestinian Arab citizens of Israel, typically referred to as either Israeli Palestinians or Israeli Arabs, comprise approximately 20% of Israel's population. They constitute a distinct minority separated from the Jewish majority by national identity, religion, language, and culture (Smooha 1998). The vast majority of the Israeli Palestinians are Muslims with a minority of Christians and Druze (Ghanem 2001; Mizrachi and Herzog 2012). Formally included as citizens, as non-Jews Israeli Arabs are socially excluded in terms of residence, land ownership, labor market participation, housing and political representation. They have long been described as the lowest socio-economic stratum (Lewin-Epstein and Semyonov 1994; Shafir and Peled 2002). Schnell and Sofer (2002) overview the literature on Jewish-Arab relations in Israel, and state that marginalisation of the Arab population can be categorised into four main aspects: discriminatory state policies, a class structure that differentiates among ethnic groups, cultural and social-structural gaps, and socio-spatial segregation in the national and geographic periphery. In addition, gaps between the Jewish and Arab population increased in areas such as socio-economic status and education. Also Mizrachi and Herzog (2012) found that the structural position of Palestinian citizens in Israeli society limits their scope of participation to instrumental relations.

Investigating configurations of integration of three very different groups in Israeli society in terms of the above-mentioned domains (economic, political and socio-cultural) can exemplify these domains as well as the interplay between them for each group. By taking into consideration the three dimensions of social cohesion and suggesting that various configurations of trade-offs are possible, we account for differences between and among groups and for particularities as well as similarities. We can thereby leave the path of a dichotomous model of state-minority relations critiqued by Migdal (2006) as not accounting for various lines of differentiations and exclusions.

In the remaining part of this chapter we look at the different domains underlying social cohesion for the three groups described above.

Domains of Social Cohesion:
Having Part, Taking Part and Being Part

Following Dickes *et al.* (2010), the economic domain of social cohesion can be measured in terms of market share capacities and equality in chances and conditions, thereby accounting for the formal inclusion/exclusion aspect and the equality/inequality aspects of "having part" of society. Data of the Ruppin Index of Immigrant Integration in Israel[1] (2010) reveal differences between the three groups investigated as to monthly average income per capita (data for 2008). Immigrants from the FSU have an average monthly income per capita of 3,222 NIS (New Israeli Shekel), which is higher than the overall Israeli average including the entire population of 2,996 NIS. Immigrants from Ethiopia have an average of 2,005 NIS and the Israeli Arabs rate lowest with an average monthly per capita income of 1,522 NIS. As to percentage of unemployment, the data reveal 3.1% for immigrants from the FSU, 12.7% for immigrants from Ethiopia and 6.2% for the Israeli Palestinian Arab population. When comparing the percentage of group members reporting difficulties covering living expenses (accounting for the equality/inequality aspect of the economic domain) the data reveal that 51% of FSU immigrants reported difficulties covering living expenses, followed by 61% of the Ethiopian immigrants and Arab Israelis with 67%. Thus, in the economic domain FSU immigrants rank highest on both criteria. They are followed by immigrants from Ethiopia, with the Arab Israelis rating lowest.

The political domain encompasses aspects of legitimacy of public and private institutions acting as mediators between a group and society, and voting behaviour expressing participation of a group in the public domain (Dickes *et al.* 2010). Data on voting behaviour of the Israeli population in general reveal a steady decrease in participation in the general elections to 65.2% in 2009.

The Arab population is represented by four political parties in the present Israeli Knesset established after the last elections in 2009. Fifty-four percent of the Arab citizens participated in the elections in 2009; 82% voted for Arab parties or for the joint Jewish-Arab party. Altogether there are seventeen Arab Knesset members, seven of them members of Arab political parties, three members of the Jewish-Arab party, and the remaining

---

1. The Ruppin Index was constructed in a way that will allow for an annual follow-up of a series of data within seven population groups including immigrants from the FSU, immigrants from Ethiopia and Arab citizens of Israel. The index focuses on those changes occurring in the various dimensions for the period from 2003 to 2008 and was published in 2010 (Semyonov et.al, 2010).

seven are members of Jewish parties of a variety of ideological outlooks. Detailed data on the voting behaviour of the Arab population show that the majority voted specifically for Arab parties and not Jewish-Zionist parties, thus choosing to differentiate themselves in the political domain but not to disconnect (Koren 2010).

Four ministers in the present government are immigrants from the FSU. With Fifteen Knesset members, the Israel Beiteinu party– traditionally representing also but not only political interests of immigrants from the FSU–became the third largest Knesset faction, thus making the party a key element in any government coalition. Altogether in the 18th Knesset of 2009 there are 14 members of FSU origin. Detailed data on political participation and voting behaviour of immigrants from the FSU show that they are highly engaged in the political arena, associating themselves with various parties. Immigrants from the FSU are a main factor in the political landscape of Israel. The Ethiopian community has one representative in the current Knesset who is affiliated with Kadima, a newly established political party located at the centre of the political arena of Israel.

The socio-cultural domain encompasses a sense of acceptance by and belonging to society (Dickes *et al.* 2010). Data retrieved by a survey on perceptions of solidarity in Israeli society (Achdut *et al.* 2012) show that 66% of the Jewish population thinks that Israeli Arabs do not contribute enough to society. About 42% consider the same for Ethiopian immigrants, and 31% think that immigrants from the FSU do not contribute their share to society. Thus it seems that economic integration, which is high among FSU immigrants, is not sufficient to be accepted into the societal mainstream by the majority. These data reflect the picture of the economic domain. When accounting for the feeling of belonging of the three groups, data of the Ruppin Index of Immigrant Integration in Israel (2010) reveal that 48.7% of the immigrants from the FSU, 60.6% of the Ethiopian immigrants and 35.1% of the Israeli Arabs reported feelings of loneliness. One could speculate that the relative lower degree of loneliness among the Israeli Palestinians can be explained by the fact that they are a separate group, not to be expected to be part of the Jewish national mainstream. This lack of mutual expectation then probably enforces in-group attachments. As to identification with society, a survey conducted in 2008 (Sorek 2011) revealed that to the question of how they define their identity, 39.9% of the Arab-Palestinian population answered "Israeli," 42.2% answered "Palestinian" and 64.1% chose "Arab" (multiple answers were possible). Data based on the Ruppin Index of Immigrant Integration in Israel (2010) revealed that 33.7% of the immigrants from the FSU define themselves as Israeli, 39.7% as Jews, and 26.6% as Russian. The same survey revealed for immigrants from Ethiopia that 18.3% define them-selves as Israeli, 59.3% as Jews and 22.4% as Ethiopians. In terms of socio-cultural integration into Israeli society all three groups investigated here show only partial identification with Israeli society.

Concluding Remarks

Having part of society means to be able to contribute and receive one's share of societies' outcomes and incomes. People then have access to work, housing, and resources and therefore are able to make a living. Taking part in society means to participate in society's institutions, which in return have to represent the groupings to which people belong. Being part of society means to be accepted and to identify with society, notwithstanding group affiliation.

When taking into consideration these domains of social cohesion, various configurations emerge, with trade-offs between the domains characterising various groups in a society. The case of Israel as presented here by investigating three groups, namely immigrants from the FSU, Ethiopian immigrants and the Palestinian Arab citizens of Israel, exemplifies these trade-offs. Immigrants from the FSU are best integrated in the economic and political domain, are perceived by the Israeli public as contributing to society fairly well, but show a higher degree of feelings of loneliness than the other two groups. The Palestinian Arab citizens of Israel rate lowest on monthly per capita income and ability to cover expenses. They take part but separately in the political sphere. They are perceived by the Israeli public as least contributing to society, but at the same time show the lowest degree of loneliness, reinforcing the notion of being a rather separate group. The immigrants from Ethiopia are ranked second in integration into the economic domain, although the data reveal that they can barely make a living with a monthly per capita income of 2,005 NIS (substantially lower than the overall Israeli average), with more than 60% reporting that they have difficulties covering expenses and with a high rate of unemployment. Probably due to the small size of the group, they lack meaningful representation in the political domain. The Israeli public accounts for their contribution to society but the Ethiopian immigrants feel lonely. Finally, when asked to rank their identity in terms of "being Israeli," for all three groups alternative identity definitions ranked higher than being Israeli.

For Israel, an economically strong and stable but at the same time highly stratified society with vast inequalities between people, the incorporation of diverse groups establishes a big challenge. Policy makers should take into account that diversity need not necessarily lead to separation.

Looking at the different domains in which social cohesion works, various configurations emerge within one society, suggesting that in order to understand the concept of social cohesion, close investigation of the three domains is needed. Having part, taking part and being part of society express various aspects of social cohesion that do not necessarily overlap, reinforcing the statement that social cohesion is not a unidirectional but rather an interactive, multilevel phenomenon.

References

Achdut, Lea, Liema Davidovitch, and Sibylle Heilbrunn. 2012. *Israeli society: What lies ahead?* Ruppin Academic Center, Israel.

Alesina, Alberto, and Eliana La Ferrara. 2002. "Who Trusts Others?" *Journal of Public Economics* 85(August):207-234.

Al-Haj, Majid. 2004. "The Political Culture of the 1990's Immigrants from the Former Soviet Union in Israel and their Views towards the Indigenous Arab Minority: A Case of Ethnocratic Multiculturalism." *Journal of Ethnic and Migration Studies* 30 (4):682-696.

Amin, Ash. 2002. "Ethnicity and the Multicultural City: Living with Diversity." *Environment and Planning* 34:959–80.

Anhut, Rolf, and Wilhelm Heitmeyer. 2005. "Desintegration, Konflikt, Ethnisierung." In *Integrationspotenziale einer modernen Gesellschaft: Analysen zu gesellchaftlicher Integration und Desintegration*, edited by W. Heitmeyer and P. Imbusch. Wiesbaden VS.

Bartam, David. 2010. "Migration, Ethno-nationalist Destinations and Social Divisions: Non-jewish Immigrants in Israel." *Ethnopolitics* 9:3.

Beauvais, Caroline, and Jane Jensen. 2002. "Social Cohesion: Updating the State of the Research." CPRN Discussion Paper No F22. *Canadian Policy Research Networks.*

Ben-Eliezer, Uri. 2004. "Becoming a Black Jew: Cultural Racism and Anti Racism is Contemporary Israel." *Social Identities* 10 (2):245-266.

Ben-Tovim, Gideon. 2002. "Community Cohesion and Racial Exclusion: A Critical Review of the Cantle Report." *Renewal* 10(2):43–8.

Berger, Peter. 1998. "Conclusions: General Observations on Normative Conflicts and Mediation." In *The Limits to Social Cohesion: Conflict and Mediation in Pluralist Societies,* A Report for the Bertelsmann Foundation to the Club of Rome, edited by Peter Berger. Boulder, CO: Westview Press.

Berger-Schmitt, R. 2002. "Considering Social Cohesion in Quality of Life Assessments: Concept and Measurement." *Social Indicator Research* 58:103-428.

Bernard, P. 1999. "La Cohesion Sociale: Critique d'un Quasi-concept." *Lien social et Politiques* – RIAC, 41:47-59.

Chan, Joseph, To Ho-Pong, and Elaine Chan. 2006. "Reconsidering Social Cohesion: Developing a Definition and Analytical Framework for Empirical Research." *Social Indicator Research* 75:273-302.

Cheong, P.H., R. Edwards, H. Goulbourne, and John Solomos. 2007. "Immigration, Social Cohesion and Social Capital: A Critical Review." *Critical Social Policy* 27:24-49.

Costa, Dora L., and Matthew E. Kahn. 2003. "Civic Engagement and Community Heterogeneity: An Economist's Perspective." Perspective on *Politics* 1, no. 1:103-111.

Dickes, Paul, Marie Valentova, and Monique Borsenberger. 2010. "Construct Validation and Application of a Common Measure of Social Cohesion in 33 European Countries." *Social Indicator Research* 98:451–473.

Gesthuizen, Maurice, Tom Van der Meer, and Peer Scheepers. 2009. "Ethnic Diversity and Social Capital in Europe: Tests of Putnam's Thesis in European Countries." *Scandinavian Political Studies* 32, no. 2:121-142.

Ghanem, As'ad. 2001. *The Palestinian-Arab Minority, 1948-2000*. Albany, NY: State University of New York Press.

Hacohen, D. 2002. "Mass Immigration and the Demographic Revolution in Israel." *Israel Affairs* 8:177-190.

Kimmerling, Baruch. 1998. "The New Israelis - Multiplicity of Cultures without Multiculturalism." *Alpayim* 16:264-308.

Koren, David. 2010. "Arab Israeli Citizens in the 2009 Elections: Between Israeli Citizenship and Palestinian Arab Identity." *Israel Affairs* 16(1)1:124-141.

Lazin, F. A. 2002. "Israel and Ethiopian Jewish Immigrants." *Society* 39:56-62.

Letki, Natalia. 2008. "Does diversity erode social cohesion? Social capital and race in British neighbourhoods." *Political Studies* 56, no. 1:99-126.

Lewin-Epstein, Noah and Moshe Semyonov. 1993. *The Arab minority in Israel's economy – patterns of ethnic inequality*. Boulder, CO: Westview.

Li, Yaojun, Andrew Pickles, and Mike Savage. 2005. "Social Capital and Social Trust in Britain." *European Sociological Review* 21, no. 2:109-123.

Migdal, Joel. 2006. "Whose State is it, Anyway? Exclusion and the Construction of Graduate Citizenship in Israel (Report)." *Israeli Studies Forum* 21.2.2006.

Mizrachi, Nissim and Hanna Herzog. 2012. "Participatory Destigmatization Strategies among Palestinian Citizens, Ethiopian Jews and Mizrachi Jews in Israel." *Ethnic and Racial Studies* 35(3):418-435.

Osberg, Lars, ed. 2003. *The economic implications of social cohesion.* Toronto: University of Toronto Press.

Peres, Y. and E. Ben-Rafael. 2006. *Cleavages in Israeli Society.* Tel Aviv: Am Oved (in Hebrew).

Putnam, Robert. 1995. "Bowling Alone: America's Declining Social Capital." *Journal of Democracy* 6:65-78.

—. 2000. *Bowling Alone: The Collapse and Revival of American Community.* New York: Simon and Schuster.

—. 2004. "Who Bonds? Who Bridges? Findings from the Social Capital Benchmark Survey." Paper presented at the annual meeting of the American Political Science Association, Chicago, September 2-5.

—. 2007. "E pluribus unum. Diversity and Community in the Twenty-First Century." The 2007 Johan Skytte Prize Lecture. *Scandinavian Political Studies*, 30:137-174.

Remennick, L. 2004. "Language acquisition, ethnicity and social integration among former Soviet immigrants of the 1990s in Israel." *Ethnic and Racial Studies* 27:431-454.

Schnell, Izhak, and Michael Sofer. 2002. "Unbalanced Embeddedness of Ethnic Entrepreneurship: the Israeli Arab Case." *International Journal of Entrepreneurial Behavior and Research* 8(1/2):54 – 68.

Semyonov, Moshe, and Noah Lewin-Epstein. 1994. "Ethnic Labor Markets, Gender, and Socioeconomic Inequality: The Study of Arabs in the Israeli Labor Force." *The Sociological Quarterly* 35(1):51-68.

Semyonov, Moshe, Yitzhak Haberfeld, Rebecca Raijman, Rapahel Bar-El, Karin Amit, Sibylle Heilbrunn, and Svetlana Chachashvili-Bolotin. 2010. *Ruppin Index of Immigrant Integration in Israel.* Israel: Institute for Immigration and Social Integration, Ruppin Academic Center.

Shafir, Gershon, and Yoav Peled. 2002. *Being Israeli: The Dynamics of Multiple Citizenship.* Cambridge: Cambridge University Press.

Smooha, Sammy. 1998. *Arabs and Jews in Israel: Conflicting and Shared Attitudes in a Divided Society.* Boulder: West View Press.

Smooha, Sammy. 2004. "Jewish Ethnicity in Israel: Symbolic or Real?" In *Jews in Israel: Contemporary Social and Cultural Patterns*, edited by Uzi Rebhuhn and Chaim Isaac Waxman, 47-80. Brandeis University Press.

Sorek, Tamir. 2011. "The Quest for Victory: Collective Memory and National Identification among Arab-Palestinian Citizens of Israel." *Sociology* 45(3):464-479.

Soroka, Stuart, Richard Johnston, and Keith Banting. 2004. "Ethnicity, Trust and the Welfare State." In *Cultural Diversity versus Economic Solidarity*, edited by Philippe Van Parijs. Brussels: De Boeck Université.

Uslaner, Eric. 2002. *The Moral Foundations of Trust*. Cambridge: Cambridge University Press.

Yuval-Davis, Nira, Floya Anthias, and Elenore Kofman. 2005. "Secure Borders and Safe Haven and the Gendered Politics of Belonging: Beyond Social Cohesion." *Ethnic and Racial Studies* 28(3):513–35.

CHAPTER SEVEN

PRACTISING SOLIDARITY: SHARING ACROSS DIFFERENCE

CLAIRE FARRUGIA

Nestled inside a 1980s-style arcade in the western suburbs of Sydney, the African Village Market is a meeting place, social enterprise, and a site of recognition. The Market was established as a means through which Australian women of African background[1] could sell their own products, provide African goods that were otherwise difficult to get, and foster a sense of community. While the Market holds a particular resonance for Sydney's Kenyan community, it also functions as a meeting place for Sudanese, Congolese, Ghanaian, and other African communities in Sydney. It is a particular space where solidarity is practiced in the everyday through the act of sharing; the sharing of space, friendship, knowledge, and support. The African Village Market is one of many examples of the social activity taking place in the western suburbs of Sydney across communities from different regions in Africa and in a range of spontaneous, informal, and more formalised spaces. This study will draw on preliminary ethnographic and interview data collected in late 2012 and early 2013 in three of these spaces: the African Village Market, Sydney's African Women's Dinner Dance, and informally organised Intercultural Exchange Programmes. Through drawing on this data, this chapter will contribute to existing critiques of social capital (Arneil 2006; Fine 2001; Spies-Butcher 2009) by exploring "sharing" as an alternative framework for conceptualising immigrant solidarity.

Popular and academic definitions of solidarity often rely on an assumption that mutual commonality or "we feelings" (Faist 2000) are necessary for the creation of a relationship of solidarity. This study will go beyond this assumption by assessing how solidarity is situated and lived in

---

1. For the sake of brevity and to accurately reflect the voices of participants, I will refer to Australian women of African background as African women from now on.

everyday social spaces by African women living in Sydney. These women have different national and ethnic backgrounds, different class status and different educational levels. They have entered Australia as refugees, migrants or through the family reunion programme. However, they often work together to provide friendship, support, and services for their community. This is not a static or bounded notion of community based on a cohesive group identity. This is a community that extends beyond ethnic and religious lines and often encompasses non-African refugees and migrants. It is a dynamic community created and recreated through everyday practices.

Within migration studies, much research into immigrant support networks has established the crucial role social bonds play in assisting newly arrived migrants to navigate life in a new country (Chelpi-den Hamer & Mazzucato 2010; Hamaz & Vasta 2009; Mazzucato & Kabki 2009; Mercer, Page, & Evans 2009; Taylor, Wangaruro, & Papadopoulos 2012; Vasta 2011). However, the majority of research on support networks has been preoccupied with the function of these social relationships. This functionalism has gone hand in hand with economic uses of social capital as well as a limited focus on bonding and bridging capital. As a result, the aim of this chapter is to shift academic focus from how solidarity functions in migrant communities to how it is practised. This requires moving beyond how individual feelings of empathy or self-interest enable solidarity to function, to how solidarity is lived collectively in everyday social spaces. Space provides the backdrop to understand how relations of power intersect in particular ways in particular places and spaces (Giritli-Nygren & Schmauch 2012; Massey 2004). In these spaces the norms, values, and identities influencing who practices solidarity, and for what reasons, are created and recreated through social practices (Swidler 2001). One example of such a practice is the everyday act of sharing. Sharing friendship, space, information, and support is a dynamic interaction that reflects the social and material realities of everyday life for refugee and migrant women. Exploring who shares, why they share and with whom they share will help unpack the complex ways African women in Sydney experience solidarity.

This chapter will begin by situating an analysis of sharing in the context of functionalist theories of solidarity, their manifestation in approaches to social capital, and popular and political discourses surrounding difference in a multicultural society. After outlining the theoretical point of departure away from functionalism, ethnographic and interview data will be utilised to demonstrate the complex ways solidarity is lived in everyday social spaces. To conceptualise this lived experience, this chapter will draw on the way that many participants articulated solidarity: as a necessary part of the struggle for recognition and/or redistribution. While the tension between theories of recognition and redistribution are beyond the scope of this chapter, drawing on Nancy Frasers's conception of these struggles as inextricably linked (Fraser 2000) will help conceptualise the environment that gives rise to solidarity and form the basis of the two subsequent sections. The first will explore how solidarity is practiced across differences and the role that intersubjective recognition plays in this process. The second will shed light on the structural conditions that influence the creative ways women engage in sharing and anchor practices of solidarity. While functionalist theories cannot alone capture the complexity of these practices, this chapter will conclude by arguing that interdependence continues to provide key insights into how solidarity is practiced and what role the state plays in influencing the social and material realities of life for migrant and refugee women in Sydney.

However, the voices present in this chapter indicate that these practices of solidarity are not wholly reducible to women's relationship with the state. Sharing provides a framework to understand the agency of migrant women in Australia. It assists us in understanding how the sharing of feelings, experiences, information and importantly, material resources, are part of the creative ways women confront the challenges of resettlement and make claims of belonging. Exploring these claims is especially important given that African Australians, while still a relatively small community, present one of the fastest growing immigrant groups in Australia, increasing from 16% of the Refugee and Humanitarian intake in the period from 1998-1999 to 70% between 2003-2005 (ABS 2012) and representing over 5.6% of Australia's population (ABS 2006). This study will not only aim to give voice to these growing communities, but also use the concept of sharing to unpack the dynamic relationships that inform immigrant solidarity in Australia.

From Solidarity to Social Capital (and back again)

While solidarity has a long theoretical tradition in the discipline of sociology, it is a term that is difficult to define. This difficulty arises from reconciling how the feelings that generate solidarity, the actions that constitute it, and the environment that gives rise to it can be conceptualised in one coherent definition. Emile Durkheim's writing in *The Division of Labour in Society* (1997) played a significant role in political and academic conceptions of solidarity. Durkheim offered two conceptions of solidarity.

The first was mechanical solidarity, where society is organised in terms of the beliefs and sentiments common to all the members of the group and in which societal cohesion is the product of the homogeneity of individuals in a defined system. The second was organic solidarity, which arises from the increasing specialisation of work in industrial societies and relies on the interdependence generated from individuals fulfilling distinct functions as a result of the division of labour in society (Durkheim 1997). Importantly, the theories of mechanical and organic solidarity went beyond accounting for the relationship between two or more people to addressing the structural foundations of that relationship (Thijssen 2012). For Durkheim, societal structure formed the basis of solidarity and solidarity then ensured the maintenance of societal structures. Talcott Parsons made this functionalist position more explicit when he defined solidarity as the "…generalised capacity to control and to bring into line the behaviour of the system's units in accordance with the integrative needs of the site" (Parsons 1971, p. 41).

Functionalist definitions have had particular consequences for studies of social solidarity in ethnically and religiously diverse societies. While Durkheim's conception of solidarity as being based on interdependence is an important way to conceptualise practices between migrant women, neither Durkheim nor Parsons incorporated a thorough understanding of how power or inequality impacts the division of labour in society (Vasta 2010). As Parsons' definition more clearly indicates, this oversight went hand in hand with an assumption that solidarity was not important in and of itself, but as a means to an end, the end being a stable and socially cohesive society. This theoretical tradition has led to an understanding that people outside the social, economic or cultural system can be a threat to societal solidarity (Putnam 2007), and that social solidarity is in decline in countries with high immigrant populations.

In Australia, the assumption that diversity threatens solidarity has not fuelled the same preoccupation with social cohesion and integration that is prevalent in western Europe (Holtug & Mason 2010; Vasta 2010). Nevertheless, this assumption did play a role in challenging the federal government's ministerial portfolio on multiculturalism in 2004 and again in 2013, when the incoming conservative government opted for the ministerial title of Immigration and Border Protection instead. Focus on social cohesion has also resulted in the introduction of a national citizenship test and values statement to help solidify a defined set of national values (DIBP 2007). Concern about integrating these values has had a specific impact on Australia's African communities. In 2007, the then Immigration Minister, Kevin Andrews, suggested that certain African communities

were not adequately integrating, and confirmed that the offshore humanitarian programme, the programme through which the majority of African
refugees came to Australia, would no longer focus on Africa as a target
region (Jakubowicz 2008). The implication was that immigrant solidarity
was threating social cohesion, a cohesion that rested on a defined national
identity.

Multiculturalism as a policy in Australia has always been as much
invested in national identity as in managing diversity (Pardy & Lee 2011).
It is a particular model of inclusion that has been challenged a number of
times in Australian history, in accordance with changing conceptions of
how best to manage diversity (Jakubowicz 2008, 1988; Vasta & Castles
1996). From the 1980s onwards, management of diversity has been
increasingly tied up with economic rationalism and neoliberal governance
structures. The rise in neoliberal policies of privatisation, competitive
tendering, and an overall increase in the role of the market has not only
impacted the provision of services for migrants and refugees, but
influenced how research into immigrant social solidarity has been
conducted. In particular, it has played a role in the increasing popularity of
social capital to describe the nature, function and outcome of networks of
support.

Like solidarity, social capital is a term that has a number of competing
definitions. However, unlike solidarity, it is a term that has dramatically
risen to prominence in the social sciences (Portes 1998). The majority of
sociological research into the social ties of immigrants has drawn on the
work of functionalist social capital research, rather than the work of sociologist Pierre Bourdieu (1985). The movement away from Bourdieu's
critical definition of social capital centred on ideas of class and relations of
power, to the methodological individualism of the more functionalist view
of social capital, presents a number of limitations for studies of women's
networks of support. These limitations relate to the question of measurement, intra/inter-group relations, and the role of the state, and are a
consequence of the underlying functionalist logic that impacts how the
concept of social capital is theoretically and empirically applied. This logic is present in the work of sociologist James Coleman who claimed that
entities of social capital "...all consist of some aspect of social structure,
and they facilitate certain actions of individuals who are within the structure" (Coleman 1990, 302). Similarly it is a logic present in the work of
political scientist Robert D. Putnam and his focus on the integrative functions of voluntary associations.

Often credited with popularising the concept, Putnam defines social
capital as the "...features of social organisation such as networks, norms,

and social trust that facilitate coordination and cooperation for mutual benefit" (Putnam 1995, 67). The first limitation of his approach relates to the use of the individual as the main unit of analysis for "capital" and a focus on what interest individuals have in cooperating for mutual benefit. Empirically, this has resulted in a focus on measuring social relationships through accounting for the formal group membership of individuals (Putnam 2000). However, quantitatively exploring the number of women attending the Market, Dinner Dance, or Intercultural Exchange, tells us very little about the complex reasons why solidarity is practised across different communities, with different needs. Putnam's analysis also suffers from the limitations of functionalist approaches to solidarity, the assumption that individuals are equally able to cooperate for mutual benefit which, among other things, denies the fact that women have differential access to resources and recognition within particular communities (Arneil 2006).

Different women are able to engage (or disengage) in practices of solidarity according to their social location in regards to class, ethnicity, gender, and position within wider structures of support. This position does not only influence how they do solidarity, but who they do it with. The first limitation comes down to how the "social" in social capital is interpreted. Viewing the social as relational rather than solely the strategic choice of individuals has implications for how social capital can be used to interpret migrant networks of support. The importance of taking a relational view of the social is highlighted by the second limitation of social capital: overuse of the terms "bonding" and "bridging" capital. Putnam argues that bonding capital is tight knit, inward looking, and important for "getting by," while bridging capital is outward looking, bridging connections which are important for "getting ahead" (Putnam 2000, 23). While bonding capital is a useful way to conceptualise intragroup networks and bridging capital intergroup networks, in practice, this dichotomy does not take account of the messy reality of the "social" in social capital. As a number of authors have demonstrated, it does not pay adequate attention to the actual resources flowing between ties or to the different kinds of relationships that develop between individuals (Anthias 2007; Ryan 2011). By assuming that the networks that make social capital possible are a possession, rather than a process, this dichotomy limits the ways solidarity can be observed in practice. Social capital approaches often take it for granted that individuals engage in bonding or bridging capital for one specific function; often in order to forward their own position in the social structure. However, solidarity can be defined as much by feelings of connectedness and belonging as by assumptions of rational, utility maximizing behaviour. In this respect, social capital often fails to capture the complexity of processes of identification and their relationship with solidarity.

The research into bonding capital takes for granted that bonds between migrants are based on a coherent group identity, based on ethnicity. However, this fails to account for the way individuals may come together in the everyday without presumptions of "being in common" or even "being uncommon" (Ahmed & Fortier 2003, 254). The women in this study are from a range of ethnic, language, and religious backgrounds, and the group cleavages that their identity as African women is meant to create are not fixed. They are interpreted and reinterpreted through everyday practices. The dichotomy of bonding/bridging limits the vocabulary to describe everyday acts of solidarity that transgress defined group boundaries. Consequently, disrupting this binary opens up more possibilities to view social bonds, ties, relationships, and practices in the social and material realities of everyday life. Viewing identity as relational (Massey 2004; Yuval-Davis 2007) and ethnicity as a culturally dynamic, mobile and incomplete process (Amin 2002) enables this to happen. In terms of migrant solidarity, relations of scarcity, inequality or experiences of exclusion play a key role in influencing processes of identification, as well the decision to practise solidarity and with whom.

These conditions relate to the last limitation of this social capital approach: how the relationship between the state and the community is perceived. While social capital presents an important shift in focus from the state or citizen to the civic space in-between (Arneil 2006), the side effect of this shift has been to abstract social relationships away from the state. The result of this abstraction is that focus on issues of employment, housing, discrimination, and racism are shifted from the responsibility of the state to provide basic necessities, to the responsibility of migrant communities to more adequately integrate (Fine 2001). This shift of responsibility onto migrant communities is part of a policy approach increasingly concerned with how to "manage" difference and engender social cohesion based on a defined set of values. As Maree Pardy and Julian Lee have argued, this approach represents a movement away from "seeing multiculturalism as state assisted and demanded *by* immigrants, to "new integrationism" as state imposed and demanded *of* immigrants" (Pardy & Lee 2011, 299). New integrationism (Poynting & Mason 2008) refers particularly to the period post-1996, which saw the rise of conservative One Nation Party leader, Pauline Hanson run on a populist, anti-immigration platform, and an increasing national preoccupation with the need for ethnic groups to engage in greater levels of social mixing. New integrationism has had a clear impact on how migrant solidarity is practised and interpreted in policy research. This impact is related to the rising popularity of social capital as a popular, political and policy term used to articulate migrant activities.

The popularity of social capital is not solely the result of new intergrationist discourses. As has been previously argued, since the 1980s approaches to migrant solidarity have been significantly informed by the neoliberal shift towards an immigration and resettlement policy which maximises the economic gains of migration while minimising the social costs (Walsh 2011). Functionalist definitions of social capital have been implicated in this regime, which has also seen the introduction of competitive tendering for service provision, an extension of reporting regimes, and an increased focus on the achievement of specific, economically productive outcomes. This focus has had particular implications for smaller service providers who are unable to compete with larger providers despite having local knowledge of communities (Darcy, Waterford, & McIvor 2009). Most importantly for African women's solidarity, this shift has also gone hand in hand with a decline in funding for ethno-specific activities.

Decline in ethno-specific funding can be seen as the product of two differing discourses. On the one hand, neoliberal economic rationalism prioritises privatisation and specific cost-cutting measures in social services. On the other is the concern that ethno-specific funding solidifies ethnic group cleavages, and that these cleavages have the potential to threaten an Australian national identity based on a defined set of values. The two discourses are not necessarily the product of competing interests. As Andrew Jakobowski has noted in an early analysis of Australian multiculturalism, the question of social solidarity is one that has "haunted Australian capitalism and the state—it is not solely a problem of multiculturalism" (Jakubowicz 1988, 37). As a result of this relationship, how women practise social solidarity is implicated in discourses about multiculturalism and how best to "manage" diversity as well as the material macroeconomic structures.

How social capital is applied in policy and academic research is influenced by this material and discursive context. While it has become an important way that migrant groups are able to situate their activity in the context of the state and articulate their relevance, moving beyond a vocabulary of social capital will open up new avenues to critically analyse sharing as a practice of solidarity. Acknowledging the complexity of social solidarity and notions of community that are linked to it requires a view on solidarity, similar to that of belonging, as more than an imagined community but as a "material practice of social containment and enablement"

(Noble & Poynting 2010, 498). As Sarah Ahmed argues, quoting Anne McClintock, imagined communities "are not simply phantasmagoria of the mind but are historical practices through which social differences are both invented and performed" (Ahmed & Fortier 2003, 257). Acknowledging the performative and inventive aspects of community enriches research into everyday practices without denying the real and meaningful way community is experienced. This perspective suggests that a focus on practices requires, at least to some extent, "disentangling 'community' from 'identity'–in both senses of 'self' (individual and collective) and 'sameness'" (Ahmed & Fortier 2003, 256). Nevertheless, the qualitative researcher needs to go further than this, taking into account the extent to which participants experience and shape the conditions for their own dis/entanglement. In contrast to the mainly theoretical work on solidarity, these conditions will be understood by drawing on the lived experience of migrant women and moving beyond a conception of solidarity that is solely determined by social structures (Calhoun 2002).

Taking into account the agency of migrant women means recognising the complexity of their social relationships, understanding these social relationships necessitates a move beyond a purely theoretical or top-down approach to social solidarity. Criticism of top-down approaches has also been levelled at research on multiculturalism, with a number of authors arguing that focus on the everyday is needed to balance out a research agenda preoccupied with the nation-state and the management and containment of diversity (Ho 2011; Noble & Poynting 2010; Wise & Velayutham 2009). This study will draw from Everyday Multiculturalism (Wise & Velayutham 2009), while taking into account how management and containment can be linked to the microsociology of how everyday practices are interpreted, experienced, and ultimately, embodied (Amin 2002; Wise & Velayutham 2009). Articulating the relationship between the macro and the micro requires drawing a link between the material, macroeconomic management of diversity and the immaterial, "the discursive, affective, and spatial regulation of cultural difference" (Noble & Poynting 2010) that influences who shares and for what reasons.

Anthropological theories of gift giving and reciprocity have paved the way to locate approaches to difference in everyday practices. Like gifts, the sharing of information, friendship, and support comes to embody particular meaning in the context of particular social relationships (Komter 2005; Komter 1996). Gift exchange has been interpreted as a mechanism that reconciles individual interests and the creation of a social system, a practice guided by self-interest (Mauss 1989), and as a key way that individual impressions are transmitted to others (Schwartz 1967): influencing the identities of the giver as well as the receiver (Taylor *et al.* 2012). Sharing builds on the literature on gift giving and reciprocity, going beyond intent and expectation of return in order to focus on how different dimensions of power intersect in practices of giving and receiving (Anthias 2006; Giritli-Nygren & Schmauch 2012; Yuval-Davis, Anthias, & Kofman 2005). Importantly, this intersection has particular significance in particular social spaces. Although this chapter will not focus specifically on space or place, the concept of sharing also draws from the work of feminist geographers that draw attention to the spatial orderings that produce moments of exclusion and/or inclusion for women (Massey 2004a; Noble & Poynting 2010; Valentine 2007). These moments influence the types of sharing taking place and reiterate the importance of situating studies of social solidarity in the lived experience of refugee and migrant women.

Sharing in Practice: Moving Beyond "We Feelings"

Research conducted at the African Village Market, African Women's Dinner Dance, and the Intercultural Exchange programme was based on qualitative research methods, methods that lend themselves readily to exploring the lived experience of solidarity. These methods are in themselves a practice that "locates the observer in the world…a set of interpretive material practices that make the world visible" (Denzin & Lincoln 2000, 8). Experience conducting ethnographic research as a volunteer at the African Village Market in 2013 made everyday practices of solidarity more visible than they would have been otherwise. Nevertheless, volunteering was not just about gaining *visibility* per se but about fostering the kind of relationship where women would feel more comfortable sharing their experience of solidarity and the meaning they ascribe to it (Archer 2009; Madison 2012).

In addition to ethnographic research, this chapter will focus on interviews conducted with key organisers of the Market, Dinner Dance, and Exchange, and draw on additional interviews conducted with a varied sample of participants. This sample includes one woman from Sudan, one from Ghana, one from Congo, three from Kenya, and one from Rwanda, as well as five government-funded Migrant Resource Centre (MRC) workers. The decision to choose a varied sample grew out of initial fieldwork conducted at events where it was clear that solidarity was being practised across a complex array of social relationships that could not be easily categorised or measured. This is the case in terms of how solidarity is practiced across different communities at the Market, Dinner Dance, and particularly, the Intercultural Exchange.

The Exchange is an informal programme organised by women from
Kenya and Sudan and involves migrant and refugee women staying with
migrant or Anglo-Australian hosts based in rural locations throughout
New South Wales. Together with the Market and the Dinner Dance, the
Exchange is one example of how solidarity is practiced among women
from Africa who have arrived in Australia from a number of different locations and through diverse methods of entrance. Women from Kenya,
Ghana, Ethiopia and Sudan comprise the majority of participants, but, as
one Kenyan organiser explained, "I take 75% Africans, 25% other wom-
en" and a large amount of effort was put into ensuring that an ethnically
and religiously diverse group of women were able to attend.

Recounting her experience of attending an Exchange, a Ghanaian participant recalled women from Afghanistan, Iran, Samoa, and Iraq
attending. When another organiser of the Exchange was asked the importance of this mix she laughed and replied:

> If you just take one group, what are they sharing? But if you take different
> people, one thing they are improving their English because they are sitting
> next to someone who doesn't speak English, you are learning about their
> culture, they are learning about your culture, by the time we reach there we
> have already learned the cultures of the people you are living with here in
> Australia.

The aim of the programme was to encourage women to communicate
despite difficulties and provide a venue where women could share cultural
experiences, information, friendship and space with one another. The
importance of this physical space was noted by nearly all African
interviewees and MRC staff. Space to organise community activities,
meetings, and social functions is in high demand for all migrant groups in
Sydney. The Exchange provided not only physical space, but an important
subjective space: simultaneously intimate, in the sense that it provides for
the sharing of personal, often traumatic stories, and public; in the sense of
being surrounded by unfamiliar faces and landscapes. Access to these
social spaces played an important role in how solidarity was practised.
While lack of transport and family commitments meant many women were
isolated from engaging with one another in Sydney, at the Exchange they
were given the space to develop relationships that did not rely on
obligations generated from membership to a family or one specific
community (Mason 2000), but on everyday practices. These practices did
not only come in the form of designated Saturday night presentations of
culture, dress and performance, but in the sharing of every-day routines, in
the "how do you do that? How do you cook that? What do you call that?"

interactions that, according to participants, gave women a sense of being recognised for their unique background. Recognition of this background plays an important role in how solidarity is practiced in these settings.

One organiser argued that working with women from different backgrounds was key to the practice of solidarity at the Exchange and beyond. It makes them:

> ...appreciate other people...because in this bus you have an Iraqi, you have an Afghani, you have an Indian, you have an African, you have an Australian...Muslims who have also never stayed with a Christian family and at the end of the day they come to realise everybody is the same.

However, sameness is not always the outcome of solidarity. Differences in attitude, values, and background also play an important role. While sharing is often expressed in positive terms, one participant recounted her experience of exasperation with the smoking, drinking and perceived aggression of another. She made a conscious decision at the Exchange to engage with this woman, where others were reluctant, and this engagement positively confronted her with her own sense of judgement. While she arrived in Australia as a student over five years ago and had a relatively easy transition to life there, the other woman had experienced a number of traumatic events prior to and after migration to Australia. She gained a sense of intersubjective recognition that impacted her relationship with other women:

> I know some people who went through hardship but the extent of damage or hardship they went through didn't sink through till you have one-on-one conversations. That's when you get to know man, some of them went through hell...it is alright to see somebody as a refugee but not until you talk to the person we can't say move on, you have to be there to know exactly.

In this instance, their differences became a key way that she began to share information, support, and friendship with those outside her immediate circle. One Sudanese organiser argued that shared participation at the Exchange would also challenge misconceptions "of a migrant and of an Australian, what they are." She believed that "instead of telling them you guys have to change your way of thinking let them experience it and decide by themselves if this is really who they thought they were."

Shared participation has often been conceptualised as a precondition for solidarity and belonging. Social contact and cooperation between members of different groups is an important element in the process of creating a common identity, a sense of belonging together as a "we," rather than an "I" (Loobuyck 2012). In the case of the Exchange, this "we" includes a number of different women who do not rely solely on collective identification based on intimate relations or common interests and concerns (Dean 1996). Instead, these instances of sharing are examples of Jodi Dean's concept of "reflective solidarity," which relies on an inclusive understanding of "we," whereby "the strength of the bond connecting us stems from our mutual recognition of each other instead of from our exclusion of someone else" (Dean 1996, 31). In practice, sharing is not solely positive and can elicit disagreements and judgement about others that can result in exclusion. However, in the case of reflective solidarity, "we" is interpreted not as given, but as "in process" where the risk of disagreement which accompanies diversity can be transformed to provide a basis for intersubjective ties and commitments (Dean 1996, 3).

The Exchange generates social and at times, emotional ties to other women, as well as commitments (however loose) to participation in community events. These ties and commitments develop and change through everyday practices. These practices play a particularly important role for newly-arrived migrants and refugees, where they are confronted with different social and cultural expectations regarding what constitutes an appropriate tie or obligation. In this context, it is interesting that some women relate to the Exchange as an experience of finally being welcomed by a wider Australian community. A Kenyan interviewee emotively argued that this was important because:

> Our people never *visit*, they have never been to rural areas, even they have never been to an Australian home most of them. And from our culture if you go to visit somewhere and people don't invite you it means they haven't welcomed you properly. I mean they haven't accepted you.

This experience of being welcomed is laden with sociocultural expectations surrounding encounters with hospitality and feelings of belonging (Lynch, Germann Molz, McIntosh, Lugosi, & Lashley 2011). Acts of hospitality at the Exchange are examples of how communities and individuals actively negotiate differences through engaging strangers and negotiating socio-cultural expectations of what it means to be hospitable. The process of welcoming plays a particular role in this process, as many women who attended the Exchange felt isolated from any sense of community when they initially arrived in Australia. While those who arrived on student visas reported that they at least had contact with other students in the institutions they were part of, all of the women interviewed had minimal contact with other African communities. They distinctly remember the experience of being without a sense of recognition of their origin, experiences or prior attachments to community. As a result of this, recognition as African women did continue to play an important role given that these women come from diverse national, ethnic and religious backgrounds. It is a term, and a process of identification, that is subject to the competing tensions generated by the resettlement environment and influences who engages in sharing, at what times and in what spaces.

How these tensions play out in the everyday becomes most apparent when exploring the relationship women have to the African Village Market. The Market is a cooperative shop run collectively by six women and frequented by a number of the African women who have attended Intercultural Exchanges. While the Market is about providing experience and income for those involved, it is also one part of a larger dream of an African cultural hub in the multicultural centre of Parramatta. This hub would house African restaurants, local shops and it would be a "learning centre, a trade centre, a shopping centre." It would act as a site of recognition that some women feel would engage otherwise isolated pockets of African communities in Sydney.

Dreams of the African hub have a significant influence on who shares and for what reasons. In practice, there is a constant tension in the shop between this dream (and its focus on selling "African products and promoting African culture") and fostering an economically viable social enterprise. How women share within the Market is influenced by these two tensions. For some, particularly those of refugee background, the priority is not whether the shop is only selling products made in Africa and remaining aesthetically "African" in appearance, but whether or not they can maintain an income from the shop ("whether selling Chinese clothes or not"). For others, they want the shop to be what Chinatown is for the Chinese and what the suburb of Cabramatta is for the Vietnamese; a place to share African culture and "a way for us Africans to identify ourselves." Extending the insights gained at the Exchange, experience at the Market suggests that for some women, sharing becomes a way to struggle for recognition as a distinct group, as well as a way to face challenges the resettlement process poses. The tension that is generated between the two is the result of how individuals practice solidarity from different social and material locations. However, drawing on feminist theorists Dorothy Smith and Sandra Harding, Nira Yuval-Davis highlights the fact that an individual's social location does not necessarily correspond with a particular identity, but rather "they both emanate as a result of specific social practices" (Yuval-Davis 2007, 8). The social practice of sharing influences how women intersubjectively draw on and perform identification (Bailey 2012, 854). Experience at the Exchange and Market suggests that solidarity does not neatly correspond with collective identification, but changes according to who is practising it and in which settings. Organisers of the Intercultural Exchange and the Market aim to share with those of diverse backgrounds and encourage solidarity through a process of intersubjective recognition. However, this recognition is influenced by the means particular women have to face challenges of resettlement. This can be articulated as a competing tension between recognition and redistribution in the resettlement context. How women choose to share, whom they choose to share with, and what they choose to share is subsequently influenced by their social and material locations within larger structures of support.

"More Than a Shop": Navigating the Resettlement Environment

Many women become involved with the Intercultural Exchange and Market primarily as a way to combat the loneliness, isolation, and lack of support that they often experience when adjusting to life in Australia. One woman actively involved in both programmes, and who also helped organise the African Women's Dinner Dance, became preoccupied with ways to connect communities because of her own experience arriving in Australia and living in a suburb with no discernible African presence. After six months she attempted to find "the Africans, any African organisation" and was eventually told about the African Community Council. The council was formed as a coordinating body for the African community in Australia, but she distinctly remembers travelling out to the suburb of Strathfield and telling the President, "there must be something very wrong if you're the President of the African Community Council and it took me six to eight months to know you or meet you."

There was clearly a gap between what the council provided and how it included newly-arrived women. This is despite assumptions that community councils are more localised and have a better chance of keeping track of newly arrived African communities, or that membership in a community council automatically indicates the possession of social capital. While initial settlement assistance is provided for newly-arrived refugees and certain categories of migrants, those interviewed noted that because of time, resources and method of provision, there is a gap between the formalised programmes of community councils and state-sponsored providers and newly-arrived women. This woman fought to close this gap, and was subsequently made Women's Officer for the council. Soon after, she began work as a community liaison with an influential state government organisation, and her time in this position confirmed that there was a large vacuum when it came to community information regarding the support services that were available for African communities. As other research into African Australian communities has demonstrated, this support was particularly needed in the areas of employment, housing, parenting, and domestic violence (Abdelkerim & Grace 2012; Colic-Peisker & Tilbury 2007; Hatoss & Huijser 2010; HREOC 2010; Ogunsiji, Wilkes, Jackson, & Peters 2012). In addition, for many women this vacuum was experienced as a loss of the time and space they once had to share with others (McMichael & Manderson 2004). As a result, this participant made it clear that when she found herself in a position to do so, she would "never stopped sharing."

The wish to have a designated space where information and support could be shared with women, and in an environment that was fun, was a key impetus behind the establishment of the African Women's Dinner Dance. The first Dinner Dance was held in 2005 and attracted over 300 women. The Dance played a specific role in filling a gap in communication between service providers and the wider community. Time was put aside from the dancing, fashion parade, and multiple courses of food for a survivor of domestic violence to share her experience and information regarding available services. One of the organisers of the Dance noted that on the Monday following the night, fifteen women contacted her for assistance reporting domestic violence and to find further information regarding the services that were available to assist them and their families. This result was partly because some women felt it was culturally inappropriate to report domestic violence to a male police officer, and others were not necessarily aware that it was against the law (HREOC 2010). Sharing information in such a unique space dealt with these barriers in a way that service providers could not replicate without the assistance of the community. Accordingly, the informal sharing of information between women played a key role in distributing knowledge of the bureaucratic, funding and legal processes of the state.

The relationship between state processes and informal practices of solidarity became particularly apparent when talking with staff of the MRCs, which are state-funded bodies equipped to work with newly arrived refugees and migrants. MRC workers recognise that the success of their programmes often relies on informal community sharing. However, complex funding and administrative processes make it difficult for these women to organise events such as the Dinner Dance. As a result of this difficulty, longer-term residents share with the newly-arrived to creatively face the challenges of resettlement. Unable to obtain adequate funding,

organisers of the Exchange found a friend of a friend to volunteer a mini-
bus for trips, and organisers of the Market found creative ways to "sell"
their idea to Pop Up Parramatta, a local council initiative that would help
pay the rent. In addition, at nearly all events the international money transfer company MoneyGram was present as a sponsor—an indication that the
corporate sector was aware of the monetary value that the sharing of remit-
tances could provide. Reliance on finding forms of assistance other than
from the state has a direct impact on the way that solidarity can be practised within and across African communities in Sydney.

Sharing cannot be separated from the context of wider macroeconomic
policies in Australia. In particular, it is important to take into account the
role that competitive tendering plays in influencing the availability of resources for smaller community networks. These networks have been
caught up in a policy shift away from funding smaller, often ethno-specific
community organisations, to larger organisations such as the MRCs
(Georgeou 2012, 56). One of Sydney's MRC Emerging Communities case
workers stated that this shift was obvious in the 2012 budget, and was justified with the argument that smaller ethnic groups were not "multicultural."
This justification rests on the assumption that migrant group solidarity
threatens societal cohesion without taking into account the dynamic ways
that sharing takes place within and across communities to build the capacity, confidence, and connection of participants in a way that larger
organisations are not necessarily able to replicate. In this respect, the
caseworker commented on the difficulty in writing activities such as the
Exchange, Dance, or Market into the government specified funding categories. This is the case because of a limited vocabulary for describing and
taking account for the value of solidarity that goes beyond one specific
function and beyond restrictive measurements of social capital.

The need to develop a new vocabulary was highlighted during my time
volunteering at the Market. It soon became clear that a number of women
simply use the shop as a place to be when they are unemployed or between
jobs. This was particularly the case for those recently arrived in Australia,
who needed assistance with English and in boosting their confidence. One
Congolese woman noted that this was a confidence that could only be
gained from giving women time to be in a space where others recognised
where she had come from. While shared experience played a vital role
here, this was also about a recognition of shared struggle that went beyond
African communities. In the Market an attempt was made to share the
space with other unemployed men and women in the area and job seekers
from Max Employment, a job seeker service in Sydney, were invited to
volunteer. This decision ensured that there were enough volunteers for

those times when regulars were busy or newly-arrived women gained employment, but also meant the space could be shared to assist others in need. There was an awareness that sharing this space could provide individuals with access to opportunities and confidence. As one woman noted, "…within one month their confidence is back and they go and get a job, so this is more than a shop."

In many ways, the Market is more than a shop because it fulfils important functions for these women. Durkheim's theory of interdependence can provide insights into these functions, despite the limitations of functionalism as a framework for analysis. Particularly for those unemployed, participation in the Market is to some degree linked to their need to work with others in order to gain work experience and potential employment. In turn, unemployed volunteers help women who have found employment, suggesting that to some degree a relationship of interdependence develops. However, for some the development of this relationship is also coupled with a simple willingness to try new things, and does not indicate that the sharing of space and opportunities is solely a product of the utilitarian motivations of individuals. The confidence people gain when volunteering at the shop goes beyond one function and is often related to the intersubjective recognition generated through the simple act of sharing time and space. For many, particularly those employed who spend their Saturdays catching up, drinking coffee, and rearranging the shop, sharing is experienced as an intangible feeling of connectedness to others. This is a feeling that does not fit neatly into either state funding and administrative requirements, or sociological theory. As David Studdert pointed out in his analysis of community, there is no sociological consensus "to the meaning experiential content and behavioural consequences of the primary condition of 'being with others'" (Studdert 2005, 9). While merely "being with others" is not alone enough to generate practices of solidarity, it is a condition that is relevant to how solidarity is experienced and, importantly, how and why it is practised. It has relevance to how African and non-African women recognise each other and how they are able to collectively occupy a space between the state and the community.

Conclusion

During the afternoon lull, between occasional purchases of waxed Ghanaian material and familiar inquiries about the whereabouts of other volunteers, one participant recounted the tightrope she has to walk when occupying a space between the state and community. This tightrope involves trying to balance a sense of connectedness and sharing with women, while simultaneously sharing information about their needs to service providers. Dismayed that she lost the opportunity to fund her own project because she had to compete with larger service providers, she resented the time and energy she was forced to put into navigating different administrative and funding processes. Despite effectively being the cultural liaison for her community and the local MRC (she helps share their programmes and they rely on her) she remains unpaid, unrecognised, and unemployed. This scenario is indicative of the shift to market-based policies that, together with the focus on social capital, have focused on performance indicators and outputs to the detriment of practices of solidarity. One MRC worker argued that the current system for working with informal migrant networks ensured that "they remain as our client, they don't become our partners, they don't do their own capacity building—they are meant to stay as our client."

The unequal distribution of power between service providers and these active community members reiterates the importance of taking into account the material and discursive role the state plays in how solidarity is practised. The African Village Market, African Women's Dinner Dance, and the Intercultural Exchange highlight the need to move beyond the functionalism of sociological and social capital theory to link social practices, such as sharing, to wider structural forces that influence who is sharing, what they are sharing and how they are sharing. These preliminary findings focus on the ways in which migrant and refugee women creatively negotiate these forces in an attempt to overcome the challenges that resettlement poses for them. Through narratives of recognition and redistribution, it becomes clear that solidarity is subject to a number of competing tensions that influence how it is practised. These tensions are part of a struggle to be recognised while also taking into account the exclusion of others, or, as Dean argued, "...a mutual expectation of a responsible orientation to relationship" (Dean 1996, 29).

Importantly, the practices of solidarity that developed at the Market, Dinner Dance, and Exchange do not only tell us something about how individuals orientate their relationships, but also about the process of developing a relationship to a wider Australian polity. Many participants strongly believe that sharing plays an important role in engaging communities and that when you "...get somebody engaged, you have moved them out of that problem and you are helping the system." As a result, moving beyond a focus on the function of social relationships to the practices, will provide new possibilities for conceptualising the relationship between sharing, belonging, and identity, and help redefine the vocabulary of immigrant solidarity.

References

Abdelkerim, A.A. and M. Grace. 2012. "Challenges to Employment in Newly Emerging African Communities in Australia: A Review of the Literature." *Australian Social Work* 65(1):104-119.

ABS. 2006. "People Born in Africa." http://www.abs.gov.au/AUSSTATS /abs@.nsf/Lookup/3416.0Main+Features32008.

ABS. 2012. "Humanitarian Arrivals." http://www.abs.gov.au/ausstats/ abs@.nsf/Lookup/1301.0Main+Features592012.

Ahmed, S. & A.M. Fortier. 2003. "Re-Imagining Communities." *International Journal of Cultural Studies* 6(3):251-259.

Amin, A. 2002. "Ethnicity and the Multicultural City: Living with Diversity." *Environment and Planning A* 34(6):959-980.

Anthias, F. 2006. "Belongings in a Globalising and Unequal World: Rethinking Translocations." In *The Situated Politics of Belonging,* edited by N. Yuval-Davis, K. Kalpana, & U. Vieten. London: SAGE.

Anthias, F. 2007. "Ethnic Ties: Social Capital and the Question of Mobilisability." *The Sociological Review* 55(4):788-805.

Archer, J. 2009. "Intersecting Feminist Theory and Ethnography in the Context of Social Work Research." *Qualitative Social Work*, 8(2):143-160.

Arneil, B. 2006. *Diverse Communities: The problem with Social Capital.* Cambridge: Cambridge University Press.

Bailey, Olga Guedes. 2012. "Migrant African Women: Tales of Agency and Belonging." *Ethnic and Racial Studies* 35(5):850-867.

Bourdieu, Pierre. 1985. "The Forms of Capital." In *Handbook of Theory and Research for the Sociology of Education,* edited by J.G Richardson, 241-58. New York: Greenwood.

Calhoun, C. 2002. "Imagining Solidarity: Cosmopolitanism, Constitutional Patriotism, and the Public Sphere." *Public Culture* 14(1):147-171.

Chelpi-den Hamer, M. and V. Mazzucato. 2010. "The Role of Support Networks in the Initial Stages of Integration: The Case of West African Newcomers in the Netherlands." *International Migration* 48(2):31-57.

Colic-Peisker, V. and F. Tilbury. 2007. "Integration into the Australian Labour Market: The Experience of Three 'Visibly Different' Groups of Recently Arrived Refugees." *International Migration* 45(1):59-85.

Darcy, M., M. Waterford & J. McIvor. 2009. *"To Market, to Market..." Competitive Tendering and Purchase of Service in the Community Sector.* Retrieved from http://www.academia.edu/194232/To_Market_to_ Market_-_Competitive_Tendering_and_the_Purchase_of_service_in_ the_Community_Sector.

Dean, J. 1996. *Solidarity of Strangers: Feminism After Identity Politics.* California: University of California Press.

Denzin, N.K. and Y.S Lincoln. 2000. *The Handbook of Qualitative Research,* 2nd edition. Thousand Oaks, California: Sage Publications.

Department of Immigration and Border Protection (DIBP). 2007. Australian Values. Retrieved from http://www.immi.gov.au/living-in-australia/values/#statement.

Durkheim, E. [1893]1997. *The Division of Labor in Society.* New York: Free Press.

Faist, T. 2000. "Transnationalization in International Migration: Implications for the Study of Citizenship and Culture." *Ethnic and Racial Studies* 23(2):189-222.

Fine, B. 2001. *Social Capital versus Social Theory: Political Economy and Social Science at the Turn of the Millennium.* London: Routledge.

Fraser, N. 2000." Rethinking Recognition." *New Left Review* 3:107-120.

Georgeou, N. 2012. *Neoliberalism, Development, and Aid Volunteering.* New York: Routledge.

Giritli-Nygren, K. and U. Schmauch. 2012. "Picturing Inclusive Places in Segregated Spaces: A Participatory Photo Project Conducted by Migrant Women in Sweden." *Gender, Place & Culture* 19(5):600-614.

Hamaz, S. and Vasta. 2009. "'To belong or not to belong'": Is that the question? Negotiating belonging in multi-ethnic London (No. 73)." COMPAS Working Papers: University of Oxford. Retrieved from http://www.compas.ox.ac.uk/publications/working-papers/wp-09-73/.

Hatoss, A. and H. Huijser. 2010. "Gendered Barriers to Educational Opportunities: Resettlement of Sudanese Refugees in Australia." *Gender and Education* 22(2):147-160.

Ho, C. 2011. "Respecting the Presence of Others: School Micropublics and Everyday Multiculturalism." *Journal of Intercultural Studies*, 32(6):603-619.

Holtug, N. and A. Mason. 2010. "Introduction: Immigration, Diversity and Social Cohesion." *Ethnicities* 10(4):407-414.

Human Rights and Equal Opportunities Commission. 2010. "In Our Own Words—African Australians: A review of Human Rights and Social Inclusion Issues. HREOC. Retrieved from http://www.hreoc.gov.au /africanaus/review/index.html.

Jakubowicz. 2008. *A Stunned Silence: The Slow Death of Multiculturalism.* Australian Policy Online. Retrieved from http://apo.org.au/node/6194

Jakubowicz, A. 1988. "The Celebration of (Moderate) Diversity in a Racist Society: Multiculturalism and Education in Australia." *Discourse* 8(2):37-75.

Komter, A. E. 2005. *Social Solidarity and the Gift*. Cambridge: Cambridge University Press.

Loobuyck, P. 2012. "Creating Mutual Identification and Solidarity in Highly Diversified Societies. The Importance of Identification by Shared Participation." *South African Journal of Philosophy* 31(3):560-574.

Lynch, P., *et al.* 2011. "Theorising Hospitality." *Hospitality & Society* 1(1):3-24.

Madison, S. 2012. *Critical Ethnography : Method, Ethics, and Performance,* 2nd edition. Washington DC: SAGE.

Mason, A. 2000. *Community, Solidarity, and Belonging Levels of Community and Their Normative Significance*. Cambridge: Cambridge University Press.

Massey, D. 2004a. "Geographies of Responsibility." *Geografiska Annaler, Series B: Human Geography* 86(1):5-18.

—. 2004b. "The Political Challenge of Relational Space: Introduction to the Vega Symposium." *Geografiska Annaler: Series B, Human Geography* 86(1):1-78.

Mauss, M. 1989. *The Gift: The Form and Reason for Exchange in Archaic Societies*. New York: Routledge.

Mazzucato, V. and M. Kabki. 2009." Small is Beautiful: The Micro-Politics of Transnational Relationships Between Ghanaian Hometown Associations and Communities Back Home." *Global Networks* 9(2):227-251.

McMichael, C. and L. Manderson. 2004. "Somali Women and Well-Being: Social Networks and Social Capital among Immigrant Women in Australia." *Human Organization* 63(1). Retrieved from http://sfaa.metapress.com/app/home/contribution.asp?referrer=parent& backto=issue,8,11;journal,34,281;browsepublicationsresults,1,2.

Mercer, C., B. Page and M. Evans. 2009. "Unsettling Connections: Transnational Networks, Development and African Home Associations." *Global Networks*, 9(2):141-161.

Noble, G. and S. Poynting. 2010. "White Lines: The Intercultural Politics of Everyday Movement in Social Spaces." *Journal of Intercultural Studies* 31(5):489-505.

Ogunsiji, O. *et al.* 2012. "Beginning Again West African Women's Experiences of Being Migrants in Australia." *Journal of Transcultural Nursing* 23(3):279-286.

Pardy, M. and J.C.H. Lee. 2011. "Using Buzzwords of Belonging: Every-day Multiculturalism and Social Capital in Australia." *Journal of Australian Studies* 35(3):297-316.

Parsons, T. 1971. *The System of Modern Societies*. Englewood Cliffs, N.J: Prentice-Hall.

Portes, A. 1998. "Social Capital: Its Origins and Applications in Modern Sociology." *Annual Review of Sociology* 24:1-24.

Poynting, S. and V. Mason. 2008. "The New Integrationism, the State and Islamophobia: Retreat from Multiculturalism in Australia." *International Journal of Law, Crime and Justice* 36:230-246.

Putnam, R. 2000. *Bowling Alone: The Collapse and Revival of American Community*. New York: Simon & Schuster.

—. 2007. "E Pluribus Unum: Diversity and Community in the Twenty-first Century The 2006 Johan Skytte Prize Lecture." *Scandinavian Political Studies* 30(2):137-174.

Ryan, L. 2011. "Migrants' Social Networks and Weak Ties: Accessing Resources and Constructing Relationships Post-Migration." *The Sociological Review* 59(4):707-724.

Schwartz, B. 1967. "The Social Psychology of the Gift." *The American Journal of Sociology* 73(1):1-11.

Spies-Butcher, B. 2009. *The Concept of Social Capital: Understanding its Economic Origins and Political Implications in Australia*. Saarbrücken, Germany: VDM Verlag Dr. Müller.

Studdert, D. 2005. *Conceptualising Community: Beyond the State and Individual*. London: Palgrave Macmillan.

Swidler, A. 2001. "What Anchors Cultural Practices." In *The Practice Turn in Contemporary Theory*, edited byKnorr Schatzki and Von Savigny, 74-92. London: Routledge.

Taylor, G., J. Wangaruro and I. Papadopoulos. 2012. "'It Is My Turn To Give': Migrants' Perceptions of Gift Exchange and the Maintenance of Transnational Identity." *Journal of Ethnic and Migration Studies* 1-16.

The Gift: An Interdisciplinary Perspective. 1996. Amsterdam: Amsterdam University Press.

Thijssen, P. 2012. "From Mechanical to Organic Solidarity, and Back With Honneth Beyond Durkheim." *European Journal of Social Theory* 15(4):454-470.

Valentine, G. 2007. "Theorizing and Researching Intersectionality: A Challenge for Feminist Geography." *The Professional Geographer* 59(1):10-21.

Vasta, E. 2011. "Immigrants and the Paper Market: Borrowing, Renting and Buying Identities." *Ethnic and Racial Studies* 34(2):187-206.

—. 2010. "The Controllability of Difference: Social Cohesion and the New Politics of Solidarity." *Ethnicities* 10(4):503-521.

Vasta, E. and S. Castles. 1996. *The Teeth Are Smiling: The Persistence of Racism in Multicultural Australia.* St Leonards, N.S.W: Allen & Unwin.

Walsh, J.P. 2011. "Quantifying Citizens: Neoliberal Restructuring and Immigrant Selection in Canada and Australia." *Citizenship Studies* 15(6-7):861-879.

Wise, A. and S. Velayutham. 2009. *Everyday Multiculturalism.* Basingstoke, UK: Palgrave Macmillan.

Yuval-Davis, N. 2007. "Identity, Identity Politics and the Constructionism Debate." In *New Ways of Knowing: Bending the Paradigm in Identity Research.* Presented at the BSA conference, UEL. Retrieved from http://www.uel.ac.uk/ipsa/documents/bsa2.pdf.

Yuval-Davis, N., F. Anthias and E. Kofman. 2005. "Secure Borders and Safe Haven and the Gendered Politics of Belonging: Beyond Social Cohesion." *Ethnic and Racial Studies* 28(3):513-535.

Chapter Eight

Negotiating Boundaries of Integration into "New Societies": The Question of Neighbours and Foreigners

Simona Zavratnik

This chapter addresses the broader questions of migration and ethnic diversity in Slovenia, the level of multiculturalism in the country, and integration policies that constitute the contemporary framework for migration management. Slovenia has a long experience of protecting autochthonous or indigenous ethnic minorities, but little experience of migrants' integration. Both these issues are today circumscribed by the long-established protection policies, attitudes towards migrants/communities/minorities from the former Yugoslavia (dubbed "suspicious *ić*" attitudes, alluding to the surname endings commonly found in other parts of the former Yugoslavia, except in Slovenia), and modern global migrations. This is also the main battlefield where the struggle for social cohesion, social solidarity, multicultural society and inclusion of newcomers is taking place.

Global migration is a key feature of modern societies and a factor of extensive social change that involves the entire spectrum of social issues, ranging from the incorporation of migrants into "new society"[1] and policies of recognising multiculturalism and citizen rights, to the challenges of achieving social cohesion in the microcosm of everyday life and preventing the construction of parallel, ghettoised worlds of migrants and the majority population. Accordingly, the question of negotiating boundaries

---

1. I use the term "new society" instead of "host society" because the latter implies temporariness and returning of migrants to the places of origin. However, the history of migration over the past decades has shown that such expectations by host societies are not realistic. "New society" implies greater openness than the deterministic term "host society."

of inclusion or exclusion of ethnic minorities and/or migrants plays a crucial role in contemporary societies. Contemporary migration trends have led to changes in identity policies and disparate responses—including populist ones—to the issues of coexistence with "foreigners," i.e. people of different identities. Since ethnic/cultural differences are factors of exclusion, the essential question is how to construct a different "we" of the kind that will include migrants as new members of our society in the "we" field.

In the Slovene context, this is particularly important in view of the perceptions of indigeneity and foreignness, and resulting discriminatory discourses and attitudes towards people who are not "ours"—not indigenous, not autochthonous. Consequently the image of a foreigner—though not just any foreigner, but specifically the immigrant worker, refugee, or asylum seeker—mainly evokes non-acceptance, if not intolerance or hate speech towards the "other" and "different." The Slovenes' attitude to migrants—who for the most part do not belong to the category of "most desirable and welcome foreigners" but are rather perceived as dubious "newcomers with (presumably) suspicious intentions"—suggests a discrepancy between the desirable migrant elites and "merely" necessary labour (Zavratnik 2012; Kralj 2011); the unfavourable conditions brought about by the economic recession have put even greater emphasis on the latter. Given this politically and economically unfavourable situation, it is all the more important to devote attention to the ways in which the frameworks of integration policies are formed in the new societies stirred up by global migration, and to the foundations of concrete political strategies for migration management.

In this text, I will begin by delineating the emerging new ethnic diversity of Slovene society. The main process that has contributed to the present ethnic diversity in Slovenia has been migration within the territory of the former Yugoslavia. In the past, it was defined as internal economic migration, but after 1991, with the changes of borders and formation of new states in the Balkans, it led to the emergence of immigrant communities, new ethnic minorities and unrecognised national minorities in Slovenia. And it is this multitude of terms used to refer to migrant groups that perhaps best reflects the inconclusiveness of contemporary ethnic diversity policies in Slovenia. It is especially evident when two concepts collide: one is the long-established protection of autochthonous ethnic minorities based on high standards (constitutional protection), and the other is the virtually unaddressed question of so-called new ethnic minorities that emerged with the formation of new states. The vagueness of their status is one of the unresolved challenges and a problem that will not easily disappear from the agenda of ethnic policies. I would also like to remark that a critical reader may find the terminology used in this text ambiguous and inconsistent, given that I alternately use the terms minorities, ethnic groups, immigrant groups and migrants to denote virtually the same group of "different" members of Slovene society. Notwithstanding the vagueness of their status, the common name for our neighbours albeit foreigners may as well be "the suspicious *ić*'s." This surname ending is the pivot around which the main tensions in Slovenia within the field of ethnic diversity revolve.

In the text I will first briefly analyse the notion of statehood, the formation of Slovene national identity, and the challenges to contemporary migration and "new" ethnic diversity created by the so-called unrecognised ethnic minorities in Slovenia and the emergence of migrant communities. In the second part, I look into the implications of global migration trends in local environments, focusing on social contacts with migrants. Since public opinion plays an important role in the process of shaping public policies, i.e. in achieving social cohesion, our point of departure in addressing the question of the public's perceptions of migrations, migrants' integration, and multiculturalism is empirical research.

Ethnic/Cultural Diversity in Slovenia: A "Suspicious *ić*," Minorities and Migrants

The establishment of Slovenia as a modern democratic state began in 1991 with the gaining of independence and the breakup of Yugoslavia. This was the time of democratisation of political life in eastern and central Europe and the collapse of the communist system. "This process was part of the global third wave of democratisation during the period 1974-90" (Rizman 2006, 3), leading to the changes to democracy in many countries worldwide (Diamond 1999). Democratic transition in Slovenia started in the late 1980s, through centrality of the civil society movements and rebels of the intellectual elites to authoritarian political regime that led to democratic changes in later periods (Rizman 2006).

Independence came with many challenges, including in the area of ethnic and cultural diversity management. New democracies were often described as "fragile" primarily because of the democratic deficit in many areas, with minority and migration policies being no exception. Here I will be concerned with the protection of ethnic minorities and new minorities, i.e. migrant communities (Komac 2003). While the collective and individual rights of autochthonous minorities had long since been secured in

Slovenia, protection of so-called new minorities is a new issue that emerged only with independence. However, regardless of whether the traditional autochthonous minorities or new migrant communities are in question, the approach to ethnic diversity should be essentially the same, i.e. based on a multicultural model which, generally speaking, promotes cultural difference and coexistence of the minority and majority cultures, with the minority members' rights guaranteed. In the case of Slovenia, the point at issue is what I named "conserved multiculturalism" to denote the predicament in which the multicultural approach has found itself. It is characterised by the dualism of the contemporary approach to ethnic issues which makes a distinction between traditional minorities and contemporary (migrant) minorities. In social sciences, the latter have been referred to as "new ethnic minorities" or "unrecognised national minorities," with the emphasis being on the attribute "new." Critics have already drawn attention to the ambiguities and unresolved issues that affect the quality of migrants' everyday life (Kralj 2008a; Medica 2004), but it is primarily legal shortcomings that have turned these groups into silent, overlooked minorities with limited options for participation in public life (Pajnik 2007).

The appearance of new ethnic minorities created even greater confusion within populist discourses. Their only palpable common denominator, and one that is widely recognisable within the public sphere, was the "suspicious *ić*" denominator,[2] denoting "people with half roof over their heads" as Kuzmanić (1999) put it. This surname ending was the point around which exclusion strategies revolved, and these ranged from making access to the labour market more difficult for migrants to discrimination against children in schools and ostracising of people who spoke Croatian/Serbian/Bosnian in public (Kralj 2008b; Medica 2004).

As a consequence, the suspicious "*ić*" surnames turned contemporary economic immigrants with work permits, war refugees from the former Yugoslavia, and the children of the second and third generation of immigrants, to name only a few groups, into "others" and foreigners who are forced to negotiate anew the crossing of social borders set up by the new Slovenian society. Negotiations of membership taking place along the lines of "us and them" and insiders versus outsiders importantly affect the public perception of integration, multiculturalism and an open society. Accordingly, concrete political strategies (of varying success) for

---

2. "*-ić*" is a typical surname ending in many parts of the former Yugoslavia except Slovenia. Moreover, the Slovenian version of the Latin alphabet does not contain "ć," but it does contain "č," so the apparent difference hinges on this missing part of the diacritic.

integrating foreigners into Slovenian society have been formulated within the context that is importantly determined by the public's acceptance or refusal of migrants, and the same context also dictates individual choices and political actors' preferences (which, in turn, influence ethnic and migration policies). All of this partly addresses the contentious question of social solidarity and social cohesion. In contemporary societies, consensus on social solidarity is one of the main issues that provokes debates over citizens' rights. It seems that the fundamental question in contemporary European societies, regardless of their socialist tradition (or absence thereof) is: how many cultural, social and political rights can a country afford to "grant" to the most vulnerable social groups? The attitude to new minorities, migrants and immigrant communities is one of the main indicators of the democracy level within contemporary societies. The bones of contention are crucial issues such as citizenship, culture, and national identity, meaning that the instrumentarium for creating potential conflicts among groups could not be bigger.

To recapitulate, ethnic/cultural diversity involves the issues of migrants' integration (quite a new issue in Slovenia) and that of the incorporation of "new and traditional" ethnic minorities. Both issues are somehow entrapped between the traditional policies of protecting autochthonous/indigenous ethnic minorities, on the one hand, and modern global migrations and attitudes towards "suspicious *ić*," i.e. migrants/ communities/minorities from the former Yugoslavia, on the other. It is the main battlefield where the struggle for social cohesion and attempts to cross boundaries take place.

Minorities and Migrants:
Traditional and "New" Minority Communities

Slovenia is defined in documents as a multiethnic, pluralist and democratic state in which the rights of ethnic and other cultural minorities are respected under the constitution. So, which model of minority protection is in use and what is the migrants' position within it? Komac (1999, 5) divides minorities into two groups: the "traditional" (territorial) minorities and the newly-formed ethnic communities (comprising mostly members of the nations of former Yugoslavia) which emerged as a result of contemporary processes of economic immigration from the former common state.

A brief look at history will show that ethnic policies in Slovenia are not of recent date. On the contrary, diversity had an important role in the process of state formation during WWII, when the new borders in this part of Europe were drawn. In both cases, the status of ethnic minorities that lived across the border was at stake: the Slovenian minority in Austria and the Italian minority in Slovenia and Croatia (then Yugoslavia), whose statuses are regulated through international agreements. To ensure the protection of autochthonous minorities in Slovenia (Yugoslavia)—meaning the Italian and Hungarian minority—a specific model of ethnic minority protection was formulated and is inscribed in the constitution of the Republic of Slovenia. Article 64 outlines special rights of both autochthonous ethnic communities,[3] and in part refers to the Roma community.[4] Accordingly, it can be said that ethnic policies in independent Slovenia, except for individual initiatives relating to the Roma, focused on the Italian and Hungarian minorities. The minority rights should therefore be read within this context described by Komac:

> A starting point for the protection of ethnic communities in Slovenia is provided by the concept of collective rights which the State grants irrespective of numerical strength or proportion of numbers of ethnic minorities on the ethnically mixed territory. Collective rights pertain to ethnic minorities as objectively existing subjects. (Komac 1999, 17)

In determining autochthonous minorities, the most important criteria are those of *territoriality* and *the duration of residence* in a specific region. This approach suggests that autochthonous minorities are defined once and for good, since it is not possible to expect that potential new minorities could meet these criteria. The number of autochthonous minorities is therefore fixed and exclusive. This is where the predicament of ethnic policy comes to light, since such an exclusive approach to minority protection automatically categorises all other, younger minority groups as "lower ranking" minorities that do not qualify for the same high-level protection of rights. Furthermore, in contrast to autochthonous ones, the "new minorities" are not mentioned in the constitution, although initiatives along these lines were put forward by both "new minorities" and part of the civil and academic public.

The situation in the year of independence, 1991, brings along the question: what are our former compatriots? The answers could be gleaned from various (conditionally speaking) newly created statuses which turned some of them into migrants and some into new ethnic/migrant communities,

---

3. Article 64: Special Rights of the Autochthonous Italian and Hungarian National Communities in Slovenia, Constitution of the Republic of Slovenia, 1991.
4. Article 65: Status and Special Rights of the Romany Community in Slovenia, Constitution of the Republic of Slovenia, 1991.

while some were erased.[5] Political designations and juggling were plenti-
ful, while dilemmas were neither straightforward nor of terminological
nature only. The issue involved broader citizenship policy, ethnic and migration policies, and these were by no means consistent. The result was the
emergence of "migrants" (and indeed, the entire migrant communities)
who in fact never moved anywhere nor had they changed their place of
residence; it was only the borders that changed. The response to this phenomenon involved the delicate topic of autochthony and protection of
minorities, on the one hand, and a more contemporary approach to regulating ethnic/cultural differences through citizen rights, on the other. Former
compatriots overnight became foreigners, migrants, members of new ethnic minorities, new minorities, people designated by their "suspicious *ič*"
surname endings. However, what is of crucial importance is that the rights
of this group of minorities are guaranteed on an essentially different level,
as described by Kralj (2008b, 236):

> Members of national communities from the former common state of Yugo-
> slavia do not possess a collective social status in Slovenia. The Slovenian
> constitution does not include particular regulations regarding the protection
> of their (collective) rights and their minority communities. When preserv-
> ing their national identity, the 'new' national communities are only
> supported by the 61st and 62nd article of the constitution determining the
> right to express their national appurtenance and the right to use their lan-
> guage and writing.

It should be noted that the differentiation between new and traditional
minorities is understandable when viewed from a historical perspective.
But social changes in the region, compounded by changes in the dynamics
and extent of global migration, led to local changes that inevitably affected
the ethnic diversity of Slovenian society. I have mentioned earlier that the
complexity of the situation of "suspicious *ič*'s" arises from the fact that

---

5. "The Erased" is a name that denotes a group of people, approximately 1% of
Slovenia's population (or, to be more accurate, 18,305 people), originating from
different republics of the former Yugoslavia, whose personal data were in 1992
unlawfully transferred from a register of people with permanent residence to a
register of people with no legal status in Slovenia. This measure came to be known
as the "erasure" and it provoked many responses among legal experts, advocates
for human rights, NGOs, and academia. The disapproval was strong, both because
of legal controversy and of resulting injustice and deprivation of these people of
legal status and related basic citizen rights. See Dedić, Jalušič and Zorn (2003):
The Erased: Organized Innocence and the Politics of Exclusion. Ljubljana: Peace
Institute.

this group consists of both present-day economic migrants (more than three quarters of the migrant population that arrived in Slovenia after 1991 came from the regions of the former Yugoslavia) and the descendants of migrants who had moved to Slovenia during the 1960s and the 1970s. One evident problem that had implications for our former compatriots was related to the building of national identity of the new, fragile state. Slovenia based its new identity on distancing itself from the Balkans and integrating into Europe ("where we have long since belonged" in the parlance of transition policies). The "suspicious –ić" was therefore an obvious signifier of Otherness that was in conflict with the new identity, and also a marker of the Balkans.

It is a fact that no matter which status is attributed to someone with a surname ending in *"ić,"* the missing half of the diacritic continues to be the basic factor of differentiation and the point around which dominant discourses of nationalism, xenophobia and stereotypes are created. Apprehensions and the fear of potential threat to cultural and national identity, which lies at the foundation of these defence mechanisms that exclude the "other," produce firm borders separating the majority from the minorities.

Shifting Borders Among "Us" and "Them": Contemporary Migration and Public Opinion

This subchapter deals with the Slovene public's perception of the issues of migration, integration of immigrants, and multiculturalism. It is empirically based on the research survey "Migration, integration, and multiculturalism—empirical data collection" (short name: Integration policies, 2007),[6] set up as a tool for longitudinal measuring of public opinion, and in many aspects comparable to similar European surveys.

When immigrants eventually overcome the hurdle posed by selective admission mechanisms, on entering the destination country they face another type of border—the social border setting conditions on their inclusion in the majority society. The inclusion of immigrants in everyday life also highly depends on the attitude of the majority population. In our research, the respondents evaluate knowledge of the language, adequate

---

6. The survey was part of the project "Integration policies—establishing an evaluation model and instruments of longitudinal monitoring," at the University of Primorska, ZRS Koper in the period 2006-2008 and repeated in a modified version in 2010 (see Kralj 2011, and for detailed results of the study Zavratnik and Kralj *et al.* 2008).

high education, and employment as the most important factor for success-ful inclusion in Slovene society, while the least important factors are race (being white) and religion (Catholism). It therefore seems that public opinion rejects racism and religious factors. However, the race factor should be relativised at least partly in a dominantly "white" environment, where nationalism and xenophobia towards foreigners from nearby environments (the former common state of Yugoslavia) have much deeper roots (Zavrat-nik 2012, Zavratnik and Kralj *et al.* 2008).

Figure 9-1: In your opinion, how important are the following factors for the successful inclusion of immigrants into Slovene society?

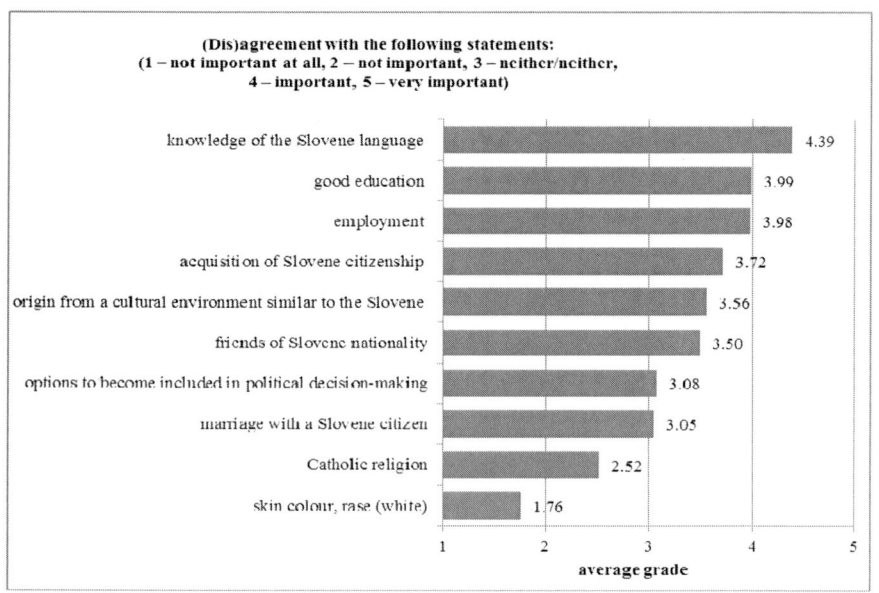

Source: Integration policies, 2007

The empirical research shows that the inclusion of immigrants in their new environment is conditioned upon clearly stated cultural and economic criteria; this model seems to hold on to a combination of a basic cultural marker (language) and economic independence. Further, the respondents evaluated expected behaviour of immigrants. Most respondents are in favour of cultural adaptation, which is a concept behind the statement that immigrants should adopt the Slovene language and customs but preserve their own language and culture in their domestic environment. A significant indicator is that the respondents completely rejected a segregation strategy, according to which immigrants should preserve their language and culture and live in separate, parallel social worlds. One of the crucial findings of empirical research in Slovenian context is that public opinion is in favour of the segmented acceptance of migrants based on their geographic origin and socio-economic status, and consequently, that integration policies are seen through the lens of segmentation. The success (or the lack thereof) of immigrants' integration into the majority society depends on several factors, among which special emphasis should be given to the attitude of the public to immigration and the majority society's attitudes to, and prejudices against, the immigrant population. The Slovene public is generally disapproving of immigrants coming from specific geographical regions, and particularly of immigrants from the territory of the former Yugoslavia, who account for the majority of the immigrant population in Slovenia and are the only numerically significant immigrant group. This is revealing of the public's strong resistance to the perceived "real threat," while the negative perception of immigrants from other poorer and culturally different (non-European) countries is indicative of the proverbial introversion of Slovene society and related perception of cultural differences as a threat to Slovene cultural identity (Zavratnik 2012, 212 and Zavratnik and Kralj *et al.* 2008).

Figure 9-3: Attitudes towards regulating migration based on the immigrants' geographical origin.

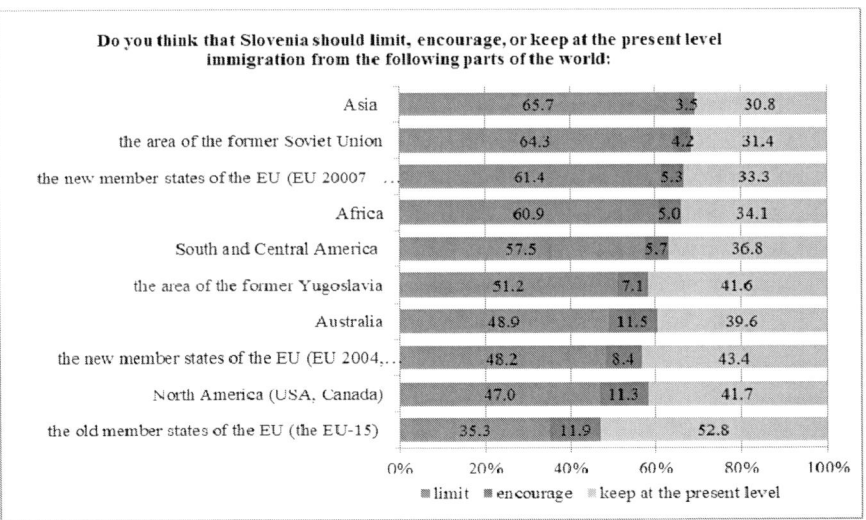

Source: Integration policies, 2007

The respondents generally support opinions that the scope of migration from different parts of the world should be limited, the only exception being migrants from the old member states of the EU. They were over-whelmingly in favour of limiting migration from Asia, the area of the former Soviet Union, Africa, and the new EU member states (2007 en-largement, meaning Romania and Bulgaria); the smallest number of respondents were in favour of limiting immigration from the old member states of the EU. Hardly any support for immigration was recorded. The percentages of respondents who think that the scope of immigration should be stimulated are very low, from a few percentage points to at most 12% for the most desirable immigrants from the old member states of the EU. The third option—immigration should be kept at the present level—is the one that, taking into account the findings of similar surveys, is valid under the assumption that the scope and structure of immigration does not change essentially (Zavratnik 2012, 213). Such attitudes are often indica-tive of people's tolerance of existing immigrants, with reasons varying from economic necessity, which the respondents recognise and accept, to cultural similarity and the like. This option is most frequently chosen in connection with the most desirable immigrants, and least frequently with those who are highest on the scale of undesirable immigrants.

Figure 9-4: Regulating migration based on the immigrants' social status.

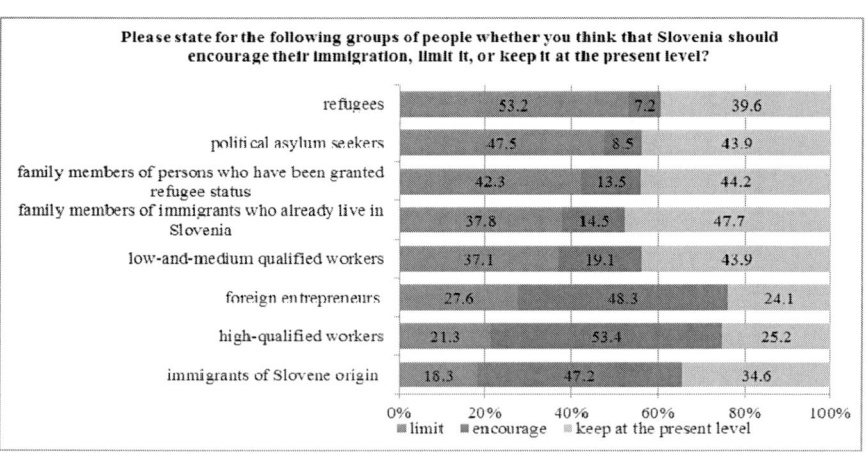

Source: Integration policies, 2007

Besides the geographical aspect, the respondents also considered the different social statuses marking groups of migrants as important, whether they be political status, ethnic features, or status variables like education, occupation, etc. (Zavratnik, 2012, 214 and Zavratnik and Kralj *et al.* 2008).

The results show a fundamental dichotomy (Zavratnik 2012, 214–216): on the one hand, they testify to the strong introversion of the Slovene public, which leads to a negative perception of all classical traditional groups of political migrants (refugees, asylum seekers, family members of migrants), but, on the other hand, when a concrete social status is involved, meaning well-educated migrants, entrepreneurs and ethnic Slovenes, the perceptions are largely positive. It seems that for the respondents the term immigration has a negative connotation in itself, and that this changes only when it refers to the immigration of elites and the ethnic/cultural "equals." The indicated dichotomy confirms the desirability of elites (the country needs them to ensure progress and social welfare), whereas unqualified workers are perceived as a "necessary evil." The combined answers in the graph illustrate the utilitarian logic of public opinion, resulting from a purposive-rational principle: the public unequivocally states that we do need certain target groups of immigrants; besides elites, these are workers with a low education level. Those who are in favour of stimulating immigration (a total of 19%) are mainly young people between the ages of 18 and 28. The respondents from the group with the highest education level are most in favour of keeping immigration at the present level. The picture is quite different if we look at the groups which "do not work for us"; refugees, asylum seekers and their families. Migration policies in modern societies operate according to the principle of classifying migrants as either desirable or undesirable, and the result is that most migrants are in the second category.

Migration management is indeed significantly defined by both external and internal borders. External selective mechanisms usually amount to restrictions on crossing the national or Schengen borders, while the internal boundaries determine membership or inclusion/exclusion along the lines of "us vs. them" or domestic population vs. foreigners. Characteristically, in the public eye, the geographical and social borders coincide when immigrants are in question: we are unwilling to encourage the crossing of borders, and when we do acquiesce to it, the crossing should be selective and should meet certain conditions. The following graph shows high support for statements that are actually in collision, but it seems that the respondents do not perceive them as contradictory (Zavratnik 2012, 215–216 and Zavratnik and Kralj *et al.* 2008).

Figure 9-5: Attitudes to immigration and integration policies.

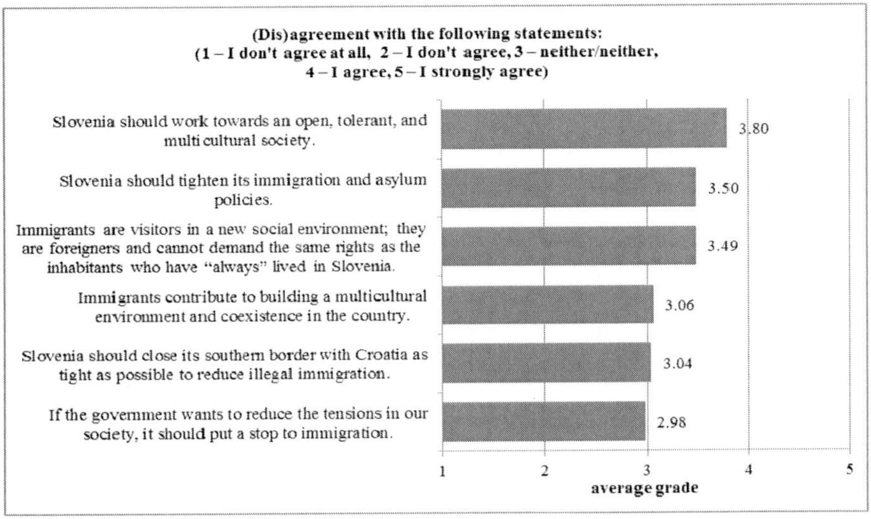

(Dis)agreement with the following statements:
(1 – I don't agree at all, 2 – I don't agree, 3 – neither/neither,
4 – I agree, 5 – I strongly agree)

Statement	average grade
Slovenia should work towards an open, tolerant, and multicultural society.	3.80
Slovenia should tighten its immigration and asylum policies.	3.50
Immigrants are visitors in a new social environment; they are foreigners and cannot demand the same rights as the inhabitants who have "always" lived in Slovenia.	3.49
Immigrants contribute to building a multicultural environment and coexistence in the country.	3.06
Slovenia should close its southern border with Croatia as tight as possible to reduce illegal immigration.	3.04
If the government wants to reduce the tensions in our society, it should put a stop to immigration.	2.98

Source: Integration policies, 2007

The first feature is the high level of agreement with the statement that Slovenia should work towards an open, tolerant and multicultural society. Another is a high level of agreement with the statement that Slovenia should apply more restrictive immigration and asylum policies. These two statements point to the fundamental contradiction: a relatively high support for cultural diversity and tolerance, but this is which is at odds with the support for restrictive migration and entry policies. It seems that the respondents fail to discern this discrepancy or do not connect the issues directly. The basic discrepancy between self-proclaimed tolerance, on the one hand, and support for restrictive migration policies, on the other, is confirmed by other answers that indeed tip the balance in favour of restrictions. Over half the respondents agreed that migrants are visitors (foreigners, newcomers) in a given society and therefore cannot enjoy the same rights as the "indigenous" population. This is an expected result, reflecting the Slovene perception of indigeneity as an important element of national identity and state building. Migrants as "temporary newcomers" do not meet the criterion of indigeneity in any way; this is particularly important in view of the fact that this concept is linked to the granting of (special) political rights. Furthermore, the agreement with the statement that immigrants contribute to coexistence and the creation of a multicultural environment varies across groups and indeed, it is not possible to expect a consensus on this issue.

Views on preventing illegal migration by imposing stricter control on the external, Schengen borders are dichotomous: the shares of supporters and opponents are nearly equal. Overall, an important signal sent out by the public opinion is that closing the European space to non-Europeans is not a matter of course. The Schengen border is perceived as the border between "Europe and the Balkans," and as such it is an important mental marker of inclusion, involving the common EU area without internal borders, and of exclusion, defining the outside population that needs permission to enter, i.e. visas and/or work permits (Zavratnik and Zimic, 2003).

The concurrence with the above-mentioned, mutually contradictory statements seems to indicate that Slovenia has "successfully" embraced the schizophrenic European attitude to migration marked, on the one hand, by proclaimed support for a democratic, inclusive, tolerant, and multicultural society and, on the other, by the implementation of repressive and selective immigration policies, which may even be in complete contradiction with basic human rights and liberties. This is illustrated by the majority support for the statement that in their new social environment immigrants cannot claim the same rights as the citizens (Slovenes) who have "always" lived here. Such counter-positioning of "newcomers" versus "indigenous inhabitants" clashes at least with the right to non-discriminatory treatment (Zavratnik and Kralj *et al.* 2008; Kralj 2011; Zavratnik 2011).

Migrants as "Neighbours and Foreigners" in New Societies

Apprehensions and the potential threat to cultural and national identity lead to various strategies for setting up cultural, social and political borders. For members of minorities (traditional and particularly "new" minorities), these borders are very difficult to cross. I argue that greater mobility and intense globalisation processes that create culturally mixed societies urgently call for the development of "good neighbour" strategies; these are increasingly important for softening the borders separating "us and them." Various empirical studies across the region have shown that keeping social distance from migrants is a constant trait in Europe. This fact should be associated with changes in global migration trends which introduce important structural changes into local spaces, including in Slovenia and other East European post-transitional societies in transition, where the contemporary issues of migration, asylum and general mobility have been contextualised in completely new social circumstances. The once closed socialist societies have become similar to western societies in this respect, where the issues of managing the effects of social migration, including migrants' integration, the management of ethnic and cultural diversity, and contemporary citizenship have been the concern, for quite some time, of various protagonists ranging from policy makers, scholars, and analysts to experts from the public and NGO sectors. The most dangerous scenario would be to leave the issue of social cohesion and solidarity between the majority society and more or less desirable social groups (among these ethnic minorities and migrants) to populist "street politics."

The intensity and increasing scope of contemporary globalised migration pose huge challenges to current migration policies. The issues could hardly be more complex: in every European society migration management is a conflict issue, whether local, national or EU policies are involved. The delicacy of the issue and policies is connected with an extreme ideological charge and new politicisation that emerged around the turn of the century, when migration turned from a classical economic issue into a paramount political issue. The disputes are taking different forms and places: that of granting citizen rights to immigrants, (dis)agreements on policies of multiculturalism and cultural difference, functioning of the welfare state, and many more.

The empirical study in our text does not suggest an admirably high level of social solidarity or consensus on values concerning migration, immigrants' integration, and multiculturalism in Slovenia. This inevitably raises the question of future trends in public opinion. Will the public opinion remain static? Will decades-old, mythicized notions on migration persist or succumb to the influence of urbanisation and globalisation processes? Empirical results point to three potential courses of development (Zavratnik and Kralj *et al.* 2008; Zavratnik 2011): the first is the so-called "European-indigenous scenario," according to which public opinion will be expectedly rational and in line with current European migration and asylum policies. Such opinions are strongly present in the survey; they represent typical "European stances" and "European values." The second trend may be called the "cosmopolitan-multicultural scenario," according to which changes in opinions will occur, as well as greater openness to migration and cultural differences. The proponents of changes are educated younger people living in urban centres. This optimistic scenario arises from the recognition that solidarity is a key social value, although data suggest only a weakly expressed trend by a minority. The third trend would be the "latent conflict scenario," characterised by a passive attitude of the public to migration or disregard for migration, both resulting from non-acceptance of immigrants. Our survey showed that the public see immigrants as a "threat to the stability" of the labour market, the welfare state, and national culture. Such un-reflected views were present in Slovenia during the decades when the country was part of Yugoslavia, and have led to latent conflicts that found expression among the descendants of the second and third generations of immigrants.

What is certain, though, is that the present situation precludes the use of any kind of instant solutions aimed at fast and easy turning of migrants into neighbours, or their fast inclusion into new societies. The line dividing a "foreigner migrant" from a "desirable neighbour migrant" is rather firm in contemporary European societies, and there are few policies based on the good-neighbour strategy that would promote respect for difference, either racial, ethnic, religious, or arising from some other cultural trait.

References

Diamond, Larry. 1999. *Developing Democracy: Towards Consolidation.* Baltimore: John Hopkins University Press.

Dedić, Jasminka, Vlasta Jalušič and Jelka Zorn. 2003. *The Erased: Organized Innocence and the Politics of Exclusion.* Ljubljana: Peace Institute.

Evropska raziskava vrednot. 2008. FDV - IDV - CJMMK: Projekt SJM 2008/1 – *Evropska raziskava vrednot / European Values Study*; http://adp.fdv.uni-lj.si/podatki/sjm/sjm081-vp.pdf.

Komac, Miran. 1999. *Protection of ethnic communities in the Republic of Slovenia.* Ljubljana: Institute for Ethnic Studies.

—. 2003. "Varstvo 'novih' narodnih skupnosti v Sloveniji." *Razprave in gradivo: revija za narodnostna vprašanja /Treatises and documents: journal of ethnic studies* 43:6-33s.

Kralj, Ana. 2008-a. *Nepovabljeni. Globalizacija, nacionalizem in migracije.* Koper: Univerzitetna založba Annales.

—. 2008-b. "When Ć becomes Č: discrimination of unrecognized national minorities in Slovenia." *Revija za sociologiju* 235-250.

—. 2011. "Ekonomske migracije in delavci migranti v ogledalu javnega mnenja" / "Economic migration and worker migrants in the mirror of public opinion". *Annales.* 21/2, 285-296.

Kuzmanić, Tonči. 1999. *Bitja s pol strešice. Slovenski rasizem, šovinizem in seksizem.* Ljubljana: Open Society Institute.

Medica, Karmen. 2004. "Perspketive medijev etničnih skupin/manjšin z območja bivše Jugoslavije v Sloveniji." *Monitor ISH*. VI/1:93-122.

Pajnik, Mojca. 2007. "Integration Policies in Migration Between National-ising States and Transnational Citizenship, with Reference to the Slovenian case." *Journal of Ethnic and Migration Studies* 33/5:849-865.

Rizman, Rudi. 2006. *Uncertain Path: Democratic Transition and Consolidation in Slovenia*. College Station: Texas A&M University Press.

Ustava Republike Slovenije / Constitution of the Republic of Slovenia, Uradni list Republike Slovenije, No. 33/1991, access: 28.12.1991.

Zavratnik Zimic, Simona. 2003. "Constructing 'New' Boundary: Slovenia and Croatia." *Revija za sociologiju*. Vol XXXIV, No 3-4: 179-188.

Zavratnik, Simona, Ana Kralj, Zorana Medarič and Blaž Simčič. 2008. *Migracije, integracija in multikulturnost - kontekstualizacije sodobnih migracij skozi javno mnenje*. Zakljucno poročilo ciljno-raziskovalnega projekta "Integracijske politike - vzpostavitev evalvacijskega modela in instrumentov longitudinalnega monitoring." Koper: Univerza na Primorskem, Znanstveno-raziskovalno središče.

Zavratnik, Simona, Ana Kralj, Zorana Medarič and Blaž Simčič. 2009. Migrations, integration and multiculturality / Migracije, integracija in multikulturnost. Ljubljana: Fakulteta za družbene vede, Arhiv družboslovnih podatkov / Social science data archives, http://www.adp.fdv.uni-lj.si/opisi/migim07.xml.

Zavratnik, Simona. 2011. "Sodobne migracije v mnenjih slovenske javnosti" / "Contemporary Migrations Through Public Opinion." *Dve domovini / Two Homelands* 33:55-71.

—. 2012. "Images of immigrants in Slovenia: insight from public opinion research." *Ethnicity studies / Etniškumo studijos* 1/2:204-223.

CHAPTER NINE

URBAN TRANSFORMATION
AND VOLUNTARY DISPLACEMENT:
THE CASE OF EGE DISTRICT
IN ANKARA, TURKEY

BURCU ŞENTÜRK

In the context of globalisation and neoliberalism, the significance of cities as "the engines of economic growth, key centres of economic, political, and social innovation, and key actors in promoting and consolidating international competitiveness" (Jessop 2002, 465) is highlighted. The cities, as the new centres of reproduction and continual reconstitution of neoliberalism, are transformed into a commodity which can be sold in the market (Brenner and Theodore 2002) and are considered "active agents when they are mere things" (Harvey 1989, 5).

Urban transformation projects have been prominent tools of creating global cities. Investments in cities, such as building sport fields, shopping malls, and the like, are used to increase the reputation of cities. All of these projects and investments are promoted as if they are for the benefit of all the people in the city. In the context of creating global cities, *gecekondu*[1] areas, which emerged as a result of rural to urban migration in Turkey, are considered problematic areas which should be transformed. For example, *gecekondu* dwellers without legal title deeds are displaced and their houses are demolished without any compensation, while their counterparts with legal title deeds are compensated and given the opportunity to live in the new apartments replacing the *gecekondus*. This is the issue under considera-

---

1. *Gecekondu* literally means "built overnight," and refers to the poor quality houses built by migrants on public land in large cities without getting permission. *Gecekondu* can refer to individual squatter houses, illegal housing or a squatter area in Turkish; however, in this study, the term denotes squatter houses in order to avoid possible confusion.

tion in this chapter. The main source of this study is based on field research conducted in the Ege neighbourhood of Ankara in 2011. Ege is one of the squatter neighbourhoods of the Mamak district, which is a typical *gecekondu* settlement populated by low-income early migrant families who came from the villages of Central Anatolia (Alpar and Yener 1991, Eroğlu 2011). For the field work, I stayed in a *gecekondu* in Ege with my parents for three months; I used participant-observation techniques which included taking part in street protests and daily activities such as baking bread, helping local children in their homework, watching TV series with women, and accompanying local people when they visited the local state authorities. I conducted in-depth interviews with 80 *gecekondu* dwellers, a city planner in Mamak municipality, and activists of NGOs and political organisations who work in Ege. I also conducted two focus group interviews with local people.

My field work included research on both the holders of formal title deeds in Ege and people without formal title deeds. However, this chapter focuses on the people of Ege with formal title-deeds, and argues that they are displaced not by police or judicial force, but as a result of pressure generated by urban rent levels. On this point, it will be suggested that although the *gecekondu* dwellers with legal titles consider these projects and the investments as the signs of development and appreciate them, they will not be able to continue living in their neighbourhood after it becomes developed. I will argue that urban reforms which do not consider the local people's needs, circumstances, and life-styles result in the displacement of the local population, transferring the problems associated with squatter areas such as poverty, insecurity, unemployment, and low levels of education, to other areas of the cities.

A Brief History of Internal Migration in Turkey

There have been two recent waves of internal mass migration in Turkey. The first one was in the 1950s and was caused by the mechanisation of agriculture, resulting in surplus labour in rural areas and necessitating the Import Substitution Industrialisation (ISI) policy. This policy created the need for labour in newly emerging industries built in urban areas. The second wave occurred in the 1980s when the development strategy of Turkey shifted from import substitution industrialisation to the structural adjustment policy (SAP), which aimed at integration with the global market. The capital owners needed a flexible and fragmented labour-force and reduced labour costs. A sharp decrease in agricultural subsidies under the SAP and the need for flexible and cheap labour after 1980 stood as the main causes behind the second wave migration.

In the absence of social policies for providing the urban newcomers with accommodation, the rural migrants had to solve their own problem. They occupied lands mostly belonging to the state and built up their own *gecekondu*. Internal migration was a chain migration, which resulted in many families from the same village or region being clustered in the same neighbourhoods. *Gecekondu* areas and communities were quite important in the sense of welcoming the newcomers and decreasing the risk of being socially excluded as a result of problems such as temporary unemployment, cultural adaptation, and lack of accommodation (Işık and Pınarcıoğlu 2009). In due course the number of rural migrants, and so the number of the *gecekondu* dwellers, increased, and it got harder to find a plot for a *gecekondu* in old *gecekondu* areas. Newcomers and the existing rural migrants who rented houses and wanted to own their *gecekondu* searched for new areas, resulting in the expansion of the city.

Physical Building of Ege

The Ege neighbourhood is a part of the Mamak district, which is one of the seven metropolitan districts of Ankara. Ege was formally constituted in 1973, according to state records, and before this it was a part of İmrahor village. The government gave the tenure of this area to the villagers of İmrahor, and they used it as pasture for feeding their animals. Ege was discovered by the dwellers of central *gecekondu* areas in the 1970s, and it became an entrance point for rural migrants who came directly from the villages of Central Anatolia. When the rural migrants came to Ege, the *muhtar*[2] of İmrahor, Mr. Fazlı, started to sell plots to the newcomers. He did not provide any written documents that proved the sale and ownership of the plots. So, it was not a formal or legal sale. Constructing a *gecekondu* on this land was not legal, and my interviewees suggested that Mr. Fazlı took advantage of the illegality of this situation and if anybody refused to pay him, he reported them to the gendarmerie. Since İmrahor Village was not a part of Ankara city centre in the 1970s, and the pasture that would become Ege district was a desolate place, there were no regular checks and controls by the gendarmerie unless there were reports or complaints.[3]

The migrant who "carries his mattress bundled upon his back along with his bag of food" (Şenyapılı 1982, 238) was a typical figure of rural-to-urban

---

2. A muhtar is the elected head of the smallest administrative unit in Turkey. Muhtars hold office both in villages and in the cities.
3. In Turkey, the police force is in charge of providing security for the city centres. For the countryside, the gendarmerie provides security.

migrants. At this point, when the first generation of migrants came to the cities, especially in the early years of migration, nearly all of them had nothing. Most of their migration stories were full of pain. Pamuk came to the city at the end of the 1960s with her family. She told me that they did not have enough money even to buy a bus ticket. They found a person in their village whose job was transporting goods to Ankara, and the family got on the back of the van. There was nothing covering it, although it was very cold. At the time of their migration, they had a seven-month-old baby. Pamuk started to cry when she told me that the baby contracted pneumonia during the migration and died a week after their journey to Ankara. For Pamuk, it was not the pneumonia, but their poverty which killed the baby. Others' stories of migration were similar. Most of my interviewees told me things like: "we came to Ankara with only a spoon," or "when we came, we did not even have a blanket."

The people of Ege, like other rural migrants, did not come to Ankara with blank minds. They brought to their destination their skills, perspectives, lifestyles, and the social relationships which they gained in their villages (Ayata and Ayata 1996, Kıray 2007, Lloyd 1979). Thanks to what they brought with them, they were able to survive in their new neighbourhood. They worked hard, were less dependent on money than the urbanites, skilled enough to solve their own problems, and collaborated with one another.

Due to economic hardship, people in Ege tried to build their *gecekondu*s step by step with the materials which they bought and collected from demolished buildings. *Gecekondu* people helped one another, particularly during the first night of building, to speed up the construction of their neighbours' houses. Ali, the *muhtar* of the Ege district, explained to me that if the population of a place was large enough they could apply to be recognised as a district, which meant an administrative unit of the city. If a place was recognised as an administrative unit of the city, it became easier for the inhabitants to apply for title deeds and harder for the demolition teams to knock down the *gecekondu*s, and the municipalities—at least theoretically— were in charge of providing infrastructure and transportation service to these areas.

Their common economic situation, the needs of their locality, and their common culture based on rural life brought them closer together, and they felt an attachment to the Ege district. This sense of community was the primary factor for their common activities. They came together and decided where there should be roads and plots for *gecekondu*s. They also shared a plot for a school and a mosque. *Gecekondu*s were poor residences without any electricity, sanitation or sewerage, in the suburbs of the city where they did not even have any public transportation or proper roads into the city centre. For water, they initially went to the fountain by the river downside of their neighbourhood and carried water. Most of the people dug a well in their gardens. For electricity, initially they pulled electricity from the street lamps in the main road. People dug a deep pit and used that for sewage and covered it with a piece of metal. Once a month, they asked the municipality to bring a vehicle and empty their sewage pits in their garden. After some time, thanks to their frequent visits to the municipality and collective struggle, they were provided with water pipes and lamp posts. The people of Ege organised themselves and installed the water pipes and lamp posts. The sewage infrastructure facility was provided by the time the water pipes were installed. In fact, providing these services was the responsibility of the municipalities, but Ege did their best to have these services as soon as possible. The contribution of the first settlers of Ege to the consolidation of the settlement shows that, as Payne (1984) would argue, rural solidarity practices were exploited by the state organisations. Ahmet came to Ege in 1981, and his account shows how the people of Ege organised to bring water to their neighbourhood:

> In those times everybody knew who lived in which houses, so we knew about who could help or not. Anyway we planned like this, for example I would dig 10 metres and my neighbour would dig 15 metres. The decision was announced by the Muhtar of that time. She visited every house. Suppose that I was not at home, she came and told my mother to ask me to dig 10 metres. So everybody dug some parts. Then the municipality came and installed the pipes in the main road.

Moreover, individual struggle would not work in forcing the state to take action to provide infrastructure services, so the district needed collaboration and collective action. The need for collaboration reinforced the relationships among the people of Ege, resulting in mutual help and solidarity. They helped one another in *gecekondu* construction, carrying water, cooking and so on. Mehmetali contributed to the establishment of Ege. His narrative is a good example in terms of explaining this help.

> The old days were different. When we came home from work, the first question we asked was how our neighbour's day was today. We visited our neighbours every night to see whether there was anybody sick or they needed anything. If they needed help in construction of their *gecekondu*, we did not even have dinner after work and went directly to their houses to help them.

Since slum areas are often viewed as urban villages (Gans 1962), the people of Ege consider the *gecekondu* settlements as an extension of their village life. Many interviewees told me that when they migrated to Ege, they did not feel many differences. It was because they thought that life in the village was not so different from life in Ege. In the early years they did not have electricity, they had to carry water, and they mostly socialised with people whom they already knew from their home towns. For example, Cemile has been in Ege for thirty years and she said that she was not surprised when she arrived in Ege and needed to continue carrying water.

Development of Ege

The *coup d'état* in 1980 was immediately followed by the SAPs, which aimed at liberalisation, establishing a flexible labour market, and shrinking the state. These policies resulted in a decrease in real incomes and exacerbation of working conditions. Under austerity measures, a series of *gecekondu* amnesties were passed in the 1980s. They legalised the *gecekondu*s constructed before 1985 and permitted construction of buildings up to four floors high. These amnesties were tools for opening public land to the urban land market and an informal redistribution process to compensate the losses of lower-class people to prevent social unrest from dominating in squatter areas (Buğra 1998, Başlevent and Dayıoğlu 2005, Keyder 1987).

In 1992, an improvement plan for Ege was prepared. This meant that Ege could be legally planned and developed and people could legally build houses and develop them. The acquisition of construction rights resulted in a significant rise in land prices in *gecekondu* areas, with the increase higher in neighbourhoods on the urban fringe (Sat 2007). Improvement plans of the 1980s and 1990s were taken as the starting point of the urban transformation projects of the 1990s and 2000s. Ege Urban Transformation Project (EUTP) was approved in 2001 and is still in process.

Ege's urban value increased in the 2000s due to three main factors. First, the building of the Çankaya-Mamak viaduct reduced transportation times to Çankaya, the most prestigious district of Ankara, with business and state institutions including the presidential palace, to ten to fifteen minutes by car. Second, since 2005, large shopping malls, business centres, and a 5,000 square metre aquarium were built close to Ege. Third, Ege is very close to the area of the Doğukent Urban Regeneration Project and İmrahor Valley recreation area. As Dündar (2001) suggests, all these developments revalued the area and left it under speculative pressure resulting in a speeding-up of its transformation. The city planner of the municipality, whom I interviewed, emphasised the significance of Ege as follows:

Ege is a very beautiful and special area. It looks towards Çankaya and it has an amazing view. So, it has potential to be developed. The Ege Urban Reformation Project aimed to develop here and Ege's development will also accelerate Mamak's development.

Currently in Turkey, TOKİ (Mass Housing Authority), the municipalities, and the large private construction firms are the main actors managing the urban regeneration projects. In practice, in prestigious urban areas, municipalities initiate urban reformation projects and leave the area to the private firms. In urban areas where the private sector does not see any potential for profit, TOKİ initiates the urban reformation. So the form of urban reformation of the 2000s in Turkey is an obvious example of entrepreneurial private-public partnership in cities, in which the "public sector assumes the risk and private sector takes the benefits" (Harvey 1989, 7). Considering the rising prestige of Ege, the urban transformation was not undertaken by TOKİ and this area was left to the private sector. The role of the municipality was restricted to preparing a plan which showed the place for public areas and described the basic features of the buildings. Businessmen and construction companies became the main actors of this transformation process.

Agreements with construction companies are based on parcels of land. Currently, in the EUTP, ten plots comprise a parcel. The usual agreement between *gecekondu* owners with legal title deeds and the firms are as follows: a person gets one flat if s/he has a 140 m² plot in the parcel. If s/he has more than this, s/he can either have one flat and some extra money, or have two flats and pay some money back to the construction businessmen/firms. People with title deeds are not legally forced to get an agreement but they told me that since everybody is getting an agreement, they will eventually have to do the same, otherwise they may have many problems. The problem is that, according to Turkish law, if the other people who have plots in the same parcel go to court, the person who has not signed an agreement will be forced to relinquish their parcel. Expropriation does not occur in Ege, where people leave their parcels to private firms and own the new flats when they are finished. This is why the people of Ege did not exhibit an extensive negative reaction.

Since the value of Ege district is increasing, luxury apartment blocks with large gardens, swimming pools, and sports areas are slowly appearing. This shows that this project is being undertaken to open Ege up to upper-class people. Since the price of these new flats is increasing day by day, buying a flat in Ege has become a tool for investing in the future (Yılmaz 2011, 86). In the winter of 2012, a new flat in Ege cost between 180,000-270,000 TL, which is more than double the price of a flat in older middle-class neighbourhoods in other parts of Ankara, close to the city centre. A *gecekondu* in good condition cost around 50,000 TL in Ege at the time of my fieldwork. So, roughly speaking, in this calculation, it seems that *gecekondu* owners will make money through this agreement.

For the residents of Ege, the recent presence of middle-class people and new shopping malls are signs of development that will benefit them. On the other hand, the older residents stress the fact that they do not mix with the new incoming middle-class people, and they are not able to shop in these malls because of the high prices. They indicated that they went to these malls just for visiting and window shopping. Visiting these shopping malls and participating in the opening ceremonies of new ones is a popular activity. The people of Ege are proud that the 5,000 square metre aquarium is close to their neighbourhood. However, they mention the fact that nearly none of the people in Ege have seen it, because the tickets are not affordable. It could be suggested that the hegemonic discourse of "development for all" is shaping the people of Ege's perspective on the recent changes in their neighbourhood. Furthermore, for them it is the first time in their life that the spaces which reflect the middle class life-style have come to their neighbourhood. For most of the people in Ege, EUTP is a kind of social service and an attempt at improving Ege, and is a part of neighbourhood development that should have been done before.

As the number of luxury apartments increases in Ege, people in *gecekondu*s start to aspire to live in apartments. They think that the ideal life is to live in the apartments, whereas living in a *gecekondu* is old fashioned and destined to disappear. Sayer suggests that a characterisation of the social field which is based on the unequal distribution of goods and commodities, as well as biases in the valuation of use-values and the people associated with them, leads to "over-valuing anything associated with the dominant" (2005, 122). The idealisation of life in apartments goes hand in hand with under-valuing *gecekondu* life, which is assumed to belong to the subordinate. In a binary construction, the *gecekondu* belongs to a peasant, poor, uncultivated, and backward way of life, whereas the apartment symbolises the urban, wealthy, polite, and progressive. The attitude of over-valuing apartment life was most obvious among teenagers and young women who were born in the city and "modern-life" oriented, discontented *gecekondu* dwellers.

My interviewees, especially women, complained about the heating and cleaning of *gecekondu*s. Most of the houses are heated by a stove, and there are generally only two stoves in each house; one is in the living room and the other in the bathroom. The stove in the bathroom is lit when the family takes a shower. They do not have more stoves in order to reduce the consumption of coal, and they even try to light the stove in the living room only during specific times of the day. Therefore the house gets cold quickly, and lighting the stove is tiring and time-consuming. The women in the study told me that, despite wiping and sweeping their homes frequently, it was barely possible to keep them as clean as they liked, due to the poor construction of *gecekondu*s. So, they would like to move to a flat to have a better heating system and to make household duties less burdensome. On the other hand, they talked about their friends who recently moved into flats from *gecekondu*s and turned on their heaters as little as possible in order to pay less. So, while they are dreaming about a comfortable house with a good heating system, they are worried about their future heating bills and are quite sure that they will not be able to afford them. On this point, it might be suggested that they will have the properties, but they will never be able to enjoy their features. Thus, in brief, the objective difficulties of *gecekondu* life are coupled with under-valuing it as an inferior lifestyle. This results in alienation from *gecekondu* houses. Aynur, a political activist who promotes urban transformation projects which fit the life-style of local people, told me that:

> Now, the *gecekondu*s are surrounded by apartments. People watch them through their windows and they dream of being there one day. People think that if they live in a flat, then they will be happy and have an ideal life.

The people of Ege are worried about the future service costs of these luxury buildings such as security, cleaning, lighting of the common spaces, and so on. Moreover, most of them are provided with one tonne of coal each year and a food pack quarterly by the district governorate or municipality. Their heating is predominantly dependent on this coal and the food package significantly decreases their monthly expenses. If they move into new flats, it is highly likely that they will not be entitled to this welfare support since the ownership of a luxury flat will prevent them from proving that they are poor. The new buildings will be heated by gas, which they will be obliged to pay for, and the coal provided by the district governorate/municipality will no longer be useful. There is a large dispute among the residents of Ege regarding some of the people who recently moved to flats heated by gas and are still receiving the coal, which they sell to other people in order to make money. This might be an initial option for people to raise money when they are in the new flats. However, once the state authorities realise this is happening they will obviously cancel the coal distributions. Thus due to the unaffordable costs of their future flats and their potential loss of benefits, many people in Ege with title deeds plan to sell them and buy more than one flat in a less expensive part of Ankara. İbrahim, who came to Ege at the beginning of the 1980s after spending two decades in Ankara, told me that:

My only income is my pension which is slightly above the minimum
wage. Now I am not paying rent and the coal is provided by the municipality welfare. If I start to live in the new flats...well, there will be a
monthly payment for the security and the cleaning of the building won't
there? There will be monthly payments for the heating... Tell me how can
I afford them all? After my *gecekondu* is replaced by a multi-floor apartment building, I will sell my flat and buy two flats in Sincan where the
prices of houses are less than half of those in Ege.

Considering the fact that *gecekondu*s correspond well to their lifestyles,
it is not unexpected that the people of Ege are concerned with the difference
between the lifestyle in *gecekondu*s and a lifestyle in the flats. The most
frequently mentioned point of difference is the freedom provided by a
gecekondu settlement, which is related to perceptions of privacy: they can
listen to loud music, beat their rugs, bake bread, cook tomato paste in their
gardens, and enjoy their gardens anytime they like. For *gecekondu* dwellers
apartment life is restrictive, and it is the primary reason that they have hesi-
tations about moving into apartments (Erman 1997). For the majority of the
people of Ege, life in a flat is like a life in a jail, so if they move into a flat
they think they will lose their freedom and privacy. Besides, they know their
neighbours and the other inhabitants of Ege. This gives them a sense of localism which is based on mutual trust and familiarity. Taking into account
the fact that the satisfaction with privacy and localism are key factors in a
sense of community (Wilson and Baldassare 1996), it could be suggested
that for the people of Ege, *gecekondu* life is the basis of their sense of community. In this sense, in addition to belonging to the peasants, the *gecekondu*
symbolises warm community ties and intimate relations and solidarity between *gecekondu* dwellers, especially for those who were born in rural
areas. In contrast, since they suppose that life in apartments requires more
formal relationships, it is frightening for them in terms of anticipated social
relations and privacy.

The residents of Ege are quite concerned with the fact that their future
neighbours will be upper-class people and they are aware of the material and
symbolic distance between themselves and the urban middle class, whom
they consider as the "other." Elvan, who was quite contented with his life in
the *gecekondu* house that he constructed in 1982, was concerned with prevailing formal neighbourly relations in apartments:

I know, in apartments people call each other "Mr.", so they will call me
"Mr. Elvan." I do not like this. What is Mr.! And why? Do not call me Mr.
Elvan, call me just Elvan. These social settings are not my cup of tea...
Look at my furniture, it is thirty years old. The construction firm told me
that a doctor, an MP and a lawyer have already bought flats in our future

apartment block. How can I invite them to my home? How can I speak to them and make friendships?

Their narratives show that they expect living in a flat requires being polite, which is assumed to be a sign of civilisation and progress. They do not know how to make friends and be neighbourly with their future neighbours. Sultan and Kiraz have been next-door neighbours for thirty years and, according to the EUTP, they will be living in the same apartment block when the project is completed. They used to call each other by their nicknames. Kiraz's nickname was "bad apple" and was given by Sultan. One day they were talking and making jokes about their future lives in the new flats:

> Sultan: When we are in the new flats I will shout "bad apple" at you as I do here.
> Kiraz: No, not anymore, I will kill you if you do so in the apartment. You are supposed to call me [she changes her voice here] "Mrs. Kiraz" and I will reply to you "yes Mrs. Sultan."

This dialogue suggests that the women may be ashamed of what they are in the face of middle-class people. Shame is related to the failings of a group or individuals in living according to the values and commitments that others will value (Sayer 2005). The people of Ege, like many other *gecekondu* people, are aware that they are different from the middle-class people in terms of consumption practices, cultural and educational backgrounds, and social class, despite their gains from the urban transformation project. Their narratives show that their way of life was not appreciated by the middle class. This feeling of difference is not value-free, but creates a sense of shame and inferiority among them. This is related to the idea that luxury is equated with people who are supposedly superior (Sayer 2005). From the very beginning of their migration, especially in their frequent encounters with the middle class after the urban reforms of the second half of the 1990s, they started to see themselves through the eyes of the middle class. With the EUTP, they are going to be living with middle-class people in the same neighbourhood and even in the same apartment building. So, although their position in the labour market and class structure of Turkey did not change as a result of the EUTP, their consumption practices in terms of infrastructure and accommodation might. Along with their immediate relationships with their neighbours, which play an important role in *gecekondu* people's life, the increase in their apprehension through comparison elevates the level of shame that they feel. As is demonstrated by their narratives, they compare their furniture, social attitude in apartments, and vocabulary to those of middle class people who move into new flats in Ege. In that comparison, it can be seen that the people of Ege identify apartment life with middle-class qualities, whereas they still feel closer to *gecekondu* life. So, they feel that they will not be able to fulfil the middle class criterion in terms of cultural and economic capital and class position, which is why they feel that they will be looked down on by their future neighbours.

The narratives that were shaped by the feeling of shame were more popular among *gecekondu* dwellers who had aspirations of upward social mobility and modern life. Karip came to Ankara alone when he was a teenager to work. He had a very difficult time, and worked hard at several jobs simultaneously until he became well-off. Currently he is retired and running an estate agency in Ege, where he used to live fifteen years ago. He celebrates the EUTP, which will gentrify the area and complains about the *gecekondu* people who replace their *gecekondu* houses with luxury apartments:

> These people do not know how to live in apartments. They are still gecekondu dwellers, what does it matter if they move to luxury houses, they are the same. Women sit in front of the luxury apartments as if they still live in gecekondus. But, you know, most of them are not able to afford these houses, so they will be moving to other areas and middle-class, educated, civilized people will come to Ege. They will be the people who will develop Ege.

The common feeling among nearly all the residents of Ege was their emotional attachment to their neighbourhood. Although they are not being forced to leave Ege, it seems that the majority of the original population will be displaced when the EUTP is completed. They think that they were in Ege when the living conditions were poor and they suffered from the lack of urban services and infrastructure facilities; nevertheless when Ege is currently "developed" they will have to leave. One of my interviewees, Fatma, who came to the Ege district when she was sixteen at the end of the 1980s, told me that:

> It was us who had to put up with all the dirtiness of this district, but when it gets developed, it will be the rich people who will enjoy it! In a way, they do not let us enjoy the improved version of our own district!

Harvey suggests that the richest would not move if they do not choose to do so, and this results in the squeezing of various intermediate groups between social pressure emerging from below and "immoveable political and economic forces above" (1993, 173). The populations of *gecekondu* areas are included in these intermediate groups and their choices are limited when compared with those of the middle-class people who will move to *gecekondu* areas after the urban reformation projects are completed. Güzey's research on thirty-one urban reformation projects in Ankara shows that the level of displacement of the original population is high in prestigious areas, whereas the percentage of displacement falls to under 50% in less prestigious areas (2009, 31). Since Ege is becoming more prestigious, the expected displacement rate could be high. Moreover, despite their aspirations of living in luxury apartments, most of my interviewees are very worried about life in a flat. Their concerns, particularly about the cost of living in the new flats and the ability to turn them into more profitable investments, may mean that the majority of them will not be living in Ege after the project is completed.

Displacing Slum dwellers and Transferring Socio-Economic Problems

The appearance of extensive *gecekondu* areas in large cities initially started a hot debate on urbanisation and development in Turkey in the 1960s. The main theme of discussion of those years was the integration of rural migrants into city life. In the 1970s, with the rise of grass-roots political activism and polarisation, the *gecekondu*s were mentioned with the potential for "terrorism." As the SAPs resulted in great loss of real incomes, exacerbating working conditions, and the *gecekondu* amnesties brought in commodification of *gecekondu*s in the 1980s, *gecekondu* studies focused on extensive poverty, social exclusion and marginalisation, informal economy, social policy, and clientelism. With the rise of political Islam in the 1990s and the forced migration of Kurdish people into large cities, *gecekondu*s were considered "dangerous" areas of radical politics. Since the 1990s, *gecekondu* areas have started to be referred to as *varoşes*.[4] While the term *gecekondu* recalled "the rural, failing to integrate into modern city life and backwardness," the term *varoş* has negative connotations of criminals and threats, although studies on crime and *varoş* have not indicated any significant relation between *varoşes* and criminal affairs (Keleş 2010). Moreover, *varoş* does not imply "a concrete spatial reference indicating the lifestyle in periphery settlements only" but is also used to denote "underground or kitsch aspects of contemporary urban life" (Demirtas and Sen 2006, 88). In brief, the squatter areas of the city have been discussed as different social phenomena. However, identification of these areas with the disorder of the city remains.

---

4. The word *varoş* originates from the Hungarian word város and means the outskirts of the city.

Since the initial appearance of *gecekondu*s, the political authorities have claimed to solve the *gecekondu* problem. *Gecekondu* demolitions, strict bans on *gecekondu* constructions, and amnesties were implemented in different political eras. While the wide range of discussions on *gecekondu* prove that the problem of *gecekondu* goes far beyond the problem of accommodation and urban planning, the political authorities have considered it a problem of low-quality housing for fifty years. Since the late 1990s, the urban transformation projects have been considered the major tool for "clearance of *gecekondu*s."[5] However, the aim of the urban transformation projects in Turkey is not to ameliorate the living conditions of *gecekondu* people and solve their problem, but to integrate the former *gecekondu* areas, which have become central and prestigious over time, into the land market, and obtain unearned urban rent. It is compatible with the general features of capitalist development which necessarily mobilises particular territories, places and scales as productive forces (Brenner and Theodore 2002). The policy of clearance of *gecekondu* areas from the cities, which are supposed to be marketed, did not only displace the *gecekondu* population to the other distressed areas, but also transferred the socio-economic and cultural problems of this population to other areas.

References

Alpar, İstiklal and Samira Yener. 1991. *Gecekondu Araştırması*. Devlet Planlama Teşkilatı: Ankara.

Ayata Sencer and Ayşe Güneş-Ayata. 1996. *Konut, Komşuluk ve Kent Kültürü*. T.C. Başbakanlık Toplu Konut İdaresi Başkanlığı: Ankara.

Başlevent, Cem and Meltem Dayıoğlu. 2005. "The Effect of Squatter Housing on Income Distribution in Turkey." *Urban Studies* 42:31-45.

Boratav, Korkut. 2010. *Türkiye İktisat Tarihi 1908*. Ankara: İmge Yayınları.

Brenner, N. and N. Theodore. 2002. "Cities and the Geographies of 'Actually Existing Neoliberalism.'" *Antipode* 34:349-379.

Buğra, Ayşe. 1998. "The Immoral Economy of Housing in Turkey." *International Journal of Urban and Regional Research* 22:303-317.

---

5. Appropriating a modernist-elitist perspective, Mr. Erdoğan, the Prime Minister, names the *gecekondu* areas "tumours of the cities to be cleaned" and the slogan of Melih Gökçek, the mayor of Ankara is "we will clean Ankara from the *gecekondu*s".

Demirtaş, Neslihan and Seher Şen. 2006. "Varoş Identity: The redefinition of low income settlements in Turkey." *Middle Eastern Studies* 43:87-106.

Dündar, Özlem. 2001. "Models of Urban Transformation: Informal Housing in Ankara." *Cities* 18:391-401.

Erman, Tahire. 1997 "Squatter (gecekondu) Housing versus Apartment Housing: Turkish Rural- to-Urban Migrant Residents' Perspectives." *HABITATINTL* 28:91-106.

Eroğlu, Şebnem. 2011. *Beyond the Resources of Poverty: Gecekondu Living in the Turkish Capital.* Surrey: Ashgate Publishing Limited.

Gans, Herber, J. 1962. *Urban Villagers: Group and Class in the Life of Italian-Americans.* New York: The Free Press (Macmillan Co., Inc.).

Harvey, David.1989. "From Managerialism to Entrepreneuralism: The Transformation in Urban Governance in Late Capitalism." *Geografiska Annaler, Series B,Human Geography* 71:3-17.

Işık, Oğuz and Melih M. Pınarcıoğlu. 2009. *Nöbeteşe Yoksulluk: Gecekondulaşma ve Kent Yoksulları: Sultanbeyli Örneği.* İstanbul: İletişim Yayınları.

Jessop, Bop. 2002. "Liberalism, Neoliberalism, and Urban Governance: A State-Theoretical Perspective." *Antipode* 34:452-472.

Keyder, Çağlar. 1987. *State and Class in Turkey.* London/New York: Verso.

Kıray, Mübeccel. 1970. "Squatter housing: Fast depeasantization and slow workerization in underdeveloped countries." Research Committee on Urban Sociology of the 7th World Congress of Sociology. Varna, 14-19 September.

Llyod, Peter. 1979 *Slums of Hope? Shanty Towns of the third World.* New York: Penguin Books.

Payne, Geoffrey, K. 1984. "Ankara." *Cities* 1:210-214.

Sat, N. Aydan. 2007. "A Critique on Improvement Plans: A tool for Transformation of Squatter Housing Areas in Ankara." *METU Journal of the Faculty of Architecture* 24:27-36.

Sayer, Andrew. 2005. *The Moral Significance of Class.* Cambridge: Cambridge University Press.

Şenyapili, Tansı. 2004. *Barakadan Gecekonduya Ankara'da Kentsel Mekanin Donusumu: 1923-1960.* Istanbul: Iletisim Yayinlari.

Türkiş. 2012. Türkiş Araştırması: Açlık ve Yoksulluk Sınırı Temmuz 2012 http://www.yol-is.org.tr/TR/belge/1-245/turk-is-arastirmasi-temmuz-2012-aclik-ve-yoksulluk-sini-.html#icerik (retrieved on 11.10.2012).

Wilson, Georjeanna and Baldassare Mark. 1996. "Overall 'Sense of Community' in a Suburban Region: The Effects of Localism, Privacy and Urbanization." *Environment and Behaviour* 28:27-43.

Yılmaz, Mahir. 2011. "An Inquiry Into Different Urban Transformation Models in the Context of Rent and Property Transfer: The Case of Mamak District." MA Thesis, Middle East Technical University.

CONTRIBUTORS

LEAH ACHDUT is currently an Associate Professor in the Economics and Business Administration School in the Ruppin Academic Center and the Head Economics and Management Department. She has been a senior research fellow of the Economics and Society Program team at The Van Leer Jerusalem Institute since 2007. During her work in the public service she directed research departments and served as a member of public committees and international projects. In the years 2001-2006 she was Deputy Director General for Research and Planning of the National Insurance Institute—the Israeli social security agency—and a member of the institute's Executive Board. Prof. Achdut has combined social policy making with research in the fields of social security, health and the labor market and on issues of poverty and income inequality. Her recent research focuses on pension reforms, retirement patterns, health finance and the impact of fiscal policies on income inequality.

SCOTT H. BOYD is a visiting faculty member teaching literature and humanities at Middle East Technical University—Northern Cyprus Campus. He received his Ph.D from Ohio University in Interdisciplinary Arts conducting research on art and identity in German twentieth century art and film. He primarily writes and conducts research in cultural theory; incorporating systems theory and adapting biological models, such as autopoiesis, to culture and paradigms of culture. He is also the co-founder of Cultural Difference and Social Solidarity Network.

LIEMA DAVIDOVICH is currently a senior lecturer and the head of the Department of Economics and Accounting at the Ruppin Academic Center. She received a MBA from Tel Aviv University and a Ph.D. from the School of Business Administration and the Department of Economics of The Hebrew University of Jerusalem, Israel. Her research areas are inequality aversion, risk aversion, ambiguity preference, and egalitarian societies. Her recent work was a survey about Social Cohesion and solidarity in Israel. The survey is addressing the most prominent and essential issues of the Israeli society such as integration, migration, minorities and multiculturalism.

CLAIRE FARRUGIA completed a degree in history and political science at the University of Sydney (Australia). She has previously collaborated with the NSW Department of Environment and Climate Change and the NSW Migration Heritage Centre, conducting research on belonging in multicultural Australia. She is currently completing her PhD in the Department of Sociology at Macquarie University (Australia), focusing on migrant women's practices of citizenship. Her research interests include the intersections between ethnicity and identity, space, place, and mobility and neoliberal structures of governance.

SIBYLLE HEILBRUNN is Associate Professor at the Ruppin Academic Center and currently head of the MA Program on Immigration and Social Integration. Heilbrunn obtained her PhD in organizational sociology from Haifa University in Israel. She was DAAD visiting professor at Bremen University, is currently visiting professor at the ISM, Dortmund and holds a research fellowship at the Institute for Research of the Kibbutz and the Cooperative Idea at the University of Haifa. Her main research interests include entrepreneurship of migrants and minorities, migration and multiculturalism and social solidarities.

ZUZANA KLÍMOVÁ is a Ph.D. student in the programme "Literatures in English." She specializes in postcolonial literature and her current research interests focus on West Indian literature. She earned her master's degree from Masaryk University in 2012. Part of her dissertation research was conducted during her stay at the University of Bristol. She has presented research at several international conferences and is a member of Cultural Difference and Social Solidarity Network. She has published her articles in the literary journal *Proudy*, in the volume *Language, Literature and Culture in a Changing Transatlantic World II* following the conference at Prešov 2012, and an essay "The Implications of Transtextuality in V.S. Naipaul's *The Middle Passage: The Caribbean Revisited*," forthcoming in *Anglica Wratislaviensia* 2013. At the Department of English and American Studies she has participated in teaching undergraduate courses Introduction to Literature and Contemporary British Literature.

JOHN MCSWEENEY is an independent scholar, based in Ireland, whose research centres on questions of ethics, politics, and subjectivity in the continental philosophical tradition, with a special interest in the political significance of the so-called "return of religion" within recent debates. He completed postdoctoral research into the nature of political act in Badiou, Žižek and Foucault in 2010 at Milltown Institute, Dublin. He was guest editor of a 2013 special issue of *Foucault Studies* on "Foucault and Religion."

PAUL REYNOLDS is Reader in Sociology and Social Philosophy at Edge Hill University in the United Kingdom. He primarily writes on issues of radical theory, ethics, and politics. His current research is focused in three areas: the ethico-politics of sexuality, ethics, and politics in Marxist theory and ethics, politics, and the role of the intellectual. He is currently one of the editors of *Historical Materialism: Research in Critical Marxist Theory*, and the *Journal of the International Network for Sexual Ethics and Politics*. He is also the co-founder of the Cultural Difference and Social Solidarity Network.

DAVID CHRISTOPHER STOOP is currently working at his PhD in Political Science about "right-wing extremist propaganda against mosques in Germany." He teaches seminars at University Cologne about anti-racist theories and right-wing extremism. His last publications include the essay "We or Sharia. Anti-Muslim Racism and Right-wing Extremism in Germany," in *Difference and Solidarity: Critical Cases*, S. H. Boyd, M. A. Walters (eds.), Cambridge Scholars Publishing, Newcastle 2012.

BURCU ŞENTÜRK graduated with a BA from the Bosphorus University Department of Politics and International Relations, and completed her MA in the Middle East Technical University's Department of Sociology. She is a PhD candidate at the University of York, Department of Politics. Her articles have been published in daily newspapers and political journals (*Radikal, Habertürk, Amargi, Feminist Politika, Ekmek ve Özgürlük*), and academic journals (*Praksis, Fe Journal:Feminist Critique, Mülkiyeliler Dergisi, SBF Dergi*). She reviewed for *International Political Science Review*, *British Journal of Religious Education* and *Fe Journal:Feminist Critique*. She gave a speech on the families of PKK guerrillas and Turkish Armed Forces soldiers in the sub-branch of the Human Rights Commission of Turkish Parliamentary on December 4, 2011.

MARY ANN WALTER received her PhD in linguistics from the Massachusetts Institute of Technology. She is currently Assistant Professor of Teaching English as a Foreign Language at the Middle East Technical University—Northern Cyprus Campus. Her research focuses on experimental phonology and sociolinguistics of the Middle East. Her current research project concerns language choice and ideology in the Arab Gulf states.

LAWRENCE WILDE received a BA and Ph. D. from the University of Liverpool and is Professor of Political Theory at Nottingham Trent University in England. For many years his research has focussed on the concept of solidarity, culminating in the publication of *Global Solidarity* in 2013. Other monographs are *Erich Fromm and the Quest for Solidarity* (2005), *Ethical Marxism and its Radical Critics* (1998), *Modern European Socialism* (1993) and *Marx and Contradiction* (1989). He is co-author of *The Marx Dictionary* (2011) with Ian Fraser, editor of *Marxism's Ethical Thinkers* (Basingstoke: Palgrave, 2001) and co-editor with Mark Cowling of *Approaches to Marx* (Milton Keynes: Open University Press, 1989).

SIMONA ZAVRANIK received a BA in journalism and a Ph.D. in sociology from the University of Ljubljana. She is currently an Assistant Professor at the Faculty of Social Sciences, University of Ljubljana, and a researcher of migrations and human rights with the faculty's Centre for Spatial Sociology. Her publications include two edited volumes, *Women and Trafficking* and *Migration – Globalization – European Union*, both published by the Peace Institute, Ljubljana. She has published different articles in the field of sociological analysis of asylum and migration, integration of refugees, public opinion towards migrants and disadvantaged social groups and ethnic minorities, and human rights. Her current research interest examines anti-trafficking policies in global scope and supportive mechanisms to the victims of human trafficking in the regions of CEE and the Balkans.

INDEX